I0120973

MODEL-MINORITY IMPERIALISM

MODEL-MINORITY
IMPERIALISM

VICTOR BASCARA

University of Minnesota Press
MINNEAPOLIS • LONDON

Chapter 2 was originally published as "Following the Money: Asian American Literature and the Preface to United States Imperialism," *Jouvert: A Journal of Postcolonial Studies* 4, no. 3 (Spring/Summer 2000); social.chass.ncsu.edu/jouvert/v4i3/con43.htm.

Copyright 2006 by the Regents of the University of Minnesota

ALL RIGHTS RESERVED. No part of this publication may be reproduced, stored in a retrieval system, or transmitted, in any form or by any means, electronic, mechanical, photocopying, recording, or otherwise, without the prior written permission of the publisher.

Published by the University of Minnesota Press
111 Third Avenue South, Suite 290
Minneapolis, MN 55401-2520
http://www.upress.umn.edu

Library of Congress Cataloging-in-Publication Data

Bascara, Victor, 1970–
  Model-minority imperialism / Victor Bascara.
      p.   cm.
  Includes bibliographical references and index.
  ISBN-13: 978-0-8166-4511-4 (hc : alk. paper)   ISBN-10: 0-8166-4511-6 (hc : alk. paper)
  ISBN-13: 978-0-8166-4512-1 (pb : alk. paper)   ISBN-10: 0-8166-4512-4 (pb : alk. paper)
  1. Asian Americans — Race identity. 2. Asian Americans — Politics and government.
3. Asian Americans — Intellectual life. 4. Imperialism. 5. Postcolonialism. 6. United
States — Territorial expansion. 7. United States — Intellectual life. 8. Nationalism — United
States. 9. United States — Relations — Asia. 10. Asia — Relations — United States. I. Title.
  E184.A75B37 2006
  303.48'273050904 — dc22   2006016448

Printed in the United States of America on acid-free paper

The University of Minnesota is an equal-opportunity educator and employer.

12   11   10   09 08 07 06   10   9   8   7   6   5   4   3   2   1

CONTENTS

There was nothing left for us to do, but to . . . educate and uplift
and civilize.

—President William McKinley, "Remarks to
the Methodist Delegation," 1898

La Jolla Playhouse, 1998: *Dogeaters* by Jessica Hagedorn

THE SETTING is Manila. The year is 1959, give or take. At the center
of the stage is a bed. On it stands Rio Gonzaga, a middle-class Ma-
nileño in her teens. In this production, Rio is played by Sandra Oh. According to Hagedorn, Rio "serves as the play's observer and sometime
narrator."[1] Rio is, after all, the quasi-autobiographical center of Hagedorn's 1990 novel *Dogeaters,* the acclaimed book on which the play is
based. To further establish Rio's alignment with an American audience, a remark made earlier in the play labels her as "the Anguished
Exile," who will eventually emigrate to California, as did Hagedorn.[2]
Atop Rio's head is a coonskin cap.

To one side of the stage, near the back, sits Joey Sands, a mestizo
hustler and the orphaned son of a Filipina prostitute and an African
American soldier. The setting is also Manila, but the year is 1982. Joey
has escorted the German filmmaker Rainer Fassbinder to a sex club.
Fassbinder came to the capital city for the Manila International Film
Festival. The event, organized by the glamorous First Lady, Imelda
Marcos, is designed to be a showcase for the cosmopolitan sophisti-
cation of a postcolonial metropolis on the rise. Fassbinder, with the
help of Sands, has wandered away from the screenings at the new and
hastily built Manila Center for the Arts in search of one of the city's

infamous sex shows. Sands has guided Fassbinder into what would otherwise be for him the forbidding, labyrinthine underworld of a neocolonial dystopia. On a catwalk at the back of the stage, two sex workers, a young man and woman, emerge to "enact a variety of sexual positions in a brisk, business-like manner."[3]

Meanwhile, Rio holds in her adolescent hands an open book, from which she is reciting a speech: "President William McKinley Addresses a Delegation of Methodist Churchmen, 1898."[4] In the speech, McKinley enumerates the four policy choices available to the United States in the wake of the Spanish-American War, when the Philippines "dropped into our laps":

> (1) that we could not give them back to Spain—that would be cowardly and dishonorable; (2) that we could not turn them over to France or Germany— our commercial rivals in the Orient—that would be bad business and discreditable; (3) that we could not leave them to themselves—they were unfit for self-government—and they would soon have anarchy and misrule over there worse than Spain's was; and (4) that there was nothing left for us to do but to take them all, and to. . . . (22)

At this point Rio's verbal delivery fails. She struggles to enunciate the American president's words and finds herself barely able to stammer out the rest of the speech. She gets as far as "to educate . . . the Filipinos, . . . and uplift . . . and civilize. . . ." She chokes on the phrases, barely able to breathe. No longer able to continue her performance, she crumples into a heap on her bed. The remainder of the speech was to have gone as follows: "and Christianize them, and by God's grace do the very best we could by them, as our fellow-men for whom Christ also died" (22, 23).

Meanwhile, in synchrony with Rio's recitation of these four options, the sex workers cycle through four different sexual positions as Sands and Fassbinder look on. For the first three positions, Rio performed McKinley with appropriate gusto. These were the options discarded as patently unacceptable. But we see that as she reads the fourth option, the one that foretold how the paired destinies of the United States and its new possession would manifest, her once-confident voice falters. After she has collapsed, sobbing uncontrollably, above her the young man from the sex show matter-of-factly speaks his only line.

YOUNG MAN (*to Fassbinder*): Okay, boss? You want us to do that again? (61)

With that line ends the sequence that would go on to be called "Sex Show Montage" in the published script of the play. We see dramatized not only the contrast between an imperialist vision and its realization, but the process by which that comparison could be made at all.

In 1998, the centennial of the Spanish-American War, this richly orchestrated moment in Jessica Hagedorn's *Dogeaters* gave dramatic form to the unburdening of empire. By interweaving two turn-of-the-century experiences, this scene staged the simultaneity of past and present, East and West, civilized and primitive, sacred and profane, colonizer and colonized, to both juxtapose differences and manifest resonance. Sex work, empire building, and an elocution exercise meet in a late-twentieth-century Asian American theatrical production. At the earlier turn of the century, the will to colonize briefly and conspicuously consumed American civilization, resulting in its famously forgotten imperial adventure in the Philippines. By bringing this history into view almost exactly one hundred years later, Hagedorn's play made newly palpable the century-old traces of the empire that the United States had long since buried. *Model-Minority Imperialism* argues that contemporary Asian American cultural politics set the conditions for the critical return of empire as an explanatory model for understanding the American Century. This scene functions as a set piece and leitmotiv for this book, which traces the history and cultural formations that draw empire back into visibility in American culture. This unburdening does not register as a celebratory moment of the truth setting one free (John 8:32) or as a long-hidden secret liberated from a dustbin or closet. Instead, unburdening comes as a trauma of disillusionment.

Apprehended collectively, the multiple performances in this scene locate us simultaneously in Washington, D.C., Manila, and La Jolla in the years 1898, 1959, 1982, and 1998. This set piece stages an especially fecund moment where Asian American cultural politics and the emergence of U.S. imperialism converge, and they converge at a point where a central speaking subject fails to speak. Constructed this way, the scene bears an emblematic trope of a "minor literature."[5] A minor literature, usefully defined by Deleuze and Guattari as a literature in a major language but serving a minor function, invokes the limits of a major discourse through a minor subject's ambivalent mimicry of its terms and logic. Through this structure of juxtaposition, this moment from Hagedorn's play makes visible the jagged contours of history and its unexpected transitions. The fate foretold by McKinley in America has become the Sex Show Montage of 1982 and the post-independence ambivalence of 1959 in the Philippines. All of this is told through the revisionist ethos of an experimental theater piece in 1998, working its way through a regional workshop at Sundance and being further tweaked at La Jolla, and eventually premiering off-Broadway three years later at the Public Theater, in a form Hagedorn calls a "leaner and meaner" version of the play. The play in 1998 lavishly dramatized and displayed the interplay of contentious histories. That contestation produces the drama that makes such displays so compelling and instructive to watch.

At the center of this arrangement of times and places is the figure of Rio, losing illusions she did not realize she had. In particular, at this moment, her weeping and collapse occasion the dismantling of American myths. Her breakdown, in other words, erupts as a new form constructed on the wreckage of the profound failure of an existing form. In an earlier scene, Rio had no difficulty reading from *The Philippines,* an 1846 anthropological study by Jesuit priest Jean Mallat. Rio's performance of the discourse of nineteenth-century primitivism readily comes out as transparently ironic and humorous.[6] To make the comedic aspects even more unmistakable, Rio was wearing a pith helmet, that powerful symbol of British involvement in warmer climes, such as Cecil Rhodes clad in khaki exploring the sun-baked Dark Continent. Mallat, who appears as a character, is openly ridiculed for his meticulous adherence to methods of physical anthropology that are now debunked, both for their questionable scientific methods and findings and for the imperialist ideologies they uncritically reinforced.[7] The soap opera star Barbara Villanueva skewers Mallat, the earnest scientist and cleric, early in the play: "Did you have fun, Father Jean? You know . . . measuring skulls and buttocks and teeth?" He responds, "Of course I did. Wouldn't you? It was the most fun I ever had." Later she asks Mallat, "Why didn't you just stay home?" To which Mallat responds, "Home? Where would civilization be, if we all just stayed 'home?'"[8] His rhetorical question can be taken earnestly. If he stayed home, there would be no occasion for this play, which critically remembers him. The colonial discourse of an 1840s missionary and scientist like Mallat is easy to lampoon, even by 1959, if not well before then.

Yet McKinley's discourse is somehow different, to both Rio and an American audience. The words of the twenty-fifth president issue as inaccurate prophecy to 1959, to 1982, and to the present. Rio is unable to read the words of McKinley's speechwriters in the same dismissive way she read Father Mallat's words. Instead of dark comedy, we get tragedy. The visions of uplift, conversion, and civilization are somehow less funny in 1959, in 1982, and certainly in 1898. But what of 1998, or for that matter, 2001? By early 2001, the production of the play at the Public Theater, as Hagedorn notes, "dispenses with the 1959 scenes and focuses on the Manila of 1982."[9] Such a disposal is understandable because the Philippines of the 1980s, with the 1986 downfall of the flamboyant Marcoses in the face of the spectacle of People Power, is arguably the most influential and enduring vision of the Philippines in American culture. Who hasn't heard of Imelda's outrageous collection of three thousand shoes? Missing, therefore, from the 2001 version is Rio's 1950s collapse while performing 1890s McKinley. Instead the wife of the military strongman, General Nicasio Ledesma, kneels beside her bed, reciting a sort of Hail Mary. The omission of McKinley's speech and Rio's centrality is the omission of Hagedorn's quasi-autobiographical persona. It is apparently the omission of the well-worn developmental narrative of a subjugated subject coming to voice. It is apparently an emphasis on the lingering traces of Spanish medievalism and a de-emphasis on formal American colonization. This moment when Rio unburdens empire becomes a fragment of a work-in-progress, a fragment deemed disposable in the development of that work in its highest profile incarnation on the stage of the Public Theater and the pages of a published script.

In effect, this book takes account of how and why such a moment of unburdening would emerge. The immediate and specific accounting would be the fact that the McKinley speech is a part of the source material for the play: the much-acclaimed 1990 novel *Dogeaters*. With its ingenious blend of formal experimentation and provocative content, *Dogeaters* created an immediate sensation when it was first published by Pantheon and it continues to be reprinted.[10] A finalist for the National Book Award, *Dogeaters* was Hagedorn's breakthrough text, despite the fact that she had been writing for decades as a poet, playwright, and performance artist. It is one of the most discussed novels of Asian American literature, particularly for its creative appropriation of colonial discourse. McKinley's speech is excerpted as one of many pieces in the novel's overt collage structure, with jagged jump cuts and apparent non sequiturs. McKinley's speech is not recited by Rio; it stands alone, shoulder-to-shoulder with shards of ethnographies, news stories, soap opera transcripts, and prayers, in addition to conventionally novelistic passages told from various first-person perspectives and through indirect free style. Putting McKinley's words in Rio's mouth is new to the play, at least in the 1998 La Jolla production under the direction of Michael Greif. This moment from the La Jolla production, then, has a specifically traceable genealogy from its source material, and it, too, is an excised moment in a genealogy of later productions. Analysis of features and histories of specific texts are crucial parts of the methodology of the model-minority myth. Such close analysis allows us to apprehend the important conditions that shape texts so that they manifest a capacity to unburden empire.

A more general accounting of Rio's moment of unburdening would suggest that the present is a product of the cultural and historical conditions of U.S. imperialism. For this history to be unburdened by Rio, it had to have happened and then been forgotten or otherwise repressed. U.S. imperialism has come to be understood as one of the great amnesias in American history, not simply because it was forgotten—so many past events are—but because it had once been so important and conspicuous. The impact that McKinley's speech has on the world that forgot it, and on Rio in particular, becomes evidence of a yawning gap between an earlier moment and a distressingly forgetful present. Therefore a crucial part of *Model-Minority Imperialism* is a consideration of what happened historically when U.S. imperialism emerged, as well as how it was, and was not, discussed.

Yet, at the same time, for Rio's moment of unburdening of empire to be possible at all, an emergent sensibility had to cohere that recognized such moments of historical recovery as indeed the unburdening of empire. In other words, the present came to find that the past had become newly significant for inventorying traces of histories that had been previously unnoticed. Rio then becomes a stand-in for emergent constituencies discovering their new and often unhappy relationship to the past. New social, cultural, and political movements form and legitimate their existence through these acts of unburdening and the revisionism those acts occasion. And thus, a new term emerges: "Asian American." "Asian American" is then an expression of, and a label for, the sensibility that makes unburdening empire meaningful and relevant to the present. Asian American cultural politics sets the conditions for a critical rearticulation of the meaning of Asian difference in American culture, and in doing so "Asian American" displaces the now maligned concept "oriental." *Model-Minority Imperialism* looks at the histories and the discourses, as well as the interests and the institutions, that made that displacement possible and necessary in contemporary cultural politics.

Back when this project was barely more than a wobbly chapter, it had one of its many new beginnings as I sat one autumn evening in that dark theater in La Jolla, probably smelling of pomade. I have since had the good fortune to pick many brains as I sought to grasp the complex of histories contained in that one fleeting sequence. I like to think that this book reenacts that moment again and again to draw connections between ideas and constituencies that might otherwise exist separately, even blissfully so. My teachers at Berkeley, especially Sau-ling Wong, Elaine Kim, Oscar Campomanes, and David Lloyd, started me on this intellectual investigation. From there, I was in the capable hands of my mentors at Columbia, Marcellus Blount and David Eng, who, along with Robert Ferguson, Gary Okihiro, and Sandhya Shukla, aided and abetted my continued work on this project as a doctoral dissertation. Throughout that period and beyond, I benefited from the generous guidance, encouragement, and example of Lisa Lowe.

Over the years, I have been grateful for the invaluable feedback provided by friends and colleagues in writing groups and by numerous strangers at many, many academic conferences. Portions of the book appeared in 2000 as "Following the Money: Asian American Literature and the Preface to U.S. Imperialism," in a special issue of *Jouvert: Journal of Postcolonial Studies* focusing on postcolonial Asian America edited by Viet Thanh Nguyen and Tina Chen. In my time at Madison, Leslie Bow, Shilpa Davé, Victor Jew, Lisa Nakamura, and Michael Peterson have given insightful and patient readings to large sections of the book. My fellow Mellon Humanities Workshoppers, Francisco "Kiko" Benitez, Michael Cullinane, and Courtney Johnson, along with Rhacel Salazar Parreñas, Warwick Anderson, and Al Mc-Coy, have been models of erudition and enthusiasm on "Empire in Transition." John Blanco, Julian Go, and Viet Nguyen each made immensely helpful comments on the introduction (which, I should say, had its genesis in a discussion of *Orientalism* with Lucienne Loh). In the final stages of revision, Helen Jun and Chandan Reddy provided me with their particular brilliances, as they have done so often in the past.

The University of Minnesota Press has been gracious and supportive. Richard Morrison has been an exemplary editor, providing not only insight and intelligence but also thoughtful encouragement and much-needed perspective.

And, of course, I am immeasurably indebted to Grace Kyungwon Hong for making this project—and the life it has led me to live—possible, sustaining, and pleasurable. It is to her and my parents, Jorge L. and Trinidad C. Bascara, that I dedicate the work here. This text is better because of the training and generous help I have received over the years. The mistakes and shortcomings are my own.

WE ARE HERE BECAUSE YOU WERE THERE

> Much of the personal investment in this study derives from my
> awareness of being an "Oriental" as a child growing up in two
> British colonies. . . . In many ways my study of Orientalism has
> been an attempt to inventory the traces upon me, the Oriental
> subject, of the culture whose domination has been so powerful a
> factor in the life of all Orientals.
>
> —Edward W. Said, *Orientalism,* 1978

IN HIS ESSAY "Postcolonial Criticism," Homi K. Bhabha acknowledges that *"Orientalism* inaugurated the postcolonial field."[1] Few
would challenge such a pronouncement that Said's 1978 study of
Western representations of the Middle East has indeed been influential for contemporary cultural politics. We might then reasonably
ask: What inaugurated *Orientalism?* For an answer, we can turn to Said
himself. In the introduction to *Orientalism,* Said describes how his
childhood as an "Oriental" under British colonialism in Palestine and
in Egypt left "traces" that he desires now to "inventory." In casting
his project this way, Said invokes an autobiographical narrative that,
like his book, traces the transition from colonialism to postcolonialism, both for himself and for "all Orientals." By going from being the
represented to one who represents himself, he lives out the refuta-
tion of the ironic Karl Marx quotation that serves as an epigraph to
Orientalism: "They cannot represent themselves; they must be represented."[2] Said foregrounds his "personal investment" in his study
to take his readers from a critique of the historical function of European representations of the Orient to, by the study's end, a critical

and historicized appreciation of "Orientalism Now." It is therefore no less important to note that he was writing in New York City in the late 1970s, in and for a world whose sun had finally set on the British empire of his youth. He was an immigrant from the East who had re-settled in the West, and he situates his critique from the standpoint of one who might be considered an Oriental American.

The presence of the "Oriental" as a constitutive part of American culture is an idea central to the project of Asian American studies, a field not usually associated with Said and postcolonial studies. Con-sidering the history of relations between East and West, the postco-lonial and the Asian American are for obvious reasons quite resonant concepts. Yet at the same time, obvious historical reasons have kept them apart, namely the chronic resistance of American culture to casting the United States as imperial. Historian William Appleman Williams, almost fifty years ago, described this "traditional view":

> [E]xcept for a brief and rapidly dispelled aberration at the turn of the century, America has been anti-imperialist throughout its history. . . . [A] unique com-bination of economic power, intellectual and practical genius, and moral rigor enables America to check enemies of peace and progress — and build a better world—without erecting an empire in the process.[3]

For confirmation of this idea, one need only turn to the fact that em-pire building is antithetical to a national culture famously founded on Thomas Jefferson's anticolonial Declaration of Independence.[4] *Model-Minority Imperialism* argues that this liberatory impulse to "check en-emies of peace and progress" becomes the very vehicle for the new imperialism, figured in the contemporary period as the convergent ideals of multiculturalism and globalization, which are the leading an-tidotes to an accumulation of historical forces and conditions antago-nistic to peace and progress, such as war and underdevelopment.

Multiculturalism and globalization have become the two guiding ideologies of the contemporary period that seek to explain the value of difference. In this capacity, they set the stage for the critiques of-fered by both Asian American and postcolonial studies. U.S. multi-culturalism emerged as the latest response to what Michael Omi and Howard Winant call the "racial dictatorship" that the United States — indeed the New World—practiced for its entire history up to the civil rights era.[5] Globalization emerged as the means by which political freedom and economic prosperity are spread throughout a decolonizing world, becoming particularly ascendant with the U.S. triumph in the cold war. What both have in common—with each other and with empire—is a will to legitimate the alignment of difference, to turn differences of gendered racialization and economic disparity into an opportunity to demonstrate better living through late capitalism.

Yet both multiculturalism (especially since the 1992 Los Angeles riots) and globalization (especially since the 1999 World Trade Organization protests in Seattle) have begun to unravel in recent years, revealing that they bear uncanny resemblance to the very ideologies and practices they had emerged to displace. From that unraveling, a history that had virtually disappeared is being redrawn into visibility, namely the emergence of U.S. imperialism. That revisionist history shows us how the postcolonial Oriental under globalization converges with the Asian American under multiculturalism.

The current ethos of revisionism, which was both occasioned and emboldened by Said's *Orientalism,* has wrought profound and lasting changes to the meaning of American culture in the world. And this revisionism has finally reached the United States, primarily taking the form of multiculturalism, with its emblematic invocations of pluralism, relativism, and the valorization of previously denigrated categories of persons, places, and cultures. *Orientalism* made possible a reassessment of the material conditions and the discursive adventures of "the West" in its vacillating confrontations with oriental difference.

And it is here that the fields of postcolonial studies and Asian American studies productively converge: struggles over the meaning of difference. Confrontation with difference is the sine qua non of empire; the management of alterity is fundamentally the project and the problem of imperialism. Difference has alternately been a source of immense fear, of irreversible corruption, of unwanted burden, of simply the unknown. It has also been a source of outrageous opportunity, for converted souls, for bottomless consumers, for ego gratification, and for inexpensive resources, human and otherwise.

The dialectic of the project of empire and the problems it purports to solve have made empire building an ambivalent enterprise, undertaken repeatedly despite a long history of glories that have consistently ended in failure. Uniquely situated in that history is the American Oriental, a figure embodying the lost hopes and dreams of a doomed empire that, at its moment of emergence, seemed like a good idea. This study examines the ways that Asian American cultural politics unburdens the emergence of U.S. imperialism and thereby burdens the present with a past it once needed to forget.

Through analysis of the cultures of U.S. imperialism, each of the chapters in this book examines the manifestations of empire. Collectively they demonstrate that attempts to assimilate Asian difference into American culture have shown not only the contradictions of national culture, but the extent to which conceptions of empire inform and indeed constitute American nationalism. Individually and collectively, each of the chapters traces the process by which empire emerged and was unburdened through Asian American cultural politics.

Emergence, unburdening, and empire itself have multiple meanings when coming to terms with the history of U.S. imperialism. In particular, Michel Foucault's notion of "emergence" (*Entstehung,* or what he describes as "a moment of arising") is important because it allows us to map genealogies for concepts in circulation, rather than retelling linear and developmental histories that reify and legitimate the status quo.[6] From grasping emergence we can revisit pasts that lay dormant, misunderstood, or forgotten until new constituencies formed to awaken, understand, and remember. Emergence, then, is useful for coming to terms with U.S. imperialism because, as W. A. Williams notes, traditional American history has routinely refused to do so. The history of U.S. imperialism therefore resists a straightforward and positivist retelling due to the tradition of the plausible deniability of empire.

In grasping the history of empire in American culture, therefore, two simultaneous operations need to take place. On the one hand, we need to remember the events and conditions that occasioned the rise of empire as an explanatory model for understanding the course of American civilization. On the other hand, we also need to reckon with the conditions and desires that prevented that knowledge from being institutionalized until the sanctioned revisionism of the contemporary period. Emergence then refers to the historical events that took place to force a moment of decision to take up imperialism, most notably in 1898, with the coming of the Spanish-American War. And emergence also means the return of the repressed in a moment that found itself needing to remember that history, most notably in the contemporary period, when new social movements radically revised history, in Said's terms, to "inventory" previously unacknowledged traces of "domination" that culturally legitimated empire.

The disappearance of empire presents both an opportunity and a challenge to counternarratives, in the texts analyzed in these chapters and in the unfolding of this book itself. I am therefore concerned with outlining a methodology for apprehending empire, and the first three chapters describe that method, while the final two chapters extend and apply that method. As a whole, then, *Model-Minority Imperialism* examines moments and conditions when empire became recognizable when previously it had not been. Consequently, this book focuses on an understanding of why the present found itself ready to see a previously unrecognized past. It focuses on the emergence of an epistemology for empire that may prove more successful at rendering U.S. imperialism visible than was possible before Asian American cultural politics. This process of representing is always dialectical. That is, Asian American cultural politics sets the conditions of emergence for these practices of reading and representation, while at the same time, these practices make possible the idea of Asian American cultural politics.

U.S. imperialism, in its own moment of conspicuous emergence at the turn of the twentieth century, arose as acts and policies in need of legitimation. As chapter 2, "An Ever-Emergent Empire: The Discourse of American Exceptionalism," discusses, the discourse of U.S. imperialism would codify American empire as a break from the then-extant imperial projects of European powers, encumbered as they were with territorial and administrative apparatuses and the charge of shouldering "the white man's burden." For America's traditional views of itself, 1898 figures as a "rapidly dispelled aberration."[7] Now, under revisionism, we can also see 1898 as a precedent for the legitimation of future practices. As aberration, 1898 then becomes a moment to redefine empire and/or to reject it. American culture did both, and the later emergence of Asian American cultural politics makes it possible to see this new empire. This new formation of empire resisted being saddled by colonization's direct methods of control and the moral ambiguities of establishing state structures for ruling, to quote the frank language of the *Encyclopedia Britannica,* "over people generally unwilling to accept such control."[8]

The year 1898 occasions, then, the unburdening of empire, the removal of the ideological and material encumbrances that make expansion hard to legitimate. In response to this challenge, American culture reinvents and redefines empire as an informal means of control that actually reinforces American ideals.[9] Indeed, the displacement of European colonial control sets the stage for the legitimacy of effective neocolonial relations under nominal postcolonialism. At the turn of the century, the putative liberations of the Kingdom of Hawaii and Spanish holdings in the Caribbean and the Pacific were therefore a precedent for an empire on the rise.[10]

Even the Philippines, despite being a formal colony of the United States, was simultaneously, even perversely *post*colonial after the banner events of 1898, in relation to Spain at least. As Amy Kaplan has observed, 1898 must be considered not as a watershed and an originary moment for American empire, but as a node in multiple and overlapping historical trajectories of American empire. Such trajectories would go through the settlement of the so-called frontier and the establishment of the racial order of the Jim Crow South.[11] This study follows Kaplan's approach to 1898 by understanding that moment as simultaneously exceptional and paradigmatic for the codification of empire in American culture. *Model-Minority Imperialism* extends that approach in a consideration of the ways that Asian American cultural politics of the contemporary period necessarily takes us through the history and discourses of 1898, or what we might refer to as the "idea of 1898."

This study proceeds from a convergence of three main fields: postcolonial cultural studies, critical American studies, and Asian American studies. *Model-Minority Imperialism* focuses on how, over time, the practices and discourses of U.S. imperialism necessarily became legible as almost forgotten memories that erupted at a time that somehow needed to remember, but routinely did not and even could not. From postcolonial cultural studies, this book derives its approaches to questions of the transitions into and out of imperialism. From critical American studies, this book derives its approaches to questions of the ever-widening contexts in which U.S. culture and nationalism need to be placed. And from Asian American studies, this book derives its commitment to generative critiques and alternatives to emergent standpoints and social movements for which these critiques and alternatives are a condition of recognized being. What links these approaches is an investment in revising and indeed remembering pasts that have eluded the contented present, but have also haunted discontented ones that have generated new social movements, such as the Asian American movement.

These acts of remembering reference the conditions of forgetting. Such newly perceptible ignorance is a site for apprehending how knowledge had seemed complete and coherent before the recognition of gaps and incoherences. Said said such ignorance was a systematic feature of imperialism, succinctly describing imperialism as "material that paradoxically cannot be overlooked but systematically has been."[12] I argue that this systematic overlooking became fundamental to the project of an unburdened empire under the stewardship of the United States. And once and future imperialisms emerge at the convergent cresting of multiculturalism and globalization. Both multiculturalism and globalization can be seen as sharing the familiarly systematic trappings of the very imperial visions they sought to displace. In culture we see how the failures and projects of the present uncannily resonate with the failures and projects of the past. The recognition of this resemblance can be difficult and painful, as we can see from the following dramatization of the process by which Asian American cultural politics recuperates the emergence of U.S. imperialism.

I begin *Model-Minority Imperialism* with Said's generally overlooked invocation of his own status as an Oriental in *Orientalism* and this lost scene of Rio's breakdown to help us grasp the look and feel of the emergence of U.S. imperialism. Each is an against-the-grain approach to their respective fields. Said is invoking his identity as an immigrant from the Orient, as would an Asian American text, and Hagedorn's play eventually downplays her formation to focus on a critique of European colonialism. These two examples are made possible and meaningful through Asian American cultural politics. The meanings of both Asian American cultural politics and the emergence of U.S. imperialism are central to *Model-Minority Imperialism* as well as to the historical unburdening of empire that this book traces. The conditions that unburdened empire—both in terms of a return of the repressed and as the historical informalization of imperialism—are dependent on each other.

Throughout the discussions of texts in this book, three main themes will emerge as the common sites for Asian American studies and the postcolonial field: (1) the project of liberation and education; (2) changing modes of representing Asian difference and therefore incorporating it into American culture, especially through new forms of abstraction and reification; and ultimately, (3) the trope of failed assimilation. Together these themes comprise the main sites of convergence between Asian American cultural politics and the critical study of empire, two revisionist fields that have made previously unacknowledged histories undeniable. This is not to say that the convergences are homologies between, say, territorial colonization and canonical inclusion or post-emancipation Reconstruction and U.S. colonization of Pacific archipelagoes. There are resemblances and there are even connections, but the specifics of these various contexts cannot, of course, be elided. To elide these differences irresponsibly would mean a repetition of imperial tendencies, masked as a benevolent liberalism. The work that this study performs is to locate moments of arresting convergence, and further, to assert that these convergences manifest as and at Asian American cultural politics.

The chapters here are arranged in an alternating chronological structure that takes us back and forth between current critiques of globalization and multiculturalism to moments in their genealogy. In tracing the three main motifs above—liberation, reification, and failed assimilation—the first three chapters outline a reading methodology, accumulating specific implications that become legible at the convergence of Asian American cultural politics and the emergence of U.S. imperialism.

Together, chapters 1 and 2 elaborate the dialectical relationship of an ethos of revisionism and the recoverable histories that revisionism makes possible. They explore the ways that these recovered histories occasioned the ethos of revisionism, as well as how that revisionism set the terms for historical recovery. Chapter 1, "Unburdening Empire: The Cultural Politics of Asian American Difference," examines the convergence of conceptions of a globally expansive empire and an assimilative national culture. From the 1890s to the 1980s, Asian difference goes from being a peril that should be excluded and exploited to being the imperiled that should be incorporated, uplifted, apologized to, and at times, literally healed.[13] The transition from menace to model minority conveniently rendered state power not only legitimate but benevolent.

Chapter 2, "An Ever-Emergent Empire: The Discourse of American Exceptionalism," turns primarily to the debates around empire at the turn of the twentieth century. It examines the ironies of the durably renewable American exceptionalism that routinely emerges in the face of overtly imperial formations. By tracking the uneven fates of turn-of-the-century representations of imperialism, such as L. Frank Baum's seemingly timeless *The Wonderful Wizard of Oz* (1900) and William Hope Harvey's dated *Coin on Money, Trusts, and Imperialism* (1899), we track not only the ways in which empire was spoken of but also the strangeness of the experience of finding empire in American culture and the strangeness of that strangeness. That strangeness is what Asian American cultural politics confronts and reanimates. Apprehending the dialectical relationship between contemporary identity politics and the history of U.S. imperialism occasions a reinterpretation of the meaning of Asian difference in American history and culture.[14]

U.S. imperialism set the conditions for Asian immigration to the West—but then it disappears. It disappears *as* imperialism proper by branding imperialism as a European problem that American culture, in various ways, has solved. The current manifestations of that solution are multiculturalism and globalization, the two ideologies that have been most effective for enabling U.S. imperialism to perform its disappearing act. This disappearing act thus produces Asian immigration to the West as *not* the consequence of imperialism. Asian immigration can fit the familiar epic of "The New Colossus," Emma Lazarus's famous 1883 poem cast at the foot of the Statue of Liberty to give meaning to the "huddled masses" of immigrants crowding at the illumined "Golden Door." Asian immigration is then free to enact the satisfying narrative of immigration from the old world to the New World, from tradition to modernity, from persecution to freedom, from darkness to the light, from "yearning to breathe free" to actually breathing free as a model minority. The material history of Asian Americans has come to militate against this very epic of America because, for most of the history of the United States, Asian immigrants were excluded.[15]

Asian American critique makes visible the links between the contradictory demands of U.S. capitalism's fundamental need to emphasize raced and gendered difference and national culture's profound anxiety around those very same bases of difference. Asian American critique questions the validity and the satisfactions of that narrative of the journey to "the West." As postcolonial theorist Edouard Glissant provocatively reminds us: "The West is not in the West. It is a project, not a place."[16] The material history of Asian Americans is an expression of both the "place" and the "project" of the West. Asian Americans have routinely struggled against being the screen for such projects by asserting the fact of material history.

A formative assertion for the Asian American movement was "We are not new here," emphasizing that an Asian presence in American history, as producers and consumers, is a long and significant one.[17] Such an assertion has the fundamental effect of rearticulating the conditions that required it to be said: that is, the movement needed to stress Asian American "not-newness" because it was not common knowledge, even among Asian Americans themselves. The history and stakes of this struggle are recounted and recast in both chapter 1 and chapter 3, "'The American Earth Was Like a Huge Heart': Old Dreams and the New Imperialism."

The chapter sequence, then, is as follows. Chapter 1 looks at the resonance between the model-minority myth and imperialism. Chapter 2 looks at the ways in which American exceptionalism confounds efforts to see connections between domestic racial politics and extraterritorial acquisitions. Chapter 3 looks at the ways that Asian American cultural politics confounds the expansion of the canon of American literature to comfortably include Asian American narratives. With the groundwork laid by these three chapters, chapter 4, "Uplifting Race, Reconstructing Empire," can argue for convergences between African American and Asian/Asian American racialization. Specifically, this fourth chapter considers the discourses of two similarly abortive episodes: Reconstruction and U.S. imperialism. The final chapter, "'Everybody Wants to Be Farrah': Absurd Histories and Historical Absurdities," examines in detail how one text, R. Z. Linmark's *Rolling the R's* (1995) manifests and reshapes the convergence of Asian American cultural politics and the emergence of U.S. imperialism. An unruly group of fifth-graders in the Kalihi section of Oahu become gloriously bad subjects of the new empire, confounding narratives of coming of age in the American Pacific under the new world order of postcolonialism and incipient multiculturalism.

With the rise of postcolonialism, another slogan has come to be significant to Asian Americans: "We are here because you were there."[18] Originally invoked by and for immigrants to England from its former colonies, that slogan erupts at the convergence of Asian American cultural politics and the emergence of U.S. imperialism. At that convergence, narratives of uplift and civilization, as well as progress and development (globalization) and inclusion and tolerance (multiculturalism), are no longer tenable because the disappeared history of U.S. imperialism reemerges to reveal contradictions embedded within American culture, in the form of underdevelopment, exclusion, and intolerance.

If Asian American culture is to displace these narratives, it must make U.S. imperialism reappear. In so doing, Asian American texts describe and dramatize the process by which they and U.S. imperialism disappeared in the first place. This recovery of U.S. imperialism emerged in the era of multiculturalism at the very moment when Asian American literature became mobilized to reproduce narratives of liberal inclusion. These comforting narratives of liberal inclusion were predicated on the disappearance of the very U.S. imperialism that emerged to manage Asian difference at the outset of the period of U.S. global hegemony that publisher Henry Luce, in early 1941, famously referred to as "the American Century."[19] In rethinking that century's opening and closing, Asian American culture functions as both a manifestation and a critique of U.S. global hegemony. In its critique of multiculturalism, Asian American culture recalls the violences and structural inequalities of U.S. imperialism. Simultaneously, in its recalling of U.S. imperialism, Asian American culture more pointedly critiques the very multiculturalism that enabled it to be recognized in the first place. The remainder of this introduction situates the three key concepts of this book: Asian American cultural politics, the emergence of U.S. imperialism, and how they explicate what it means to unburden empire.

On Asian American Cultural Politics

"Asian American Cultural Politics" is the phrase that figures prominently in what has emerged as the most important book on the study of Asian American culture, Lisa Lowe's *Immigrant Acts: On Asian American Cultural Politics* (1996). Her book rescued the category "Asian American" from being unproblematically connected to and contained by pleas for inclusion in a liberal pluralist mosaic of multiculturalism. Her book is decidedly *not*, as its title might suggest, an exploration of the experience of Asian immigrants, treading the well-beaten path of departure from a sending country to resettlement and adjustment on the shores of a resistant new homeland. Lowe avoids the pitfalls of making a case for Asian American culture as an affirmation of hegemony—whether liberal, conservative, or cultural nationalist—or as a site of ceaseless postmodernist play. Instead, her study emphasizes the cultural politics that produces the idea of the Asian American in a dialectical relationship with the histories that become not only newly significant to these emergent subjects, but even visible at all because of them. "Asian American critique" emerges as the emblematic process and product of the Asian American cultural production worth our consideration.

Her study synthesizes the ways in which the development of modern capitalism must reckon with the material and ideological stakes of the encounter between U.S. national demands and the abortive management of Asian difference. Asian American cultural politics involves a critical account of class formation and gendered racialization, direct and implicit engagement with the state structures, and the return of repressed histories, as well as the critique of identity politics, the devil's bargains of institutionalization, and the ongoing struggles to rethink movements and their co-optation by hegemony.

Lowe's rich and compelling formulations intimate, but do not quite pin down, what "Asian American cultural politics" means as a concept in circulation; her work in *Immigrant Acts* coins rather than tracks the concept. Inspired by Lowe's work, I therefore begin by breaking down the phrase "Asian American cultural politics" into its constituent parts: *Asian American, cultural, politics.*

First, *Asian American.* Broadly speaking, this concept emerged, as the well-rehearsed story usually goes, as the antidote to the exotifying, objectifying, imperialist term *Oriental.* From this self-naming, those who had been represented show that they can indeed represent themselves. *Asian American* holds out the possibility of the self-determination that begins at self-naming. An ongoing challenge to progressive organizing is ensuring that, once a name has been decided on, the struggle does not effectively *end* at self-naming, and the paralytic quibbles over inclusion, exclusion, and the quest for additional modifiers.[20] That obsession with finding *le mot juste* for an identity category has come to be the hallmark of identity politics, concomitant with its fundamental belief in the viability of representation through cultural and political institutions.[21] More specifically, Asian American becomes a site for "claiming America," whether through earnest appeals to the state for, say, reparations or access to resources, or as an ironic performance designed to demonstrate the state's inability to redress wrongs.[22]

Next comes *cultural*. It is customary and useful to turn to literary scholar Raymond Williams, who reminds us that culture is "one of the two or three most complicated words in the English language."[23] It ranges from its most literal uses, referring to the growing of plants, to the formation of subjects through education. This process of formation is immanent, therefore, in other meanings of culture, as in the aestheticians' notions of beautiful and sublime high art, as well as culture being the stuff of ethnicity that concerns anthropologists and other social scientists. Williams's discussion of culture is particularly useful for its emphasis on the implicit and explicit processes relating to something that is often thought of as a product. Culture comes to be reified as a thing that a person or a group possesses, distinct from its becoming and the subjects that it produces. By emphasizing culture as a process, the struggles that take place through, with, and over culture can be more precisely appreciated. Indeed, the politics of culture becomes manifest at the breakdown of these processes, resulting in what Louis Althusser has called the "bad subjects" of an "ideological state apparatus."[24] The cultural politics of new social movements recuperate and revise *bad* from meaning bad to meaning, if not exactly good, at least no longer bad in the same way.

Finally, *politics*. Politics, curiously absent from Williams's *Keywords*, conventionally concerns the state and governance. Politics, broadly and generally understood, is simply power and its legitimated and unequal distribution. It references social and economic relations, the public sector, and the notoriously not-personal. This latter conception of politics has led to residual yet still powerful notions of the "separate spheres" of culture, economy, civil society, and the state. Less conventionally, politics concerns all social institutions and "governmentality," the generative term coined by Foucault to describe the ways in which all aspects of knowledge and behaviors came to be invested with an importance that reinforced existing institutions of control and led to an endless proliferation of new ones.[25]

The notion of "cultural politics" is important for situating the interventions of "Asian American." Cultural politics invokes simultaneously the separation of the spheres of culture and politics and their synthesis. As the phrase "cultural politics" emerged, it was used in British cultural studies to emphasize the displacement of deterministically class-based mobilizations, as in the important early work of Stuart Hall and Paul Gilroy.[26] Cultural politics and its related formation, cultural studies, are both products of the New Left, a shift allowing an appreciation of the "relative autonomy" (Althusser) of base and superstructure that refused to resolve all struggle to being a manifestation of class conflict, as with the Old Left. Under this new epistemology, gendered racialization, national (dis)identification, and class formation all have the status of being both symptomatic *and* determining of relations of production.[27]

In the contemporary U.S. context, however, with its blatant and subtle racism and its legacy of imagining itself as classless, "cultural politics" has meant the infusion of historical materialism and political economy into critiques of such racial formations as genocide, slavery, segregation, and exclusion. Much important scholarship on either side of the Atlantic, or the Pacific, was devoted to explicating the complex relationship of race and class, particularly dealing with the post-emancipation period onward, as the link between race and labor under African American slavery is rather unambiguous. The challenge after emancipation is to demonstrate that race and class persist, despite the end of legalized enslavement based on race. The work of such scholars as Edna Bonacich, Alexander Saxton, and Lucie Cheng has explored the complex racial order that emerged in the late nineteenth century, as Asian difference became increasingly—and at times disproportionately—important to American lawmakers, labor leaders, and captains of industry.[28]

Asian American cultural politics emerges from these conditions and critically rearticulates them. Asian American cultural politics sets the terms for describing the process by which Asian difference was and is managed in American culture. It references and remobilizes the history of gendered racialization, the unstable dictates of national culture, and the shifts in the mode of production that are visible at sites of contradiction emblematic of Asian American cultural politics. In an attempt to situate Asian racialization amid the historical discourse of the turn-of-the-century race "problem," chapter 4, "Uplifting Race, Reconstructing Empire," looks at the convergences between the burdens of empire and the dominant discourse of otherness in circulation at the time: the so-called "Negro Problem."[29] For the discourse of U.S. imperialism at the turn of the century, the post-emancipation incorporation of African Americans was the elephant in the room. The resonances between discourses of Asian and Asian American assimilation and African American uplift demand that we rethink blackness and Asianness simultaneously and comparatively, as mutually constitutive discourses. That is, rather than rearticulating the conventional notion that the racialization of Asians is, in a strict adherence to chronology, always reducible to being an epiphenomenon of black alterity, this chapter demonstrates how the crises and resolutions of American empire in the Pacific recast the failures of Reconstruction.[30] In doing so, this chapter traces the ongoing struggles of American culture to manage forms of difference that must both affirm the civilizing mission of the United States to reform the Other into the same and ensure the profitability of its capitalist development through the reproduction of Otherness as a site of exploitation. This dilemma becomes the emergent dilemma of U.S. imperialism. And the solution to empire emerges to figure the possible solution to all race "problems."

The Emergence of U.S. Imperialism

"U.S. imperialism" is a once provocative phrase that is now more currently in circulation.[31] But like many once provocative hypotheses, it has a history of conceptual struggle. That is, the phrase is occasionally voiced, followed by qualification and explanation, with a hint of apology, or the conspicuous lack of contrition, as chapter 2 discusses. U.S. imperialism describes the ideologies and attendant discourses of how the United States imagined and explained its varieties of growth. At times it alternately excused, glorified, excoriated, bemoaned, self-pitied, and puzzled. It went by numerous and well-documented aliases and euphemisms: errand into the wilderness, settling the frontier, Manifest Destiny, interventionism, keeping the world safe for democracy, finding a Passage to India, ferreting out weapons of mass destruction, exercising dollar diplomacy, and advocating neoliberalism. Each of these is a form and a moment in what can properly and somewhat broadly be called U.S. imperialism.

Despite this broadness of interpretation, the explanatory power of this concept has managed to remain, particularly because empire remains conceptually at odds with the dominant ideals of U.S. nationalism, yet undeniably pervasive in the material history of American civilization. Such a contradiction becomes the engine of cultural politics in general and Asian American cultural politics in particular. The capaciousness of the notion of U.S. imperialism is what keeps it so compelling, especially in its more grandiose form, empire.

To better grasp the process of unburdening empire, this book is organized to promote a dialectical understanding of the revisionism of the present and the pasts that it reanimates. The sequence of the chapters here seeks to maintain this dialectical approach in the inevitably linear form of a monograph. The chapters can certainly be read separate from each other, as extended discussions of a particular problematic or theme. Nevertheless, their sequence is designed to destabilize unidirectional flows of influence that might unduly posit that the past made the present possible. A central contention of *Model-Minority Imperialism* is that the fractured conditions of the present necessarily made, and make, the past recognizable, while these new pasts maintain those conditions of possibility.

A dominant progression that *Model-Minority Imperialism* seeks to complicate is the notion that American nationalism "came of age" through its engagement with—even its repudiation of—empire.[32] As Gauri Viswanathan notes in the British context, narratives of national maturation through empire building neglect to account for the uneven but multidirectional flow of influence between colonial periphery and metropolitan core.[33] Asian American cultural politics, with its problematic position between the metropolitan West and the colonized East, emerges, then, as a site for appreciating this dialectic. That is, from Asian American cultural politics we can appreciate the intertwined relationship between ostensibly domestic struggles for civil rights, on the one hand, and geopolitical contests between putatively unified fronts of nations on the other. For this book's account of the emergence of U.S. imperialism, the practice of empire emerges both before and after its legitimation, in a dialectic made uneven and unstable by the politics of national and imperial memory. Amnesia emerges as perhaps the highest form of legitimation so that the present is filled with, to invoke Avery Gordon's suggestive image, "furniture without memories." That is, the process of production is lost amid the force of the present's presence. Asian American cultural politics makes remembering possible and meaningful.

A few words should then be said about the way this book is put together. The structure of the chapters attempts to dramatize the alternation between an emphasis on the emergence of a revisionist subjectivity and an emphasis on the emergence of recovered history. Therefore, chapters 1 and 3 concern identity politics and canonical demands, respectively. Chapter 1, through a reading of the ambivalences that accompany the official recognition and incorporation of Asian difference into American culture, examines the unintended consequences that emerged from recent and successful mobilizations for civil rights and other institutionalized forms of recognition. These mobilizations, and to some extent their limits, set the conditions for the historical revisionism that Asian American cultural politics performs. Asian American cultural politics comes to need to routinely figure Asian American difference as plotted onto a spectrum of damage and repair that comes to resonate with and serve conceptions of U.S. imperialism. Particularly with the rise of the "model-minority myth," struggles against past discrimination are used to legitimate the evacuation of Asian American difference.

Chapter 3, "'The American Earth Was Like a Huge Heart': Old Dreams and the New Imperialism," thematically examines the ways that Asian American narratives inhabit and fail to be contained by the assimilative models ascribed to them in dominant culture. The failures of assimilation are a common trope of both Asian American and postcolonial texts. Chapter 3 argues that this shared critique becomes an opportunity for remembering the emergence of U.S. imperialism. Through an analysis of the critique of assimilation in famous and studied endings in the Asian American literary canon, we can see how narratives of domestication and Americanization are unlearned, by characters and by readers. Along with chapter 1, these chapters focus more on the critical revisionism forged in the contemporary moment as setting the stage for the possibility of retelling imperialist pasts. They serve to situate the cultural politics of the contemporary moment.

Chapters 2 and 4 focus on the emergence of the empire question at the turn of the twentieth century and the meaning of race after Reconstruction, respectively. These chapters examine imperial pasts to establish the past's uncanny resonance with the crises and conditions of the present. Chapter 2 makes a case for the paradoxical abundance, not absence, of empire in American history. Indeed, empire's ubiquity is its invisibility as it hides in plain sight in forms that are both frank and subtle. We need to grasp how empire is at once an allegorical structure of intelligibility and a material history and trace. Using a related methodology, chapter 4 is concerned with both finding empire in unexpected places and finding in the discourse of empire resonant histories previously unnoticed. For chapter 4, that specifically means finding the discourse of Reconstruction, and its failures, in the discourse of U.S. imperialism and its failures. It also means finding the discourse of U.S. imperialism in the discourse of Reconstruction.

The final chapter, "'Everybody Wants to Be Farrah': Absurd Histories and Historical Absurdities," explores the implications of these reading practices through an extended treatment of a central text that reinvigorated Asian American cultural politics with its brilliant humor: R. Z. Linmark's *Rolling the R's* (1995). Chapter 5 uses postmodernist strategies of juxtaposition and nonlinear narration to revisit the emergence of U.S. imperialism, as both tragedy and farce. From the sassy queer adolescents of Linmark's paean to 1970s Hawaii, we see how a mission can begin with the best of intentions to uplift, civilize, and Christianize, but lead to futures neither intended nor imagined. What might simply be a text of endless play instead leads to a wickedly funny dramatization of historical revisionism. From our vantage point, equipped to juxtapose McKinley's colonizing rationale from 1898 with the spectacle of the sex show from 1982, we see clearly that those intentions were never realized. The detours of history have become our present.

U.S. imperialism becomes newly visible when we recognize the present's queer connections to a lost moment of emergence. From that moment, a genealogy of modernity can be mapped. We are then able to connect a recovered past to the present that somehow needed to remember, to reopen a cold case and retell history. Walter Benjamin wrote that "to represent the past historically is not to recognize it the way it was. It means to seize hold of a memory as it flashes up at a moment of danger."[34] This study is concerned with inhabiting that everpresent moment of danger produced through memories that have flashed up, seemingly of their own volition. However, those flashes both illuminate and are the products of subjects, almost lost to both the present and the past. From this examination, we can consider why a memory could and did flash up when it did, as well as the nature of that particular danger. That emergence—or reemergence—renders an object meaningful because it establishes a pattern based on formerly unrelated events. That emergence is concretized in the contemporary moment through Asian American cultural politics.

The subject and the memory meet and become newly visible at sites of unburdening, as we see with Rio Gonzaga in the Sex Show Montage from the play *Dogeaters*. As she inhabits McKinley discoursing on the unfit–for–self-government Filipinos, she finds herself living out that description by being unable to govern herself. She is face-to-face with herself as an uncanny figure, at once familiar and frightening. The same could be said for Edward Said, recalling his Oriental childhood at a moment when he is about to foment a crisis in the West's self-perception. Like Rio, he, in his own way, chokes on the alterity that he cannot reconcile with the material conditions in his midst, and the result is "Orientalism Now."

Empire Unburdened (ca. 1899)

In his poem "The White Man's Burden" (1899), Rudyard Kipling describes the "thankless years" and the "dear-bought wisdom" that have made the meaning of empire clear: namely, it is a bloody burden. *Model-Minority Imperialism* examines the changing meaning of U.S. colonialism at the turn of the twentieth century by considering the relationship between Asian American cultural politics and the emergence of U.S. imperialism. At the same time, this book also traces how this famously forgotten episode in American history has made a resurgence in the late twentieth century. Almost a century earlier, in the wake of the events of 1898, a new vocabulary for speaking about the United States as an empire fleetingly emerged. Imperialism and the language of empire, however, lost their legitimacy as the movements for decolonization dictated the codification of an alternative vision of modernity to lighten and displace the "white man's burden." Rather than own up to the sheepish embarrassment at having become an empire in 1898, the United States must share in Europe's imperialist self-pity.

Kipling certainly did not invent the phrase "White Man's Burden" when he composed his rhyme of that title, but his is probably the most famous articulation of its meaning.[35] He published his infamous doggerel in *McClure's* magazine in February 1899 to coincide with the U.S. Congress's debate over the fate of the United States and the Philippine Islands. Indeed, the subtitle to his versification is "The United States and the Philippine Islands." It is not considered one of his better works.

While Kipling's poem clearly calls on the United States to colonize the Philippines, it does so in a rather ironic fashion: by describing how unpleasant and burdensome the job is. The imperatives of the first stanza alone convey the miserable labors of administering an empire: "Take up," "Send forth," "bind," "serve," "wait . . . On." Rather than extolling the glories of having an empire on which the sun never sets, the poem makes a martyr of the colonizer. Kipling can then end the poem by challenging the United States to rise to the occasion and join the colonial powers at the height of the period Eric Hobsbawn rightly dubbed "the age of empire."[36]

> Comes now, to search your manhood
> Through all the thankless years,
> Cold, edged with dear-bought wisdom,
> The judgment of your peers!

Based on the British model, self-pity rather than glory will be the likely result of the colonial project in the Philippines, or anywhere else for that matter. Nevertheless, the choice to colonize is not exactly preferable; there simply is no choice. As President McKinley put it, "[T]here was nothing left for us to do."[37]

After vociferous debate, the United States eventually, though uneasily, took up the burden that Kipling famously described, and which other contemporaries warned against.[38] So uneasy was that burden that American history would soon forget that the United States held colonies. The burdening and unburdening of America with empire constitute what may be the great amnesia of the twentieth century.

Yet there were populations within American culture who did not share the same luxury of forgetting, peoples for whom the question of empire was not merely a political debate but a visceral and transformative experience and memory. This study examines how memories of the emergence of U.S. imperialism—or perhaps more precisely, the scarcity of them—structure the meaning and practice of empire today.

At the turn of the century, the United States became a frank and subtle imperialist beyond its contiguous borders. The frankly imperial status faded away amid a chorus of its contradictions with core

American values, but the subtle empire was only getting started. Arguments for and against becoming a "saltwater empire"—an empire based explicitly on European models—once spoke with a now forgotten frankness about the civilizing mission of the United States.[39] Gone is the fleeting legitimacy of the "benevolent assimilation" of "little brown brothers," or the uplift and Christianization of the heathen, or even the opening of "the China market."[40] That arrogance has since been displaced by a different type of arrogant conception of modernity that champions development and globalization, as well as multiculturalism and its forms of diversity management. Only in recent years have the cracks in that ideology begun to make headlines, as the uprising at the World Trade Organization summit in Seattle made abundantly clear in 1999. Such events showed that the subtlety of the new imperialism was becoming frank again, and the United States could no longer deny that it was a key player, a denial that was more legitimate a century before.

In *Orientalism*, Said announced to a stunned world of cultural historians that, by 1914, 85 percent of the earth's surface was under the control of colonial powers.[41] Of that vast 85 percent, only a paltry few holdings in the Caribbean and the Pacific could be officially claimed as extraterritorial additions to the United States. And of those locations, only the Philippines was imagined as something more than just a naval base beside some plantations and bordellos. The Philippines was a colony in the proper, modern, flag-flying, European sense. This new extraterritoriality became a problem because it both challenged and affirmed the frontier thesis of American history, articulated so influentially by Frederick Jackson Turner in 1893.[42] American national identity and prosperity were built resolutely on the idea of settler colonialism, with its westward expansion and its removal of a defeated and nearly annihilated indigenous population. Extraterritorial colonialism was a new formation in American culture. The United States was in a quandary over its fundamental anticolonialism—of being, in the discourse of the Age of Revolution, "an empire of laws and not men"—alongside its expansionism.

Even as late as the 1970s and 1980s, when Said's *Orientalism* radically recast the British literary canon as a rationalization of imperial policy, the revisionism of American literature was taking shape as multiculturalism. Multiculturalism was, and is, an ideology traditionally bounded by the nation-state. It seeks to codify a comfortable sameness amid difference, and a tolerable difference amid sameness.[43] The undeniable but inadequately explained racial and ethnic heterogeneity of the United States demanded, and still demands, an explanation: why does so much difference remain a source of discord and exploitation, rather than producing unity, equality, freedom, and—to quote a 1980s recruitment slogan from my alma mater—"excellence amidst diversity"? The meaning and persistence of that burdensome discord is what this study explores.

This study examines the unexpected convergences between contemporary conceptions of plurality under liberal multiculturalism and the discourse of the colonial project of the United States at the turn of the century. Those convergences appear not only at visions of peripheral incorporation emblematic of these projects, but more tellingly at their shared contradictions and the alternatives that become discernible through their contradiction with that project. Considering the history of relations between East and West, a particularly revealing site for appreciating those contradictions and alternatives is Asian American cultural politics. These concerns are always a question of the meanings we make of history and its telling. Ranajit Guha, venerable historian of the celebrated Subaltern Studies Group, reminds us of the need for a new conception of history:

> There is nothing that historiography can do to eliminate . . . distortion, for [distortion] is built into its optics. What it can do, however, is to acknowledge such distortion as parametric—as a datum which determines the form of the exercise itself, and to stop pretending that it can *fully* grasp a past consciousness and reconstitute it. Then and only then might the distance between the latter and the historian's perception of it be reduced significantly enough to amount to a close approximation which is the best one could hope for.[44]

Model-Minority Imperialism outlines the ways that Asian American literature and culture came to recuperate the emergence of U.S. imperialism, parametric distortions and all. From this history, we can ask and even answer the question, with due deference to W. E. B. DuBois, how did—and does—it feel to be a burden?

U N B U R D E N I N G   E M P I R E

THE CULTURAL POLITICS OF ASIAN AMERICAN DIFFERENCE

> We have been trying to make a Filipino over into an American.
> As well expect to turn a palm tree into an elm!
> — Henry Parker Willis, *Our Philippine Problem,* 1905

> [F]actors that contribute to discrimination against Asian
> Americans and create barriers to equal opportunity for Asian
> Americans . . . (1) Viewing Asian Americans as a Model Minority.
> — U.S. Commission on Civil Rights, *Civil Rights Issues*
> *Facing Asian American in the 1990s,* 1992

DESPITE STRENUOUS EFFORTS to debunk the model-minority myth, there is perhaps no idea that remains more dominant about Asian Americans than the conception that Asian Americans are a group that has managed to achieve economic, political, and cultural success in the face of adversity. Asian Americans, according to the myth, have transformed themselves from menaces into model citizens, from an industrial reserve army into entrepreneurs, from unassimilable aliens into decorated allies, from classed subjects into rights-bearing individuals, perhaps even undergoing an extreme makeover from "a palm tree into an elm." It is an inspirational story, and that capacity to inspire is precisely the problem as the putative success of Asian Americans is used to discipline other minority groups seeking social and economic justice through majoritarian means.[1] The modern Asian American movement has invested much of its energy in critiquing the model-minority myth to the point that, with the exception of hate crimes, no other issue has been such a visible priority for Asian American mobilization.

At the heart of the model-minority myth is the notion that American culture can adapt to absorb persons and populations who had once been deemed explicitly, in the language of the Alien Land Laws, "ineligible for citizenship" and, in the language of colonization, "unfit for self-government."[2] The model-minority myth has functioned as a way of reading progressive historical change. That is, the present has reckoned with uncomfortable pasts and is doing right by the wronged by incorporating them, or, more precisely, by allowing a putatively color-blind and gender-neutral market to sort things out. The resulting vision is the smooth and compliant incorporation of Asian difference into American civilization. This chapter argues, therefore, that the critique of the model minority can be understood as a critique of U.S. imperialism. At the intersection of the model-minority myth and U.S. imperialism is a critical account of how the incorporation of Asian difference into American culture can serve questionable ideological needs.

In particular, this chapter considers how Asian American cultural politics has recovered lost histories that the present can no longer deny. Yet the recovery of those pasts — of labor exploitation, of injustices suffered, of colonial projects undertaken — is also a point of access into the needs and desires of the contemporary moment to continue to manage and contain difference. By analyzing the various ways that success stories of Asian Americans have been used, we can critically examine the justification for the means by which Asian difference is, in effect, transcended in the service of the new terms of empire. When we recognize that service, the terms of the old empire become newly visible.

Righting Wrongs in the 1980s

Like Rio Gonzaga reciting President McKinley, we see another Asian American subject reading the words of an American president when Koto "Jack" Tanaka reads a letter from President George H. W. Bush at the end of his daughter's 1992 film documentary, *Who's Going to Pay for These Donuts Anyway?*

> A monetary sum and words alone cannot restore the lost years or erase the painful memories, and neither can they fully convey our nation's resolve to rectify injustice and to uphold the rights of individuals. We can never fully right the wrongs of the past but we can take a clear stand for justice and recognize a serious injustice that was done to the Japanese Americans during World War II.[3]

Jack is representing himself by inhabiting the voice of the one most officially empowered to represent him: the sitting president of the United States. And like Rio, Jack's delivery is similarly tinged with ambivalence. He is being claimed by America, at long last, as an individual. But in this act of reading "words alone," and of accepting "a monetary sum," is he claiming America? At the ostensible end of a protracted and hard-fought struggle, his difference is being put to use by American culture as finally assimilable. The traumas of the past have been unburdened and addressed, reified and redressed.

The triumphs and limits of the redress movement have been a paradigmatic instance of Asian American mobilization for grasping the urgency of historical recovery. I have argued elsewhere that a close examination of Japanese American discourse on internment and redress shows a resistance to the idea that redress would fully right the wrongs of internment.[4] This chapter examines the ways that Asian difference in American culture has routinely functioned as a means for unburdening troubling pasts that have remained unresolved. What the present does with these pasts has been a test of the changing meaning of Asian difference for American civilization. In the contemporary period, the model-minority myth has cast Asian Americans as an aggrieved population that has tested the capacities of American culture to do right by doing very little. This mobilization of difference sets the stage for the recovery of earlier instances when Asian difference was used in the service of what we now recognize as a kind of imperialism. That is, we see the capacity of American culture to absorb persons and histories that once embodied a form of difference that American culture needed to repudiate and exclude. This chapter argues that this feature is at once structural and historical. Specifically, I trace here the contemporary conditions that situated Asian American difference politically as a form of damage in need of repair. For in understanding the appeal and the limits of this narrative of the meaning of Asian difference to American civilization, the narratives' uplift, incorporation, and healing come to figure the meaning of Asian difference in American culture.[5]

Asian Americans are indeed a minority in terms of raw numbers, and this minority status set the stage for their status as a model.[6] Asian Americans, as a category of difference, have also gained a significance beyond those small numbers. The symbolic power of the successful incorporation of Asian difference serves to discipline any other group that has similar grievances. In the contemporary period, the Asian American movement has been defined by its struggle to fight against the questionable uses of its difference.

In February 1992, the United States Commission on Civil Rights issued a 234-page report called *Civil Rights Issues Facing Asian Americans in the 1990s.*[7] The report identified seven "factors that contribute to discrimination against Asian Americans and create barriers to equal opportunity for Asian Americans." Sitting at the top of the list is "Viewing Asian Americans as a Model Minority."[8] This perception implies that Asian Americans have recovered from histories of exclusion, internment, exploitation, and colonialism, and that Asian Americans are therefore not entitled to reparation. To critique the model-minority myth is to assert that the effects of that history are ongoing, despite, as the report states, "statistics revealing the high average family incomes, educational attainment, and occupational status of Asian Americans" (19). Critically examining these often dubious statistics has been an important political activity for the Asian American movement.[9]

Yet in both the assertion and the debunking of the model-minority myth, there are shared conceptions of the nation-state and the meaning of the emergence of a minority category. That is, *Asian American* has political meaning only insofar as it is a category for appealing to the state for addressing inequalities. At issue in this debate is a conception of the state as either laissez-faire or affirmatively acting to undo systemic inequalities.[10] Emerging in the 1960s, the model-minority myth arose as an effective tool for legitimating the dismantling of affirmative action and welfare programs in the conservative 1980s.[11] Asian Americans were trotted out, as demonstrated by the appropriately derisive language of *Aiiieeeee!*, as "miracle synthetic white people," who, to cite the report's third factor, were "unaggressive" and were achieving the American dream through self-reliant pluck rather than agitating for rights.

The model-minority myth therefore served the need of the hegemonic U.S. culture to portray the nation-state as ineffective, bolstering the case for smaller government and privatization. Understood as an argument for the changing role of the nation-state, the model-minority myth has uncanny similarities to emergent notions of globalization. That is, globalization is both celebrated and denounced as signaling the end of the sovereignty of the nation-state as the privileged and irreducible institution in the global order. Entities such as the transnational corporation and the "global city" have purportedly displaced the nation-state as the site for agency, particularly in economic affairs.[12]

The notion of a model minority also places that minority into a developmental trajectory as its best fruition. Members of that minority are a testament to the success of the incorporative capacities of the United States, politically, economically, and culturally. The model minority has become integrated, modernized, and civilized. Beyond the satisfactions of the Horatio Alger narrative of ascendance into the middle class, the power of the model-minority myth, from the fictional Brooklyn Heights obstetrician Heathcliff Huxtable, to writers Richard Rodriguez and Stephen Carter, to strikebreaking linguist S. I. Hayakawa, lies in the ruminative and highly visible overcoming of the history of American racism, whether manifested in slavery, territorial annexation, or wartime internment.[13] Success in conventional terms is taken as a tacit form of forgiveness for the past.

In the quotation above, Jack Tanaka reads words written by the American president. The letter in his hands fills the frame of the screen while he reads the apology. Apologies as a genre of speech reckon with past deeds and thoughts and manifest actions and ideas over which the present now feels guilt-ridden. An apology is an invitation, indeed a plea, to forgive. An apology sets the terms by which forgiveness can be given.[14] In this case, the contrite letter from the chief executive bestows the status of an "individual" whose rights are upheld. The president is in effect declaring, as far as Executive Order 9066 is concerned, that being a "person of Japanese ancestry" is displaced, if not effectively erased, by the "monetary sum and words alone" that transform Jack Tanaka into a wronged individual. In other words, Jack Tanaka can finally become unmarked, his record effectively expunged. He can become what Lisa Lowe calls the "abstract citizen," an entity unmarked in the eyes of official national culture and politics by anything that would mitigate being a voter and a free agent in the market.

Indeed, the will to abstract has been and continues to be a compelling narrative for managing difference, not only in the political sphere, but in culture and economics. Yet abstraction directly contradicts, and erases, a history of the interested mobilization of difference. Lowe writes,

> Abstract labor, subject to capitalist rationalization and the logic of equivalence through wages, is the adjunct of the formal political equality granted through rights and representation by the state. Yet in the history of the United States, capital has maximized its profits not through rendering labor "abstract" but precisely through the social productions of "difference," of restrictive particularity and illegitimacy marked by race, nation, geographical origins, and gender.[15]

Whether it goes by color-blind constitutionalism, assertions of gender-neutrality, or invocations of objective selection criteria, the capacity to render difference as abstract is the antidote to illegitimate forms of discrimination.[16] It should then be no surprise that the official discourse of a 1988 apology, from an era that has been called the "age of apology," would champion abstract citizenship for a population that had lived through a concrete history of being officially different.

Perhaps no single event in Asian American history—not just Japanese American history—was more defining than the internment of "persons of Japanese ancestry" during World War II. Not only were Japanese Americans singled out for persecution, but the fact of corporeal misrecognition prompted a need to differentiate between "Oriental" groups that might otherwise be lumped together.[17] This tenuous coexistence of lumping and splitting is emblematic of the ever-fluctuating category "Asian American." Not only was internment the crucial moment for putting Asian Americans into discourse, but it is also a classic example of how an event falls out of, and then returns to, history. As internment is written into the telling of U.S. history, a shameful and forgotten chapter reaches new generations of Americans. If we take seriously Walter Benjamin's notion that "to articulate the past historically does not mean to recognize it 'the way it was,'" but rather "to seize hold of a memory as it flashes up at a moment of danger," what do we make of the conditions that made long-repressed memories of internment—or any occluded past—flash up? What are these moments of danger that now make it possible for the present to recognize a past that previous generations had blissfully ignored? As Benjamin also wrote, "[E]very image of the past that is not recognized by the present as one of its own concerns threatens to disappear irretrievably."[18] For internment, the issue is more of culpability than guilt.

The question of what to do with this newfound capacity to recognize the past led to the Civil Liberties Act of 1988, of which President George Bush's apology was a part. Even before the passage of House Resolution 442, the government had formally acknowledged that Executive Order 9066 was wrong through such documents as Presidential Proclamation 4417 from President Gerald Ford, dated February 19, 1976. HR 442, with its number shared by the celebrated "Go for Broke" battalion of Japanese American soldiers, owned up to "racial prejudice, wartime hysteria, and a failure of political leadership" as unfortunate factors motivating the mass incarceration. HR 442 not only made a formal apology as a reckoning with the past, but it also offered to pay $20,000 in redress to those who were interned and survived long enough to collect. The government admitted its culpability in perpetrating an injustice and sought to do right by the formerly interned.[19]

Fundamental to what made internment so disturbing is that it was essentially written out of the past and had to be recovered by activists, cultural workers, and scholars.[20] The historical revisionism of the age of multiculturalism has radically restructured the present's relationship to the past. The path from internment to redress is a story of the ways that national culture seeks to reckon with the past. In the wake of this acknowledgment of collective guilt, national culture seeks to accomplish many important tasks of recognition: to recognize the past, to recognize that this past was nearly lost to history, to recognize that this past and its loss produced subjects who deserve to be compensated in some way for past injustice. And in the end, as Bush implies, if injustice is to be "rectified," the recipients of reparations will become "individuals" with "rights upheld." Asian American cultural politics resides at the confrontation between deeply fraught terms, one quite old and the other relatively new: *civil society* and *globalization*. Multiculturalism has been a casualty of these incommensurable terms, as the ostensible similarities between cultures are overshadowed by widening difference. In other words, East and West, and for that matter, North and South, are not as important as global North and global South.[21]

Responding to this confrontation, Asian American cultural politics emerges out of the possibilities and pitfalls of multiculturalism in the United States. Although the cresting of multiculturalism may be behind us, it continues to be an undeniably powerful force for reshaping what Cornel West calls "the new cultural politics of difference" in the wake of the civil rights era.[22] "Racial formations" came to be embraced in an institutional valorization of diversity and an enabling critique of hegemony.[23] A sense of atonement pervaded the many measures taken by individuals and both governmental and nongovernmental organizations to promote a comforting sense of diversity. It is now difficult to see this celebration of diversity as anything other than the interested magnification of some differences to serve as a comforting distraction from others. What matters is not the new differences, but the new samenesses that become recognizable as we look back on the era that James Kyung-Jin Lee calls "the long decade" of the multiculturalist 1980s.[24]

This is the era that mapped out and institutionalized the terrain of cultural categories now in circulation, such as Asian American and Asian Pacific American (and even at one time, Oriental American).[25] The question of what constitutes Asian American culture is an oft-rehearsed but necessary matter to resolve when approaching literature with the increasingly familiar prepositional, "by and about" a particular population, in this case, Asian Americans. The emergence of the category of cultural production called Asian American literature is fundamentally a return of the repressed. In particular, we are at a "moment of danger" when the strange history of American colonialism in the Pacific is flashing up, in and through Asian American cultural production.

Asian American literature performs this act of "unrepression" not only by invoking specific historical details of the birth of American empire at the turn of the century, but more tellingly by critically examining the terms through which we do or do not recognize American imperialism as such. Asian Americans are living proof of America's expansionist history and the literature of Asian Americans fundamentally bears the traces of that history.[26]

The historicity of Asian American texts, then, gives form to what we can recognize as the confrontation between civil society and the lingering traces of the incorporation of difference that marked U.S. colonization projects. What made erstwhile colonization an appealing project was the ironic narrative of liberation that pervaded its discourse. Acceptance of the well-deserved compensation of redress could be cast as acceptance of the possibility that the nation-state could indeed right the wrongs of the past.

The world that Asian Americans would later occupy, and help build, generated formations that would test the limits of this narrative of the incorporation of alterity. Asian alterity would put such a strain on modernity's and America's narratives for resolving difference that many of the writings and their terms of intelligibility would go virtually unnoticed in their moments of literary and cultural production and they would be quickly forgotten.

While earlier generations of Asian American revisionism would radically airbrush Chinese labor back into the photograph of "the joining of the rails" and testify to the fact of internment, the current project of revisionism is the branding of the United States as an empire.[27] So fundamental is this narrative that epistemologies for the nonrecognition of American empire won out.[28] Indeed this vision of American civilization as not imperial—as even anti-imperial—has been so historically influential that if we are to grasp the ways in which the turn-of-the-century era comprehended empire, questions of epistemology need to be addressed. To recover this past, we have to imagine a consciousness that may not have the present as its telos. Arguments for and against imperialism are discourses that, despite their wide circulation a century ago, demand a process of contextualization inspired by Benjamin's pronouncements from "Theses on the Philosophy of History," quoted above. To radically contextualize means to grasp both the meanings lost to history and the reasons our modernity had to lose them. It means understanding our radical *dis*connection from texts of the past because the epistemological standpoints for apprehending them had to disappear.

To reanimate these lost histories, we need to imagine alternatively mapped futures that profoundly question the destiny we have inherited. Asian American cultural politics enables this critical act by showing us the manifestations of the course of American empire: exclusion, segregation, and the international division of labor alongside life, liberty, and the pursuit of happiness. Asian American literature reverse-engineers the past to speculate on the possibility of alternative presents.

The Absent Presence of Empire in Asian America

Pronouncements, such as Amy Kaplan's, about "the absence of empire in the study of American culture," also fit the study of Asian American culture when subordinated to the same national and domesticated visions of the American studies that Kaplan identifies. This absence becomes especially conspicuous in the wake of the rise and fall of multiculturalism.[29] This is not to fault Asian American priorities specifically, but rather to call attention to the conditions in which Asian American studies began to be institutionalized out of the 1970s and into the 1980s. The earlier formations of the Asian American movement made a more explicit connection to geopolitics, neocolonialism, and Third World consciousness.[30] U.S. imperialism appeared to escape critique in rather satisfying ways in an Asian American canon populated by narratives of finding voice, debunking stereotypes, assimilation problems, related manifestations of identity politics and, as Viet Thanh Nguyen points out, the understandable identification of the "crisis of representation" as the root problem for Asian American cultural politics to address.[31]

To begin to grasp the pervasive invisibility of empire, we need to consider the lingering appeal and the growing inadequacy of multiculturalism as a means for managing difference. From appreciating the critique of multiculturalism articulated by Asian American literary criticism, we simultaneously critique the terms and conditions of American empire. For in these narratives that are critical of Asian American assimilation into American culture, we can also read for formations of what Lowe calls "countersites to official national culture."[32] Countersites exist as such to reference both the resemblance to national culture and the oppositionality it produces from this productive disidentification. We see that which the nation-state has historically and constitutionally been both drawn to and unable to resolve. In these lingering contradictions we find traces of the legacy of U.S. imperialism. To make that legacy legible, Asian American literary texts draw into visibility conceptions of empire that resist being named as such.

Under American imperialism, the most effective form of empire turned out to be one that would not be so easily recognized. As chapter 2 discusses, modern empires of Europe were proving an uncomfortable fit for American culture, itself a kind of postcolonial formation. American control and incorporation of the world would require a less overt and indeed less burdensome mechanism of domination. Rather than seeing the world as subject to an imperial monarch, American culture imagines itself as a shining beacon of freedom and free trade, its civilizing mission nothing more or less than modernization and order, progress and development. Despite some colonial missteps in the Philippines in the first half of the twentieth century, the course of American empire did indeed proceed, in an effectively less formal way. The conception of Asian Americans as a model minority is therefore in direct contradiction to that failed colonial project.

Model-minority standing paradoxically eliminates minority status and renders formerly concrete difference abstract. The ideal of abstraction thus becomes useful for legitimating American expansion and incorporating difference: in other words, the will to make political, cultural, and economic differences abstract, as Lowe explains above. Assimilation comes to be figured as not necessarily American, but as an Enlightenment ideal, along with freedom, equality, and upholding the rights of individuals. American culture does not want the rest of the world to become American, as such, but rather to become individuals in a world ordered by American ideals. In "The Citizen Subject," Etienne Balibar persuasively asserts that, with the Enlightenment and its political manifestations, "the citizen is the subject who rises up."[33] In our current moment, that citizen-subject may have been supplanted by a being we might call the abstract citizen-consumer, defined as inhabiting a site for export market expansion. These new subjects assert their agency through their purchasing power, rather than, under the old empire, through their unfitness for self-governance. As Gayatri Spivak has observed, the international division of labor emerged out of "the displacement of the divided field of nineteenth-century territorial colonialism" to ensure that nothing would "impede the growth of consumerism."[34] The felicitous subject of the developed and deindustrialized world becomes the consumer.

History has shown that the process of becoming this citizen-consumer has been quite messy. As recent and extensive critiques of globalization by scholars and activists have shown, the unequal distribution of resources and opportunities is not only an unfortunate fact of life; it is a necessary condition of reaping profit under the current, highest stage of capitalism.[35] Formal equivalence, Lowe tells us, is doomed from the outset because it is based on the willful denial of persistent and profitable practices that mark populations as raced, classed, and gendered. From the coexistence of these two contradictory demands—one for unmarked equivalence and the other for indelible difference—emerges what Lowe calls "Asian American critique," a subject embodying contradictions that neither official national culture, nor political economy can resolve.

Asian Americans, with their historically tenuous relationship to American citizenship, know intimately the processes that have kept them at a distance from the promises of equality and equivalence under citizenship. Gendered racialization has produced populations that have defined "American" by being its other, while also providing a necessary stratified labor pool that has made the material development of the United States possible.[36] Asian American cultural politics articulate an aesthetic characterized by a radical critique of the civilization that produced the Asian Americans who make that critique.[37] Asian Americans exacerbate contradiction not only by voicing these critiques, but by being the raced, classed, and gendered embodiment of contradiction itself.

As Lowe states above, abstract citizenship means formal equivalence in the political sphere, and abstract labor means formal equivalence in the economic sphere. Abstraction emerges as a screen for claims of equality on the terrain of civil society. From the beginnings of the republic, the category "free, white persons" inherently invoked the various unfree, nonwhite ones against whom the enfranchised defined themselves.[38] Asian difference has been differently used by American capitalist culture at various moments in U.S. history. That difference has strategically taken two main forms: (1) as a symbol of America's ability to absorb difference in the form of civilizing and indeed "purchasing" our "little brown brothers,"[39] penetrating the seductive China market, and parading the model minority; and (2) as a specter of what marks the limits of the nation in the form of military and/or economic Yellow Peril abroad and subversive enemy aliens at home. This historically contradictory condition fueled much of the important early work in the Asian American movement and in Asian American studies.[40]

Asian American cultural politics focuses on the ways that the incorporation and assimilation of Asians came to be figured and practiced. Asian American literature critically grasps American methods of absorbing Asian difference by animating the limits and contradictions inherent in those methods. More specifically, this project proceeds from the notion that because U.S. imperialism marked a genuinely new phase in capitalist production, conceptions of economic practices were central to the rationale of American empire, particularly its not being seen as one.[41] *Globalization* is now probably the most widely used term for this practice, and this book confronts its emergence at the turn of the twentieth century. Specifically, the Asian American literary texts analyzed in this book mount an indirect critique of globalization by showing us the bastard epistemologies in its genealogy.

From the 1980s to the 1890s

At the turn of the twentieth century, the United States first became an old-style empire, forcibly acquiring lands beyond its borders and unfurling Old Glory conspicuously above them.[42] At this same time, the new empire had already begun to take root. This transition marks and is marked by a shift in ways of unifying the globe, particularly through the new conceptualization of commerce and markets. While imperialism has often been considered the incorporation of "new caught sullen peoples," or benevolent assimilation, or the civilizing mission, it is also always an economic system. For the United States especially, the turn of the century was also the period in which the question of a newly global economy—and its truly global currency—arose and was temporarily settled. The struggles over these issues in American history have been forgotten or, at the very least, have been seen as anomalous detours on the path to the present. Competing conceptions of American empire circulated in diverse arenas of culture and politics. While the conspicuous events of territorial acquisition occupied the attention of pundits at the turn of the century, money itself underwent profound global changes that promoted the image of its ever-increasing reach.

In *A History of Money from A.D. 700,* John Chown chooses 1896 as his history's endpoint. The year 1896, he writes, was "the year which saw the end of 'The Great Depression' and (effectively) of the Silver Wars. This ushered in a period of stable prosperity which, even though it lasted only eighteen years, is looked back on as a Golden Age by those who yearn for the (apparent) simplicities of the gold standard."[43] At the turn of the twentieth century, money's contentious history more or less ends. The eighteen years following 1896 ended with the establishment of the Federal Reserve System, which was instituted to centralize and therefore stabilize monetary mechanisms.[44]

Indeed, with the adoption of the dollar-based Euro and the so-called "dollarization" of now defunct small currencies, money is still undergoing changes that facilitate the infrastructures of globalization. In the name of stability, the American dollar continues to be the de facto gold standard. An international gold standard was seen as the tonic for global economic instabilities. With exacting tests, economist Marcello de Cecco characterizes the nineteenth century as "the century of great price oscillations."[45] Such instability, he argues, led to a belief that the international gold standard would unify market forces globally.

Yet the international gold standard failed to become a world currency that could transcend national specificities and vagaries. The actual globality of the global economy was overrated during this Golden Age of the gold standard, as it turned out to be more important as an idea than as a practice.[46] For one thing, the convertibility of notes to a measurable substance of putatively intrinsic and universal value would make sense if such a substance actually existed. Today, the American dollar has become the next best thing as a growing number of world currencies are "tied" or "pegged" to it. But that was a future not yet known to those turn-of-the-century folk grappling with the money question, as I examine further in chapter 2.

The monetary issue still boiled down to three choices for standards: silver (the outmoded "dollar of the fathers"), gold (the far-sighted "dollar of the sons"), and bimetallism (democratic and therefore too messy to actually work).[47] Late nineteenth-century advocates of gold money ridiculed silverites with cartoons depicting the heavy equipment that any large transaction in silver would require. Yet most people were suspicious of adopting paper money because of the risk of the as-yet inconceivable idea of inconvertibility. The ultimate triumph of inconvertibility is demonstrated by the fact that it is our current state of things. Precious metal reserves have long ago proven too limited and too cumbersome for the speed and scale of global capitalism.

The idea of unifying the modern world under a single monetary standard was the innovation of the turn-of-the-century era, and that single money has come to be the American dollar. The unification of the world under the Union Jack or the *Tricoleur* is something quaintly nineteenth century. But what does it really mean for the American dollar to be the thing that has the power to bind us all together despite our myriad differences? What is its power to level and abstract?

As I have argued above, the hallmark of American imperialism is its appeal to a will to be abstract, the ideal that we can all inhabit a political, cultural, and economic position of universal equivalence that surmounts, or at least circumvents, our differences. Asian American cultural politics makes visible the dialect of abstraction and marking that recalls the watershed transformations from the turn of the century, when the United States faced its call to be an empire. Asian American literary texts are a point of access for refracting that period's epistemologies for a modern empire. Asian American cultural politics questions these processes of incorporating difference.

Abstraction is therefore a simultaneously economic, political, and cultural process. In "Marx, Nietzsche, Freud," Michel Foucault locates the crisis of representation in resonant ideas emerging in the late nineteenth and early twentieth centuries.[48] For Nietzsche, Foucault argues, the point at which representation began to show its malevolence was moral categories; for Freud, it was symptomatology. For Marx, that concept is money. Foucault writes,

> I mean that there is in the sign an ambiguous quality and a slight suspicion of ill will and "malice." Moreover, insofar as the sign is already an interpretation that is not given as such, signs are interpretations that try to justify themselves, and not the reverse.
>
> Thus functions money as one sees it defined in the *Critique of Political Economy*, and above all in the first book of *Capital*. Symptoms also function in the same way in the works of Freud. And in the works of Nietzsche, words, justice, the binary classification of Good and Evil, that is to say, signs, are masks. (65–66)

Money is not simply an instrument of capitalism; it is also the concept that is both the site for the creation of modernity and the site for its undoing. Indeed, the symbolic as well as the economic significance of money is one of the main preoccupations of Marx's writings. He writes: "Money is 'impersonal' property. It permits me to transport on my person, in my pocket, social power and social relations in general: the substance of society. Money puts social power in material form into the hands of private persons, who exercise it as individuals."[49] To dissect the operations of money is to produce a deep critique of knowledge itself and the sovereign subject of knowledge and the Enlightenment.

More specifically, "interpretation," and representation more generally, can be seen as participating in the actual triple operations of money, which are traditionally measure, circulation, and hoarding. And further, what we might think of as the epistemology of money is constitutive of textual representation and interpretation in general.[50] That the question of monetary reform emerged as these representational developments were reaching a critical mass was more than coincidence. Can it be a coincidence that as these money controversies were raging, there was also the waxing and waning of realism and naturalism and the emergence of modernism and postmodernism? Jean-Joseph Goux has remarked on this very "coincidence":

> Was it purely by chance that the crisis of realism in the novel and in painting coincided with the end of gold money? Or that the birth of "abstract" art coincided with the shocking invention of inconvertible monetary signs, now in general use? Can we not see in this double crisis of money and language the collapse of guarantees and frames of reference, a rupture between sign and thing, undermining representation and ushering in the age of the floating signifier?[51]

Money goes from being a tangible material object (specie) to being just another sign (a cyber blip), perhaps even aspiring to the status of a transcendental signifier. The paralleling of such troubled pairs as reality and representation, signified and signifier, and specie and note, engendered material and epistemological crises in this era that American political culture sought to resolve.[52]

Such crises did not simply touch the issues of money and economy, but they furthered the very processes and institutions of meaning-making themselves. Foucault argues that we must question not simply the interpretation of representations, but the newly assailed interpreter him/herself. The object of interpretation ceases to be a textual object mimetic of history. Instead the act and actor of interpretation are made knowable only through interpretation; interpretation then can be seen as the fundamental condition of subjectivity itself. How we situate and contextualize interpretation (i.e., the text) reinvokes historical meanings, even ones that had been relegated to history's proverbial trash heap. The terms of modernity demand major and minor formations and the institutions made by this distinction, as well as institutions for making determination of major and minor, or in Willliams's terms, "emergent, dominant, and residual." Any historical moment and any text contains these elements in struggle; the point is to interpret them interestedly.

A Successful Failure to Assimilate

I return to Janice Tanaka's personal documentary, *Who's Going to Pay for These Donuts Anyway?* (1992), for its subtle renderings of abstraction and reification of difference—politically, economically, and culturally. The video, which aired on PBS in 1993, deals with the disappearance of Tanaka's father at the outbreak of World War II and her quest to find him. As she researches and investigates his story, she tracks the ways in which her father's objections to internment were deemed a threat to national security and how he subsequently spent the rest of his life institutionalized as mentally ill. When she finds him, what she encounters is a semicomprehensible old man who may or may not recognize her. The video is an attempt to come to some sort of resolution, both over the mysterious circumstances that took her father away and the matter of whether she can ever really get him back.[53]

A voiceover holds the video's disparate parts together by tracing a narrative of Tanaka's process of coming to terms with her father's vanishing and her life without him. She compares her absent father to her present uncle, exploring the reasons for one's disappearance and the other's persistence. The resistance that Tanaka's father immediately expressed to internment resulted in his immediate repression: first he was imprisoned as subversively dangerous and later he was institutionalized as mentally ill. Whether medically or politically motivated, the toll that institutionalization took on the elder Tanaka is undeniable. We see him unable to recognize his own daughter standing in front of him as he speaks incomprehensibly about his traumatic experiences.

The video ends with Tanaka's father reading the letter that accompanied his 1991 check for reparations for the internment of Japanese Americans during World War II. Ambivalent images of recovery, if not repair, are arrayed at the video's conclusion. While he reads, we see images of Janice Tanaka's daughter and her new husband fox-trotting at their wedding to Nat King Cole and Natalie Cole's "Unforgettable" duet. A father and daughter have been reunited. A mother gives her daughter away in a marriage ceremony. An apologetic nation makes restitution.

In that letter of apology, George Bush points to the formal limits of tort law for producing adequate compensation for the internment of Japanese Americans during World War II. The president understandably conveys that a sum of money and words cannot replace what had been lost. In the etiquette of apology, it would be inappropriate for Bush to say that the trauma of that experience and its systematic erasure from official national culture could be bought for twenty thousand dollars.

And yet, that trauma cannot *not* demand compensation. Something must be done to address historical injustice, he seems to say, just not this only. What then is left to be done? Tanaka is not unhappy to have gotten the check, but he is not quite happy with it either.[54] With that sum of money and a letter of apology, he is supposed to have been given back his status as an "individual." But the very occasion and purpose of the letter itself is an acknowledgment of his not being one; he was, and is, a Japanese American whose experiences trace the changing fortunes of that particular category of racialization. He has found himself, with the blessings of President Bush, at a site of contradiction. The use, not only of literal economic practices such as damage awards, but also more broadly of an economizing logic for rendering historical legacies measurable in money, points to the dilemma of a desire for formal abstraction and the reality of historical markedness. The meaning of that markedness is where we can find Asian American critique.

Rendering anything as money carries with it the possibility for whitewashing, or laundering, to use the term for the familiar criminal practice. George Bush's statement acknowledges both the desires and the limits of monetary compensation. Money is an age-old idea and instrument found in every culture, a veritable fact of social life. In basic economic theory, the three defining characteristics of money are (1) unit of measure, (2) substance of hoarding, and (3) medium of exchange. When money works properly, it is a mechanism of social contract, a substance that makes possible the pricing of anything valued, from widgets to labor to historical injustice. Just as the question of whether Tanaka has really found her father in this broken man is left unanswered, the question of whether the reparation settlement is formally up to the task of repairing wrongs remains unresolved.

Money is supposed to wash, but it, too, needs washing to function properly. That is, in its most basic function, the further an exchange-value gets from its use-value, the more abstracted and unmarked by specificity that sum of money becomes. But behind the history of what has come to be money and its power to represent everything, we can find the residue of vanquished alternatives that had to be jettisoned. Money may be a form of speech, but it can also be accused of hushing. And Jack Tanaka is not going quietly. Clearly Tanaka's video does not directly reference histories of the Silver Wars and the Philippine Insurrection. Yet Japanese American internment and its legacy share with those histories America's totalized and legitimated ascendance as the preeminent global power, built on unresolved vestiges of pasts that were thought to have been managed.

The momentous significance of redress marks both the apex and the endpoint of multiculturalism, of embracing difference. Traces of those histories remain when the resolutions to contradiction fail to operate and, in particular, a sum of money falls just short of its ideal function: to resolve the marked groups to the nation as individuals. We find these repeated failures in the Asian American literary texts constellated in this book. These moments are therefore points of rupture between the logic of incorporation and its concretized actuality. Asian American cultural politics exacerbates that contradiction and in doing so calls for alternative means for confronting unsettled pasts. That historical confrontation has cohered and has been institutionalized as a body of cultural production called Asian American literature.

Periodizing Asian American Literature

In assembling an interested diversity of histories and texts, Asian American cultural production constitutes what Sau-ling C. Wong calls a "textual coalition," one that purposefully constructs a palimpsest meshing both periods and genres—the two conventional bases for mobilizing a cluster of texts.[55] An unconventional and interdisciplinary approach is necessary for a critical understanding of how the United States as empire became an idea that failed to outlive the decades surrounding the turn of the century. That periodized layer of the palimpsest serves not so much as a point of origin from which we can narrate a linear chronology of why Asian American cultural politics became what it is, but rather it is a historical pivot point we can reassess for its lingering, but obscured significance. The 1890s mark an epistemic shift that we have only begun to appreciate. Cognizant of the contours of this shift, we can better grasp what did not make that shift and the significance of its failure to do so. That is, not only are disconnections between eras and issues emblematic of the scars of historical struggles, but further still, our profound inability to even recognize that there may have been a connection becomes evidence of lost possibilities that manifest themselves nearly unintelligibly and hysterically. In other words, we witness cognitive failures that register in the literature as abortive incorporation. These failures register through invocations of economy, especially through curious conceptions of money.

The significance of these failures extends beyond Asian American literature to have ramifications for American culture and history as a whole. The turn of the twentieth century was both a manifestation of U.S. development and a time of crucial cultural, political, and economic transitions that made the world what it is today. With a recontextualized grasp of the turn of the century, we can map a genealogy of American imperial culture by charting the transitions and recuperating the possibilities that got lost as one regime defeated another in the contest to represent the meaning of modern American civilization and its desire to gain the world.

Despite the lack of Asian American literature as such, the turn-of-the-century era was crucial to Asian American literature, as it is the era when U.S. imperialism formally emerged.[56] The specific terms through which American culture sought to explain its imperial project became the discourse against which Asian American literature would need to be articulated. Even though that imperialist discourse seems to have died a natural death, Asian American literature resuscitates that discourse for a critique of U.S. imperialism, both past and present.

Asian American cultural politics sets the conditions for remembering how the late nineteenth-century emergence of U.S. empire made new challenges to the institutions of American politics, economics, and culture. The political sphere had to reconcile empire with conceptions of republicanism and democracy, and the economic sphere had to reconcile empire with the free market. The cultural sphere, however, has a different burden, namely that of managing the myriad contradictions that the other spheres fail to contain. To understand U.S. empire, new conceptions of empire and of the United States have to displace the explanations of American civilization that have become hegemonic.

Asian American cultural politics orchestrates the dynamics of hegemony and counterhegemony. Hegemony is as much the manifestation of the ascendancy of a "historical bloc" as it is the representation of the reality of what happened.[57] Hegemony makes it difficult to recognize anything outside of it. Consequently, references to U.S. imperialism in Asian American literature come across as oblique, perhaps necessarily so. Furthermore, these references need to recuperate not only the existence of U.S. imperialism, but also its contested emergence. Voices of discord, dissent, and contradiction were necessarily squelched by the rise to dominance of a new regime, one both political and epistemological. Asian American literature, as such, recuperates discordant voices to establish formerly unrecognizable resonance with later sources of contradiction.

Colonized immigrant Asian Americans seek to voice their abortive attempts to assimilate themselves to the tradition of American narratives of assimilation. The cultural contestations of the turn of the twentieth century mark the point at which American culture began to put into discourse the transitions taking shape in the political and economic spheres, as well as the contradictions that emerge. That era's own self-conscious attempts to make sense of its status as an era of transition provide fertile accounts of the power, as well as the limits, of hegemony.

The reading practices enabled by Asian American literature seem at first to resemble those of New Historicism. That is, Asian American literature demands the recovery of ways of interpreting literary texts that history has forgotten. To borrow from Stephen Greenblatt, the key New Historicist figure, we see how cultural poetics manifested in a literary text exhibit the "resonance" and "wonder" of the literature.[58] Texts *resonate* with our cultural conditions because of their readily recognizable form and content. And these texts provoke a sense of *wonder* at their profound and subtle differences from what we in our present find familiar.

The New Historicism took much of its inspiration from postmodern anthropology, particularly the conscious textuality and ethnocentrism of the participant-observer in the interpretation of cultures. In their rereading of canonical literature, New Historicist critics defamiliarize other periods that were formerly thought of as of-a-piece with the present. Just as, say, Balinese cockfighting is a cultural formation worthy of status as radically other from the Euro-American metropole, the early modern period is like an exotic civilization that we are not equipped to apprehend. A text's historicity can make it like a foreign country.

Such reading practices require the acceptance that a distant historical period, despite its being Western, has cultural practices that cannot be translated to fit a narrative of history that has the present as its telos. As Walter Benjamin—an influential theorist for the New Historicism—writes in "Theses on the Philosophy," the flight path of what has come to be known as "the angel of history" leaves mountains of detritus in its self-obscured wake.[59] New Historicists focus on that babbling wreckage and what its noisiness can tell us.

Asian American cultural politics appreciates the ways that literary texts, for all their transcendent and transhistorical aura, speak to us across gulfs of time and space, as well as make us aware that there are some things we have lost the ability to see. While texts give us access to the past, the past does not always meet us halfway. These gaps make us feel more keenly the present's particularities and interests, which willfully numb us to that which our modernity cannot make its own.

As a population around which American culture has had both willful blindness and hysterical concern, Asian Americans have historically presented problems to official national culture. Whether invoking American imperialism in Asia or capitalism's dependence on racially segmented labor pools that are easily exploited, the corporeal and ideological presence of persons of Asian descent in American territory has generated a literature that exacerbates the contradictions of America. The radical contextualization of Asian American literary texts is more than a New Historicist approach can handle because a minor literature text cannot be wholly explained by the social and cultural conditions of its moment of emergence. As the New Historicist formulation goes, we grasp simultaneously the historicity of texts and the textuality of history. Radically minor literature fails to achieve either that textuality or historicity.

The field of Asian American literary studies has understandably focused on illuminating the conditions of emergence and the consumption of the texts of the Asian American canon. Such scholarship, particularly that of the field's spearhead, Elaine Kim, performs the necessary and important work of tracking the struggles for Asian American self-representation and the epistemic shifts that made the literature visible and possible.[60] The emergence of her study is a moment as worthy of critical attention as the publication of any literary text.

Kim's book quite deliberately seeks to introduce the writings and their social context to a scholarly community unequipped and perhaps unwilling to grant that a category such as Asian American literature did indeed exist. Shrewdly, her study offers an underappreciated accounting of American culture's fascination with Asian imagery before she begins to discuss writings by Asian Americans. She exhaustively shows us what the literature had to displace to achieve recognition as what Raymond Williams calls a "new formation."[61] She tracks for us the movement from minor *object* status to minor *subject* status.

This narrative arc from object to subject is contained in every piece of Asian American literature. Whether referred to as "gaining one's voice" or "breaking silence," this feature is what makes this insurgent body of writing recognizable as a new and distinct aggregate.[62] But shedding silence is not the shedding of the history of having been silenced—of having, and perhaps keeping, minor status.

For all its pejorative connotations, minor status is not something this book takes lightly. This study builds on the activist scholarship of Kim and others by looking not only to a text's moments of emergence, but also to its consumption. Unlike the New Historicists, who use the texts of a given period to illuminate that era's lost specificities, I use a "minor literature" to illuminate the period in which that minor *status* had its emergence.

Minor literature, as Deleuze and Guattari theorized the concept, is a literature in a major language that serves a minor function.[63] Being minor is not a stigma; rather, it is a condition for counterhegemony. The interpretive methodology of this book extends their conceptualization by asserting that the manifestations of and articulations by those bearing that minor status cannot be considered on the same timeline as a history whose telos is modernity.

Asian American literature, and indeed Asian American history, is not necessarily a literature of a group of people; rather, it is a literature of a category of marginalization, as well as of the resistance and alternatives to that marginalization. Therefore, a Filipino American text produced, say, in the late 1980s, can tell us new things not only about the late 1980s, but about the turn of the twentieth century, for that was the period when the category Filipino American emerged. Epistemologies from the *1890s* remain significant, even if they are no longer in wide circulation. Indeed, their disappearance is what is most telling about what American culture wants to forget and what Asian American culture cannot *not* remember.

Asian American literature resuscitates that discourse by critically animating its cockeyed rationale. This first chapter is also an example of the ways in which the ideology of the turn-of-the-century era, in forms that are no longer recognized as having connections to that period's specificities, can be read in Asian American literature. We can then appreciate how a text such as Jessica Hagedorn's *Dogeaters* can emerge to refute the claims of the American imperial project by corporeally inhabiting its contradictions. Through a similar strategy we saw when Janice Tanaka's father read the words of George Bush, the presidential embodiment of William McKinley in a performance of Hagedorn's Rio Gonzaga critically illustrates the abortive attempt to make "Americans" out of "Asians," or to make individuals out of those whose internment made the category of the individual meaningful at all (as the noninterned).

On the surface, this colonial disciplining bears no explicit reference to the new modes of capitalism and the monetary unification inaugurated under U.S. imperialism. But what joins this colonial disciplining and that economic history is how the hallmark of American imperialism fails; the abstract and unmarked remains concrete and stigmatized. As desirable as it would be to become the abstract citizen, the material and ideological conditions of being historically resituated make that abstraction ultimately doomed. Rio cannot be rendered abstract in the face of historical difference. Her sobbing and Jack Tanaka's ambivalent delivery are evidence of alternative presents in need of remembering those alternative pasts. Asian American culture dramatizes moments of transition, epistemic shifts that both inaugurated and were made possible by a return of the emergence of U.S. imperialism. In seeking to make sense of the past, the coherence and closed status of a period are best assured by the manifest irrelevance of that past to the present. For that irrelevance would be its resolution, its no longer mattering to today. But a monetary sum and words alone cannot perform that act.

Such a hermetically sealed past becomes an object not for the historians, but for the antiquarians and archaeologists. The turn-of-the-century period had been relegated to the irrelevant past. What makes this fact remarkable is not its truth; after all, any historical moment yields artifacts that are assuredly ephemeral and unintelligible to eras not its own. The remarkable aspect of this amnesia is that it concerns historical conditions that have manifest relevance to the present.

Yet the methods of the archaeologist are nonetheless necessary to tell this history. Whether under the banner of postmodernism or postcolonialism or perhaps even the avant-garde, cultural politics today is the site of an ongoing struggle to represent the past without recourse to co-opted mimesis or impracticable subalternity.

Multiculturalism was an oddly masochistic impulse, as evidenced by political events like HR 442 and cultural developments such as the institution of Asian American cultural studies.[64] To reckon with the past historically does not mean to narrate what happened, but rather to appreciate the return of the repressed and the conditions that made that return possible. Out of the still functioning institutions of multiculturalism—particularly ethnic canons and strategically assumed-and-discarded identities—new formations have emerged that make visible residual old ones. And neither the emergent nor the residual need rely on the guilt of the dominant to have historical significance.

To say that Asian American cultural politics is profoundly concerned with historical revision and recovery is at once very simple and quite complicated. The centrality of the critique of the model-minority myth in Asian American cultural politics has set the terms and stakes for critically remembering the emergence of U.S. imperialism from a century ago. In appreciating this, we see the simultaneity of a synchronic and diachronic critique. That is, Asian American cultural politics critically expresses both the contemporary epistemologies and the multiple histories that attend the abortive incorporation of Asian difference into American culture. In the next chapter, I turn specifically to the proliferation of discourses that accompanied the emergence of U.S. imperialism. These discourses show us the ways that Asian difference came to be uneasily scripted into American civilization as empire explicitly, much to the continued surprise of the very American civilization built on those imperial designs.

AN EVER-EMERGENT EMPIRE

THE DISCOURSE OF AMERICAN EXCEPTIONALISM

> We took up arms only in obedience to the dictates of humanity
> and in the fulfillment of high public and moral obligations.
> —President William McKinley, 1898

> We've never been a colonial power. We don't take our force and
> go around to the world and try to take other people's real estate.
> . . . That's just not what the United States does.
> — Secretary of Defense Donald Rumsfeld, interview with
> Jamil Azer on Al Jazeera television, February 2003

The Year 1898 as Exceptional and Paradigmatic

THE IDEA that modern empire is distinctly European and decidedly un-American has cohered as an ideology of American exceptionalism.[1] The spoils of 1898 achieve the status of "a brief and rapidly dispelled aberration" in William Appleman Williams's critical phrasing.[2] This chapter examines the ways that American exceptionalism set the stage for the interventions of Asian American cultural politics by being precisely that "rapidly dispelled aberration" that made exceptionalism possible. The idea of Asian Americans as a readily incorporable model minority gave the lie to exceptionalism by transforming the oriental other into the triumphant individual. Consequently, Asian Americanist critiques of the model-minority myth occasion critiques of American exceptionalism.

In chapter 1, I argued that the management of Asian difference in the contemporary period, particularly through the logic and instruments of multiculturalism in the post–civil rights era, has simultaneously obfuscated and reopened the question of empire in American culture. In doing so, Asian American cultural politics has begun to dramatize the ways that empire has been an "absent presence" in mainstream American culture. The management of difference is fundamental to the idealized self-image of the United States, and the model-minority myth for Asian Americans feeds an emergent notion of a low-maintenance empire. Indeed the maintenance is seen as so low, mainly through the consent of the governed, that the label of *empire* can be and has been avoided. Until recently perhaps, whenever *empire* is invoked to describe American activities around the world, American culture responds with denial, shock, disappointment, and a studied innocence.[3]

This chapter now turns to the overlooked but overt presence of empire in American culture. From the many valid pronouncements about American imperial amnesia made by Williams, Amy Kaplan, and Oscar Campomanes, one might understandably imagine that the record and archive of deliberately imperial discourse in American culture would be small and difficult to find.[4] On the contrary, there is no shortage of material, from Henry Parker Willis's *Our Philippine Problem* (1905) to some of the earliest uses of the cinema.[5] And certainly the archival and theoretical scholarship of Williams, Kaplan, Campomanes, and others has demonstrated the ubiquity of empire in American culture. But if there is an abundance of materials on American colonization projects, why has this history been paradoxically so hard to see? The shortage, if it may be called that, is in the epistemological limits that prevent American culture from recognizing its imperialism.

In the conclusion to Matthew Frye Jacobson's *Barbarian Virtues: The United States Encounters Foreign Peoples at Home and Abroad, 1876–1917,* Jacobson quotes popular historian David McCullough in his documentary on Theodore Roosevelt: "America, like it or not, would have to play a large part in the world."[6] This quotation seems to provoke some irritation in Jacobson, as it is yet another characterization of America as a reluctant imperial power. For historians like Jacobson, the disjuncture between abundant documentation and scant ideological revision is indeed irksome, to say the least. He writes:

> *Like it or not.* This is the real significance of the disappearance of the Philippine-American War from national memory; this is what is at stake in forgetting what was once proudly adopted as a grand imperialist design. When we recall and squarely face U.S. conduct in the Philippines at the dawn of the

Pacific empire in 1899, we can neither utter the phrase "like it or not" nor pass off the U.S. rise to global predominance as blind, unintentional, or accidental. Despite some opposition, the United States consciously chose imperial power along with the antidemocratic baggage and even the bloodshed that entailed; and many Americans—none more than Teddy Roosevelt—*liked it*.[7]

It has become increasingly common and necessary to remind the present of its investment in misremembering or forgetting this past, especially what Jacobson calls U.S. nationalism's "Coming of Age in the Philippines."[8] John Carlos Rowe and Amy Kaplan go one step further, not only reminding the present of this forgotten history from the turn of the century, but showing that those events may be more the rule than the exception. The year 1898 is then a particularly conspicuous manifestation of what came before and what would follow in increasingly occluded ways.[9] Considering the well-established inability of an imperial conception of America to take root in dominant understandings of American culture, it is therefore understandable that the subtle and unexpected manifestations of empire would occupy the attention of revisionist scholars.

This chapter, and indeed this book, is not therefore a straightforward retelling of the tangled history of American colonization projects, as such a history cannot quite be told in a straightforward way.[10] American colonization projects were uneven at best, ranging from eventual Hawaiian statehood to protectorate status for Puerto Rico to nominal independence for Cuba to formal colonization in the Philippines. This chapter looks, on the one hand, at the dialectic of the bracing bluntness with which empire was discussed a century ago, and on the other it looks at the oblique manifestations of imperialist tendencies in the way that history managed to go unnoticed or at best unremarked on. Recovering this discourse makes it possible to begin to make a case for imperial prescience through what Williams paradoxically calls "imperial anticolonialism."[11]

While the focus of this book is on how contemporary Asian American cultural politics makes American empire newly visible, this chapter examines how the frankly imperial discourse of a century ago resonates with the subtly imperial discourse of today. The ideological struggles over imperialism, which composed what E. Berkeley Tompkins grandly referred to as "The Great Debate," were neither that great, nor that debatable. The developments of the contemporary period demonstrate that the similarities between the two official sides in the debate were more aligned than they seemed to be at the time. Both envisioned the destiny that came about: a putatively nonimperial form of incorporating difference into American culture.

As president during the Spanish-American War, William McKinley seems to be the obvious figure to turn to to grasp the arguments in favor of U.S. imperialism. But his status as an imperialist is actually ambiguous. Even in his most overt articulations justifying the acquisition of the Philippines, he is consistently hesitant and defensive. As early as 1905, commentators noted that the late President McKinley was, prior to 1898, actually more aligned with anti-imperialism.[12] Even Theodore Roosevelt, for all his bluster, had been ambivalent about certain forms of conquest.[13] But the imperialism that both McKinley and Roosevelt were against was that of the nineteenth-century empires of Europe. That is, they were opposed to extraterritorial conquest, the kind that Secretary Rumsfeld is quick to deny that the United States is engaged in. In the kind of imperialism favored by McKinley and Roosevelt, armed territorial conquest would only be undertaken with great reluctance. As McKinley stated in 1898, "We took up arms only in obedience to the dictates of humanity and in the fulfillment of high public and moral obligations."[14]

For McKinley, status as a "world power" was only incidental to the commercial opportunities that extraterritorial state activities made possible. Already in a speech from 1898 he stated:

> Incidental to our tenure in the Philippines is the commercial opportunity to which American statesmanship cannot be indifferent. It is just to use every legitimate means for the enlargement of American trade; but we seek no advantages in the Orient which are not common to all. Asking only the open door for ourselves, we are ready to accord the open door to others. The commercial opportunity which is naturally and inevitably associated with this new opening depends less on large territorial possession than upon an adequate commercial basis upon broad and equal privileges.[15]

"Large territorial possession," he suggests, is of secondary importance to Americans. The most important reason for entertaining "tenure in the Philippines" is "an adequate commercial basis upon broad and equal privileges." By espousing these policies eschewing special tariffs, McKinley advocates for what was at the time called "most favored nation" clauses, which would establish nondiscriminatory relations between trading partners.[16] The "American Century" would unfold not only *despite* a lack of direct American control throughout virtually the rest of the world, but *because* of it. Such a policy is a testament to the realization of McKinley's vision. In 1898, he envisioned a world opened for American commercial activity. Historian Thomas McCormick has remarked, "In contemporary jargon, the main thrust of America's commercial policy in China at the turn of the century would be described as 'neo-colonial.'"[17] William Pomeroy even went so far as to say, "In simplified terms, the anti-imperialism of that time is the neo-colonialism of today."[18]

Direct colonization was at best a needless extravagance and at worst a contradiction of American ideals. Direct colonization involves the incorporation of subjects who were, as both sides of the debate often agreed, unfit for self-government. But do we want them to become a part of the United States? One exasperated pundit, Henry Parker Willis, suggested in his 1905 study, *Our Philippine Problem: A Study of American Colonial Policy*, that incorporating the Filipinos was a fool's errand:

> The natives of the Philippines are entirely foreign to the inhabitants of the United States in all their ways of thought, action, and prejudice. What we have consistently done thus far has been to try to force upon them methods and institutions with which they were wholly unacquainted and for which they had no natural aptitude.[19]

Neocolonialism would become the answer to "our Philippine problem." Back in 1898, McKinley had described the commercial opportunity as "incidental."

By 1901, with the ongoing Philippine-American insurrection (ca. 1898–1904) failing to be as tidy as the Spanish-American War, commercial opportunities came to be the central project and suggestions to take up arms to secure those opportunities were made only very reluctantly. McKinley's final speech, given in 1901 shortly before anarchist Leon Czolgosz assassinated him at the Buffalo Pan-American Exposition, was about the wonders of technology and its capacity to enable a truly global economy. By that time, McKinley was already downplaying the imperial grandiosity of the "splendid little war" of 1898 by playing up the communications and transport innovations that made it possible to wage the war:

The quick gathering and transmission of news, like rapid transit, are of recent origin, and are only made possible by the genius of the inventor and the courage of the government, with every facility known at the time for rapid travel, nineteen days to go from the city of Washington to New Orleans with a message to General Jackson that the war with England had ceased and that a treaty of peace had been signed. How different now.

We reached General Miles in Puerto Rico by cable, and he was able, through the military telegraph, to stop his army on the firing line with the message that the United States and Spain had signed a protocol suspending hostilities.[20]

How different now. McKinley marvels at the new age inaugurated by transport and communications technology. A truly global age was dawning and he announces its arrival at Buffalo by emphasizing the reluctance of the United States to take up arms.

The question of the bottom line was also becoming a sore point in the debates over the prudence and feasibility of empire. Edward Atkinson, an anti-imperialist businessman, remarked, "We may not compute the cost of our military control over the Philippine Islands at anything less than 75,000 dollars a day.... I leave to the advocates ... to compute how much our export trade must be increased from last year's amount, to cover even the cost of occupation."[21] Implicitly, if colonizing the Philippines were to increase export trade, the project would be defensible. If export trade were to increase without actual colonization, as say, in Cuba, which was a protectorate, then presumably Atkinson and his interests would find expansion more acceptable.[22]

McKinley's discourse leaves room for this possibility. This deft hedging was nothing new to McKinley, a consummate politician. Even his oft-cited 1899 remarks to the Methodist Delegation, for all their resolution about the divine call to "uplift and civilize and Christianize" the Filipinos, produce, on closer scrutiny, a rather tortured narrative. "There was nothing left for us to do," he tells the clergymen, "but ... by God's grace to do the very best we could by them, as our fellow men for whom Christ also died."[23] We see then, even in the discourse of empire of the American president who oversaw this pivotal overseas colonization, considerable ambivalence about the meaning of empire in American culture. The ambivalence over empire manifests itself as ambivalence over taking on a burden. Contemporary Asian American cultural politics would inhabit that burden by questioning the uses to which that difference was being put.

The remainder of this chapter revisits the overt and oblique formations of empire from the turn of the century to examine how past uses of Asian difference resonate with the contemporary usage described in chapter 1. I look primarily at the anti-imperialist discourse to find how the ambivalences of taking up the white man's burden at the turn of the century bear an uncanny resemblance to the ambivalences over the same mission up through the end of the twentieth century. These ambivalences, I argue, are symptoms of the globalized, neocolonial empire yet to come, now legible to the present in the discourse of empire at the turn of the century.

Allegories of Empire: Return to Oz

> The Winkies were not a brave people, but they had to do as they were told.
>
> —L. Frank Baum, *The Wonderful Wizard of Oz*, 1900

In a 1964 issue of *American Quarterly*, Henry Littlefield argued that *The Wonderful Wizard of Oz*, Lyman Frank Baum's tale of a little girl from Kansas transported to and from the dazzlingly colorful land of Oz, is an allegory of turn-of-the-century political debates, particularly over monetary standards; regional, class, and race divisions; and the question of empire.[24] Since Littlefield's article, a quiet but increasingly audible group of scholars has used Baum's phenomenally popular children's book as a wedge into its era.[25] That such a triumphantly oblique and transhistorical text as Baum's should be saturated by (alleged) historical meanings is evidence both of the pervasiveness of these interpretive possibilities and their virtual invisibility to a present that may find them hard to believe. Allegorical readings show both the lengths to which one may have to go to find the discourse of U.S. colonialism, and the obviousness of that discourse in texts that had to be recovered. On the one hand, there are the voluminous pronouncements for and against empire, and on the other there is the manifest strangeness of these articulations when they are rebroadcast a century later. The dialectic of obscurity and the self-evidence of the discourse of American colonialism have become structuring features not only of Asian American cultural politics, but of American cultural memory of its colonization projects.

As the nineteenth century came to a close and the twentieth

century began, one of the most beloved classics of American literature was published, *The Wonderful Wizard of Oz* (1900) by Lyman Frank Baum.[26] The book was immediately and immensely popular for nearly forty years before the globally influential 1939 Victor Fleming film starring Judy Garland was produced.[27] For these reasons alone, *The Wonderful Wizard of Oz* is a document of the late nineteenth century that continues to speak to the present, despite its historically specific conditions of emergence. As such, it provides access to that pivotal era of American history in both obvious and obscured ways.

Historians and literary critics have argued for the allegorical meanings of Baum's narrative, suggesting that it is an allegory for late nineteenth-century politics.[28] After all, for any fantastical narrative to be intelligible, it must necessarily resonate with the social and cultural conditions out of which it emerged and within which it is consumed. While scholars have been wary of overly neat parallels between specific histories and analogues in the text, they have endeavored to show how lost meanings in the text parallel lost meanings in history. Toward that end, they argue that *The Wonderful Wizard of Oz* functions as a parable of the turn-of-the-century monetary debate, with sympathies leaning toward the losing bimetallic side.

To decipher the ways in which this fantasy about Dorothy Gale's odyssey from Kansas to Oz and back again is a roman à clef for turn-of-the-century American politics, the long-since forgotten and defunct components of the monetary reform issue need to be remembered and reanimated. Financial issues had dominated national politics in the United States since the Civil War, and the turn of the century saw a particularly heightened contestation over the Greenback issue.[29] With the election of William McKinley and the defeat of William Jennings Bryan in 1896, the highly contested question of monetary reform was fast on the road to resolution: the financially conservative gold standard bearers trounced the antimonopolist bimetallic and silver advocates on the populist side.

Historians have offered a variety of keys to Baum's referentially opaque text. Gretchen Ritter, in her recent history of the money question, *Goldbugs and Greenbacks: The Antimonopoly Tradition and the Politics of Finance in America,* includes a provocative appendix decoding Baum's story for its allegorical meanings.[30] For instance, *Oz* is the abbreviation for *ounce,* the common measure of precious metals, still bearing intrinsic value before they are monetized through minting.

Dorothy is the American everyperson. The Scarecrow represents farmers who no longer trust their own common sense. The Tin Woodman is the worker mechanized into heartlessness. The Cowardly Lion depicts Bryan with all his ineffectual bluster. The Wizard is William McKinley, the American president himself, aloof and ruling through intimidation and illusion. The Wicked Witch of the East represents Eastern industrial capitalism, while the Wicked Witch of the West stands for Western capitalist interests, especially mining. The Good Witches of the North and South typify the good people of the agrarian northern Midwest and Southeast. The Yellow Brick Road is a path of gold leading to the Emerald City, our nation's capital. And importantly, that golden road is trod upon by Dorothy in silver slippers as a metaphor for the bimetallic route to prosperity.[31]

As a representation of the American political landscape, Baum's story rightly includes racialized populations. The Winged Monkeys are Native Americans, and Ritter argues that the Winkies, the yellow people enslaved by the Wicked Witch of the West, reference Asian immigrants who came eastward to the U.S. West as miners and railroad workers beginning in the middle of the 1800s.[32] Economist Hugh Rockoff disagrees. Rockoff argues that if the parable is to operate properly, the Winkies are Filipinos, recently colonized by the United States.[33] Chinese laborers were not beloved by either of the main political parties. Organized labor's anti-immigrant sentiment was just a part of a general anti-Asian racism, especially prevalent in the American West.[34] Bryan, the figure under whom populist and mainstream democrats unified, was outspokenly anti-imperialist. For Baum's allegory to function consistently as sympathetic to populism and free silver, the Winkies could not be Chinese and therefore had to be Filipino.

Yet in a narrative of salvation through the money question, why did Filipinos enter the field of representation at all? To address this question, we need to begin by tracing the emergence of the money question and its displacement by the empire question in American political culture. More than any other era before or since, financial questions dominated national electoral politics at the end of the nineteenth century. Built on the questionable "quantity theory of money," the issue of what basis of coinage the U.S. monetary supply would adopt dominated debates and defined constituencies.[35] But the events in Cuba and the Philippines in 1898–99 forced the question of American empire into the minds of an electorate formerly divided by their different feelings about precious metals. The strange convergence of these issues gave rise to the serendipitous inevitability of empire and its debated connection to monetary reform.

Bryan sought to link the money question and the empire question, and in doing so to link the American people to anti-imperialism. Seven years after his constituency-galvanizing "Cross of Gold" speech at the 1896 Democratic National Convention, Bryan sought again to unite a movement with his orations. At a Jackson Day speech in Chicago in January 1899, he made the following argument, which indicates how he tried to sell this link to his constituency:

> The democratic party stood for the money of the Constitution in 1896; it stands for the government of the Constitution now.
>
> It opposed an English financial policy in 1896; it opposes an English colonial policy now. Those who in 1896 were in favor of turning the American people over to the greed of foreign financiers and domestic trusts may now be willing to turn the Filipinos over to the tender mercies of military governors and carpet-bag officials.
>
> Those who in 1896 thought the people of the United States too weak to attend to their own business may now think them strong enough to attend to the business of remote and alien races; but those who, in 1896, fought for independence for the American people will not now withhold independence from those who desire it elsewhere.
>
> We are told that the Filipinos are not capable of self-government; that has a familiar ring. Only two years ago I heard the same argument made against a very respectable minority of the people in this country. The money loaners, who coerced borrowers, did it upon that theory; the employers who coerced their employees did it for the same reason.[36]

Seeking to make his anti-imperialist position intelligible, Bryan makes the empire question not simply an analogous formation to the money question, but one directly related through the various "familiar ring[s]" he emphasizes between the question of empire and the question of monetary reform. He begins with an account of how both empire and the gold standard are seen as unconstitutional and anti-republican.[37] To rouse the American nativist and anti-European sentiments of his populist constituency, Bryan likens the Republican party to a de facto aristocracy and monarchy, not unlike decadent England. And Bryan struggles to make his audience identify with the colonized Filipinos;

just as the government had acted against your wishes in 1896, he says, so also it is acting against the wishes of the Filipinos.[38] Despite being in Chicago, the so-called New York of the West, Bryan can play to sectionalist tendencies by resurrecting the villains of Reconstruction, the military governors and carpetbaggers, to make an oblique parallel between the devastated post–Civil War South and the post-Spanish Philippines.[39] Yet he also warns the American people that they may not want to take up the white man's burden of absorbing and "attending to the business of remote and alien races." Like McKinley, Bryan uses the term "business" to describe the course of action to take regarding the Philippines.

Bryan transformed the persistent question of Filipino fitness for self-government into a question of the fitness of the American people to maintain a democracy. Was the American public ready to make such identifications, to hear the "familiar ring"? Were Americans going to grant the same degree of autonomy that they valued for themselves to Filipinos, to yellow Winkies? (The question of whether Filipinos sought to identify with Americans, however, hardly came up in U.S. colonial discourse.)

Not surprisingly this transition proved to be a hard sell, especially as the depression of the early 1890s finally gave way to expansion.[40] Bryan, in his third run for the presidency, was again trounced by McKinley in the 1900 election, and subsequently, the United States adopted a gold standard and officially became an imperial power not unlike the "decadent" nations of Europe, such as England and France.[41] Another factor that made this shift so difficult was that an already shaky constituency, the ambivalently pro-silver Democratic party, was even more difficult to mobilize around an issue that did not seem to affect their daily lives: the seemingly extravagant question of empire.

With his prominent position in party politics and his oratorical prowess, Bryan is the central figure for mapping the abortive transition from money to empire. To one lost cause was added another.[42] And history has shown that within a few decades, the debatability of these two issues, individually and collectively, perished from the earth. The transitional discourse between these two issues sought to explain what was at stake in becoming an empire to the laymen who needed the translation as a kind of imperialism for beginners.

Bryan, of course, was not alone in his efforts to make this transition intelligible to the masses. William Hope Harvey, author of the million-selling free silver tract, *Coin's Financial School* (1894), also tried to pass the populist torch from free silver to anti-imperialism with *Coin on Money, Trusts, and Imperialism* (1899), his sequel to *Coin's Financial School*.[43] Bryan's famous 1896 "Cross of Gold" speech is considered an encapsulation of Harvey's ideas in Coin's Financial School.

Filled with such provocative illustrations as anthropomorphized coins, *Coin's Financial School* consists of six "lessons" by "Coin," a ten-year-old economics prodigy who explains the key issues of the monetary debate to an audience of both boys and men. Like Harvey himself, Coin is based in Chicago, a hotbed of Democratic and Populist activity. Some of the audience members are prominent Goldbugs, who Harvey sets up as straw dogs for Coin to knock over. By the end of the sixth day, Coin has won over the reluctant members of his audience, especially the boys, the frightening target of much reform literature of this period.[44] As a critique of imperialism pitched to free silver advocates, Coin's 1899 text is a study in failure, the failure to make an already opaque and virtually lost issue, the money question, a persuasive narrative for the critique of empire.

Coin's Financial School was wildly successful. It became the bible of the Populist free silver cause, and therefore the object of much critique and ridicule by Goldbugs.[45] *The Wonderful Wizard of Oz* is a part of this tradition of discourse, albeit in its waning moment. Coin's (and Baum's, for that matter) use of a child to educate the putatively ignorant masses, who, like Baum's Scarecrow, had lost their ability to trust their own intelligence in a world far too complicated for them, presented an appealing image to the common folk. Populist in its pedagogy as well as its political platform, the book assured its readers that the complex economic matters of the day were utterly graspable by the layperson. Coin, in 1899, captured the political ethos of the defeated people in the early 1890s: "Many of them regarded the money question as beyond their comprehension. So they looked in other directions as to how they could better themselves."[46] Coin, however, thinks that money is precisely where these defeated people need to look and he says he will demonstrate that money is not beyond their comprehension. Furthermore, Coin's lectures show that those who purport to be experts are misguided and misguiding. Seemingly counter to trends such as Social Darwinism and laissez-faire, Coin implicitly explains that poverty is not necessarily a natural defect of the impoverished, but a defect of national financial policy.

In the sequel, *Coin on Money, Trusts, and Imperialism,* Harvey has the "young financier and statesman" return to the site of his former lecturing triumphs four years later. This follow-up text uses the same format as the first. The first four chapters take up the main arguments of *Coin's Financial School,* recapping his arguments about the nature of money and the subsequent need for monetary reform through bimetallism. Coin devotes the sixth lesson to a critique of the United States' recent colonization of the Philippines, making arguments quite resonant with those of Bryan. Coin pontificates on the meaning of American civilization and, in the process, he makes little meaningful connection between his conceptualizations of money and his account of empire. Like many of the anti-imperialists of the era, Coin argues that empire is in direct opposition to American political ideals, without making an explicit link to economy.

To emphasize the decline of American civilization, Coin stages a touching, though hypothetical, diplomatic meeting between Abraham Lincoln and Emilio Aguinaldo, leader of the Philippine nationalists. Coin asserts that Lincoln, as the Great Emancipator, would have gladly granted freedom to the Filipinos in an exchange that ironically echoes and extends the Monroe Doctrine: "Mr. Lincoln would have answered him, saying: 'Go to the telegraph office and cable Aguinaldo that the great Republic of the western world sends greeting to the young Republic of the Orient, and will protect it from the other nations of the world.'"[47] Then Coin abruptly reminds us that McKinley refused to recognize the Filipino government and therefore refused to see the visiting delegation from the deposed Filipino nationalist government.[48] Coin goes on to refute the main arguments against formal recognition of the Aguinaldo regime, including the argument that the nationalists were nothing more than a "Tagal [sic]" hegemony.[49]

Coin warns his readers that they are on the verge of backsliding from a republic to a monarchy. He makes the case that, as a monarchy, the United States would need a large professional standing army, not a volunteer corps. He closes the chapter by warning us that, in the hands of the Republicans, the United States is declining as it stealthily slouches further from democracy and moves closer to a monarchy that seeks to emulate the decadent British.[50]

These arguments against empire were quite in line with the arguments other anti-imperialists had been making.[51] Yet Coin makes what is probably an inadvertent link between economic and political developments. The lesson on "the fifth day" of the 1899 text, the day preceding the empire lesson, gestures toward a conceptualization of the transition from the money question to the empire question that more closely resembles how the United States came to practice empire. Coin describes the new form of American capitalism that emerged in the late nineteenth century, which historian Alan Trachtenberg has aptly called "the age of incorporation," an age characterized by the contestation between labor and capital, in which capital emerged victorious.[52]

The very sequence in Harvey's title, money-trusts-imperialism, as well as the seemingly serendipitous sequence of Coin's lessons, captured the means by which U.S. imperialism would come to assert its global management.[53] While antitrust legislation eventually did emerge, the global transformations of the so-called "modern world system" were already being set up in terms of military and political structures, as well as in business practices.[54]

Coin's critique of trusts was couched in the pro-small-producer rhetoric that was the bread and butter of the Populist movement. While these critiques may have been somewhat naive, provincial, and deludedly nostalgic for an idealized past that was actually built on slavery and genocide, the ways that new developments in capitalism were being explained by the free silver movement show that the new capitalism was really the new imperialism. Coin speaks fondly of such dying figures as the traveling salesman, the country editor, and the small shop owner, who were forced to struggle to make ends meet in the face of their respective replacements under the new mode of capitalist production: the mail-order catalog, the professional (and presumably disinterested) printing house, and the department store. Coin states rather bluntly: "[A] department store is a trust."[55] He is aware that the justification for these trusts is efficiency, but he finds trusts to be an enterprise militating against the freedoms that the founding fathers had codified.

While he may seem to be blaming an effect for a cause, he does present an analysis that links his antitrust argument with the issue that was seen as the panacea for the era's ills: a change in monetary policy. Money, to Coin, was the basis of all other trusts. Eventually, he believed, all industrial and other trusts would be absorbed by the financial trust or "money power." "Money power" to Coin was an *ur-*

trust because of the growing role of finance capital in every phase of economic development that was going on in the age of robber barons and incorporation and their economies of scale.[56] Here Coin invokes the "crime of '73" that surreptitiously demonetized silver.[57] An audience member asks Coin to tell him "when the first Trust was formed":

> "In 1873," replied the little teacher, "when silver was struck down as a competitor with gold. The Money Trust began forming soon after the war to control the volume and issue of money, the same as Industrial Trusts have since sought to control the products in which they deal. The Money Trust may be said to have succeeded and fastened itself upon the country in 1873."[58]

Coin makes visible the almost parasitic money trust as the source of the more visible industrial trusts. To illustrate, he personifies gold and silver as business competitors, with gold achieving a monopoly, thereby allowing it to control the products in which it deals, i.e., money. In other words, finance capital needed first to control the money supply: "The Financial Trust will own all the other Trusts," replied the little teacher.[59] With the emergence of economies of unprecedented size, productive capital had become unprecedentedly dependent on finance capital and its cultures of speculation and investment.[60] To convey this idea, Harvey used a cartoon of a fat sow printed with the words "Money Trust" nursing her piglets, each labeled with the names of the various industrial trusts that were driving the small producer to extinction.

While both mainstream history and popular memory have designated such antimonopoly financial reformists as being on the losing side and historians have branded them as well-intentioned crackpots, the critique of the form that capitalism was taking at this time was quite prescient.[61] Necessarily pitched for the layperson, Coin's sweeping assertion that the principal trust was the financial trust resonates with the developments in American capitalism.[62] Coin indicts not monetary policy in general, but one piece of legislation in particular; he locates the origin of the people's, nay humanity's woes, in a particular graspable moment: the demonized and demonetizing crime of 1873. If the law had created this unnatural monster, he reasoned, then the law could also kill it. Just as foreign financiers (usually British) had taken over the economy of the United States, so also was their ideology infecting the political decisions of the state. The extravagant drive to colonize the Philippines is narrated as simply a further extension of this rift between the haves and the have-nots.

That such anti-imperialist sentiments would find political expression in financial reform should not be as surprising and odd as it may seem to us now. That monetary reform or anti-imperialism would be popularly debated issues individually is strange enough. Debating them together is even more remarkable and wonder-provoking to the present.[63] Harvey and his supporters were still trapped in the nostalgic culture of the myth of the small producer, the same myth that Frederick Jackson Turner in 1893 had theorized in his explanation of America as a perpetual frontier society with multiple safety valves to create opportunity for the not-yet middle class in conditions of overproduction.[64] What we can recover and learn from the small producer's dissatisfaction with capitalism offers a critique of imperialism that shows the genuinely new historical formation that U.S. imperialism inaugurated. In the curious resonances between anticolonial colonizers of the turn of the century and the anticolonial colonizeds who came after, we can generate the terms and the subjectivities for critiques that the triumph of imperialism made nearly inaccessible.

Small producers, who are not at all synonymous with the growing industrial proletariat of late nineteenth-century America, are really a waning part of the petite bourgeoisie. Their furthest left fringe was made up of those who shared a liberal toleration for quasi-socialist reform; in the jargon of the 1930s, these people would be called "fellow travelers."[65] They yearned for an older, idealized capitalism that was on the way out as "economies of scale" smothered the competition. The burden on the shoulders of corporate America was—and still is—to show that incorporation marks the new and improved America that will provide what the older capitalism could not and would not.[66] The main opposition that corporate capitalism actually had to put down was the emergent proletariat. Yet, perhaps counterintuitively, the liberal Populists were the easier enemy to mobilize against because their defeat affirmed the validity of traditional party politics, even with third parties.[67]

We can see this struggle between moderates being played out in Coin's specific objections to trusts and imperialism. Instead of envisioning a workers' struggle, he claims that the current regime is sliding further back into history, that is, all the way back to European-style monarchy and oligarchy. In the struggle over the meaning of modernity, empire fell squarely on the side of an alarming return to feudalism. With monetary reform essentially a lost cause even before 1900, the Populist arguments that critiqued imperialism and new economic developments would have been unconvincing and not feasible to most (even a young W. E. B. DuBois).[68] Though Coin is an antimonopolist fighting financial conservatives, he is essentially a conservative critiquing the decadence of so-called captains of industry. These robber barons, instead of representing the common person's mode of production, exploit the common person through a new organization of production, namely the trust. Coin seeks a strong state to face down corporate greed at a time when the state had become too weak to regulate the new breed of "very large" corporations.[69]

Capitalism was still seeking to come up with internal correctives. As the global division of labor would later keep corporate centers in the United States and recruit more and more industrial labor from the hard-to-organize racialized proletariat in the underdeveloped world, such critiques linking antitrust and anti-empire would be sparse as the ills of monopolies and empires seemed to merit condemnation in their own putatively distinct arenas. As we have seen, recuperations of the neglected writings of this era show the inklings of abortive efforts to make manifest the conspiracy of capitalism and imperialism to an America that still seemed to be in a position to prevent imperialism in the name of true capitalism. The replacement for bad capitalism was, in the eyes of both sides of the debate, good capitalism. (Marxist writings would soon make the relations of empire and capitalism visible and recognizable.[70])

Who Are the "Real" Yellow Winkies?

The Wonderful Wizard of Oz serves as a useful point of access for understanding American imperialism and the ways that Asian American culture emerges to generate subjectivities and critiques that even sympathetic turn-of-the-century cultural formations like Baum's, Harvey's, and Bryan's could not have.

But the terms of that sympathy are an important means for making sense of why that sympathy vanished. Is Baum's 1900 "monetary allegory" an anti-imperialist, proletariat tract valiantly going against the grain of soon-to-be dominant ideologies? Or is it a fantastical justification for America's benevolent imperial designs? That it has been read for generations as neither is revealing for how resistant America's empire is to codification.

The recuperative act involved in making plausible allegorical interpretations for what is for all intents and purposes a piece of children's literature illuminates the extent to which the course of American development had been contested. More than just children's literature, the text is a watershed instance of what can be lost when an American cultural text makes the transition from popular culture to mass culture. Conventionally, cultural artifacts as historical evidence have been given the status of reflectors of reality, points of access for apprehending some graspable reality of a specific time and place. But with the emergence of what Benjamin has called "the age of mechanical reproduction," works of art, because of their wide proliferation, have become more productive than reflective of their reality in unprecedented and unprecedentedly large-scale ways.[71] We can then see how Baum's 1900 text escapes the bounds of its historical moment, only to be imprisoned in a new interpretive hegemony.

As we find our own way back from Baum's 1890s Oz, we can begin to see that Winkies conveniently uphold U.S. colonialism's justification of serendipitous inevitability. Dorothy liberated them in a quest for her own salvation. This interpretation, emerging from the pivotal 1890s, and the neglect of this interpretation show how later cultural and political formations recuperate what the mainstream had to lose in order to remain the mainstream. Money was still on the people's minds despite empire's demands for attention—and America imagined it could reconcile them.

Was monometallism really the reason that so many were so poor and the reason that empire could become an American reality? To assess the historical validity of Populist claims, we must resolve a number of basic questions about our political decisions. Is it profitable to run an empire? Are immigrants and wards ultimately a burden or a boon to the citizens of the host country and colonizer? To cast the gold standard as a scapegoat issue while some more "real" factor goes unnoticed is not the point in this inquiry. One thing is clear: money was *the* issue in the early 1890s.

The somewhat historically misguided question of whether the

critiques voiced by the antimonopoly reformists had any merit emerges in attempts to valorize or repudiate the financial reformists. Leading historians, most prominently Richard Hofstadter, have understandably branded Populists as ignorant yokels, and, judging from the extensive pamphlet tradition they left as a record, clearly many of them were just that. But their writings did possess recuperable, and radically alternative, aspects for mounting genuinely prescient assaults on the wages of corporate capitalism, primarily on the home front, but eventually even globally, as the late 1890s made necessary.

If the money question did not really matter, why did so many care about its fate? These questions serve as access points for making sense of an era, theorizing our connection to it, and wondering about the limits of our comprehension. What genealogies do we have to articulate to ensure that what happened is not, as Benjamin put it, "lost for history"?[72]

Who, then, were the "real" yellow Winkies? There is, as yet, little hard historical evidence to determine definitively that they were colonized Filipinos or Chinese American laborers in the West, in any clearly referential way. Even the monetary allegory in Baum requires a willing suspension of disbelief. Rockoff's main argument for Filipino Winkies is based on their being subordinated and then benevolently, if unintentionally, emancipated by the United States. The Winkies, though they do attack Dorothy and the others, are seen as nonmalevolent, as merely doing the bidding of she who commands them. Once Dorothy douses the Witch with mop water, the Winkies immediately rejoice and thank Dorothy. She just happened to liberate the Munchkins and the Winkies, and even the Winged Monkeys, on her circuitous path toward bimetallic bliss.

The connections between these narratives of serendipitous liberation and fortunate domestic prosperity reveal the ways that the subjectivity of the colonized could and could not be given expression. As the narrator tells us, "The Winkies were not a brave people, but they had to do as they were told."[73] *The Wonderful Wizard of Oz* is far from being a realist representation; it demands that we allegorize. While we do escape the grayness of Kansas by going to multicolor Oz with Dorothy, that fantasy world's curious resonances with our own give it meaning. The literature necessarily presents to us its conceptions of the way of the world.

Yet what is left out of the allegory is as telling as what is included.

Two missing elements of the era emerge to show the limits of Baum's allegory: (1) the trusts and how they operate, and (2) African Americans and the era's "Negro problem."[74] The narrative seems to dispose of trusts in the political landscape of the 1890s by conveniently having Dorothy's house land on the Wicked Witch of the East. And the South, allegorized primarily as the site of poor white farmers, is presided over by one of the good witches. With such omissions, these elements of the allegory are left out; the fantasy narrative shows us the fantasies of a Populist's wishful thinking about the political, if not also the cultural, representability of the world.

How the Winkies could achieve the status of being liberated from their colonized state offers us a conception of America's mission in the world. Tellingly, the economic conditions and infrastructures that made colonization presumably possible and desirable are absent. The market-expanding benevolent assimilationists' cry of "philanthropy and five percent" does not enter the picture; instead we get the McKinleyesque providential randomness of freeing a people while in search of another goal. The result is the serendipity of the American imperial project, so eloquently captured in McKinley's remarks to the Methodist Delegation.

Attempting to access a subjectivity for the colonized in the colonial narrative in Baum's text would be a misguided pursuit. Instead *The Wonderful Wizard of Oz* points more to the limitations of American culture in the late 1890s. The Winkies exist only to make Dorothy heroic, albeit inadvertently. That Winkies were liberated is important and progressive, but the question of what to do with these putatively liberated people is left unresolved. Upon such a conception of Asian and Asian American liberation, narratives of Asian assimilation to America have been built.[75]

Due to its conditions of historical emergence, *The Wonderful Wizard of Oz* is a text in which we could say U.S. imperialism is immanent.[76] While such a statement is not inaccurate, it is imprecise. Baum's text may more usefully and appropriately be considered a text of anti-imperialism for its sympathy for the oppressed, even though that sympathy resulted in the displacement of one colonizer in favor of another. In its anti-imperialism, the book does not much trouble the standard anti-imperialist arguments of the day. Attempting to build on its silverite constituency, the antimonopolists had to produce a connection between the formation of corporations and trusts and the economic inequalities that shaped their daily lives. Opposing empire was a method of advocating for the have-nots in America, as much as it was about recognizing the sovereignty of Filipinos, or Cubans, or Hawaiians, or Puerto Ricans, or Guamanians, or Samoans, or any indigenous peoples, other than American Indians, who had been dispossessed of their land and sovereignty in the name of American imperialism coded as progress.[77]

In the public debates over how to have an honorable peace in the Philippines, "Who shall take down the flag?" was the rhetorical question that imperialists used against the anti-imperialists when they branded the latter as un-American. It was the slogan that the anti-imperialists needed to address.[78] Historically the colonized had been the ones who, for starters, tried to take down the flag.[79] But in American culture at the turn of the century, the *who* of this rhetorical question was a pronoun for un-American anti-imperialist Americans. After all, Winkies did not liberate themselves.

In the aftermath of such military and epistemic failures, the subjectivities forged from that literal and figurative effort to take down the flag test the limits of the ability for American incorporation, via the colonized immigrant subject. Debates over empire emerge to displace the money question because these issues came to be considered distinct instead of related. American culture sought to make distinct the economic sphere (money) from the political sphere (empire).

Culture can either manage or make unmanageable this fictitious borderline. Asian American culture emerged in the delicate condition of having an unrecognized legacy of resistance achieve recognition through the very contradictions of American culture.[80] The irony and persistence of Asian Americans as the "model minority" is a testament to the depth and power of American narratives of assimilation.[81]

Asian American culture shows the ways that both official and informal colonial disciplining constructs them not only as deviant or "bad" subjects, but as subjects at all, assimilated into a worldview that finds these subjects deviant.[82] In going back over the inculcation of this disciplining, we can first recognize imperialism and then its legacies. Asian American culture demonstrates the dilemma American culture faced when it decided whether to liberate or to assimilate Asians. America felt that it could do both.

Like the liberated yellow Winkies, Asians and Cubans and Puerto Ricans at the outset of American empire found themselves freed from a prior colonizer while America had been preoccupied with other matters. Moments later, America awoke to find itself in the curious predicament of freeing these formerly colonized populations from their own child-like backwardness—in other words, of colonizing. American culture needed to produce both the serendipity and the inevitability of American empire to consolidate the triumph of capitalist development, and its (perceived as) necessary gold standard, over the masses forming to bring it down. Culturally and materially, capitalist development, on the other hand, did indeed need American empire in Asia to expand markets, to achieve militarily strategic purposes, and to find and maintain sources of cheap labor and natural resources. To put matters another way, Asia happened to become the new frontier just in time, because the frontier appeared to be closed.

Articulating narratives of Asian assimilation under both colonization and immigration, Asian American literature and history show us that American empire was neither serendipitous, nor inevitable. Literature is a double-edged institution that teaches emancipation while it also imprisons. The writings by those who speak, to borrow Ralph Ellison's famous phrase, "on the lower frequencies," seek to negotiate the possibilities and the limits of taking up representation, seizing the means of production and generating discourses forged from that which official culture cannot contain or fully repress.[83] Asian American culture, with its historical roots in diverse transformations of U.S. capitalist and imperialist development, makes discernible not only the dominant and occluded history, but the forms of resistance to the narration of history. Locating this resistance requires an understanding of the transitional discourse first used to make it visible, the transition from the money question to the empire question.

Rio's sobbing as she tries to enunciate McKinley's words plays for us the new language for articulating American imperialism. But where, geographically, historically, and bodily, this new language is housed makes all the difference in the meanings we give those words. While the sympathetic likes of Bryan and Harvey were against the monetary and imperial policies of McKinley, their platform did not account for the radical subjectivity necessary for Asian American critique. Asian American literature, like Rio Gonzaga, absorbs the odd blend of serendipity and inevitability imposed by McKinley at the outset of American imperialism and finds it contradictory. And, as we shall see in the next two chapters, recognizing the ill-fitting mantle of the colonized has repercussions not only for the saltwater empires, but for the ongoing and historic crises over American heterogeneity. Chapter 3 turns specifically to the institutionalization and canonization of Asian American narratives that strategically manifest failures of contemporary multiculturalism. Multiculturalism occasioned the turn to Asian American narratives that routinely dramatize the failures of multiculturalism. Those failures then resonate with the failures of the project of U.S. imperialism. With a recognition of this aesthetics of failure, chapter 4 examines the contiguity of emergent overseas empire with Reconstruction in retreat. This historical contiguity and epistemological convergence allow us to see how both of these episodes are similarly misunderstood and forgotten failures in the modern American management of difference.

3

"THE AMERICAN EARTH WAS LIKE A HUGE HEART"

OLD DREAMS AND THE NEW IMPERIALISM

> That identity shit, man, that's old news, man.
> — Steve in Wayne Wang's *Chan Is Missing*

Assimilation and the Ends of Asian American Literature

A CULTURAL CANON, as such, has become a maligned tool of assimilation because of the exclusions necessarily involved in canon formation. Yet canons also hold out the temptation of inclusion, as well as exclusion.[1] An ongoing challenge to advocates, teachers, and practitioners of emergent literatures is how to expand the imperium of American literature and knowingly confront the defining and delimiting necessarily involved. This dilemma is particularly fraught when advocates construct canons composed of historically excluded texts. The irony of practicing exclusion while simultaneously trying to recover from exclusion has led to a curious and perhaps new formation of literary canons—not wanting to be a member of a club that would have you as a member. That is, texts achieve inclusion for resisting the terms of assimilation. This resistance to canonicity, particularly in American literature, becomes a site for critiquing U.S. imperialism in Asian American cultural politics.

This book began with a consideration of the convergences between Asian American studies and the critical study of colonial discourse. In addition to their common interventions into notions of East and West, a central overlap between these two fields is the question of assimilation. The question of assimilation is the cornerstone of Asian American cultural politics, as notions of immigrants, aliens, and "strangers from a different shore" have been the traditional figures structuring Asian American cultural politics.[2] But specifically, the failure of assimilation has been an important element marking Asian American literature as distinct from and unassimilable by mainstream American culture. This chapter focuses on the uses of this failure of assimilation, along with the other two related themes that this book has been examining: (1) the project of education, salvation, and liberation, and (2) the changing modes of representation and their implications for incorporating Asian difference. Asian American cultural politics has, perhaps ironically, been sustained by vigilant resistance to assimilation to even a much changed mainstream, which now claims to recognize and accept Asian Americans. Considering the history of Asian exclusion, such a recognition and acceptance have been regarded with well-worn suspicion.

As alluded to in the introduction to this book, "We are not new here" emerged in the early 1970s as an important rallying cry for the Asian American movement. That statement asserted a claim on America through a claim on its past.[3] A constituency was forming, based both on a common history of exclusion and, more fundamentally, on a common history with those who may not have realized that commonality. "We are not new here" is a complex demand for recognition that assimilates Asian difference in America along coordinates of revised history ("not new"), material presence ("here"), and emergent subjectivity ("we"). With such a claim, the altered cultural landscape leads one to question whether there is a "here" here, once that difference has been assimilated.

In other words, taking up the question of assimilation has meant a critique of assimilation. Consequently, a productive irony of both canonical Asian American culture and postcolonialism is the narrative of thwarted assimilation. The irony generally manifests itself in one of two ways: (1) finding acceptance in a social formation historically defined by your exclusion, or (2) waiting for the social formation that would not accept you to become worthy of your inclusion. The famous and studied end of Carlos Bulosan's 1946 *America Is in the Heart* is just such a moment when Asian American and postcolonial impulses converge.[4] This ending is something of a Mona Lisa smile for Asian American studies; its ultimately undecidable meaning provokes compelling speculations.

The scene is early 1942. After being turned away from enlisting in the United States military after the attack on Pearl Harbor, Bulosan is on a bus, yet again on the move and looking for work:

> I glanced out the window again to look at the broad land I had dreamed so much about, only to discover with astonishment that the American earth was like a huge heart unfolding warmly to receive me. I felt it spreading through my being, warming me with its glowing reality. It came to me that no man—no one at all—could destroy my faith in America again.[5]

The material conditions of Bulosan's difficult life as an exploited migrant worker, rather than contradicting a notion of a receptive America, ironically fuel his unshakeable faith in American. He describes this faith as

> something that grew out of the sacrifices and loneliness of my friends, of my brothers in America and my family in the Philippines—something that grew out of our desire to know America, and to become a part of her great tradition, and to contribute something toward her final fulfillment. I knew that no man could destroy my faith in America that has sprung from all our hopes and aspirations, *ever.* (326–27)

Bulosan ironically imagines his inclusion into America as being a product of his being excluded from it. His relationship to American incorporation is defined not by his incorporation into a "final fulfillment," but rather by his incorporation into a structure of lack and desire. Viet Nguyen and Rachel Lee have insightfully noted the gendered language that emerges when Bulosan describes his ongoing hope for a consummation in the final two sentences of his "personal history."

By juxtaposing his intense optimism with his clearly dire conditions, Bulosan can manage to eschew the despair he might feel in the face of this contradiction by producing terms for assimilation that actually celebrate colonization by the United States. His "sacrifices and loneliness," rather than being evidence of exploitation and oppression, are instead his very existence as the dispossessed become the continued opportunity for America to become America. He seems to have fully internalized and regurgitated the logic of colonization, and he does not collapse into a sobbing heap, as did Rio Gonzaga.

It should be noted, however, that the conception of America that Bulosan may well be describing would be that of the 1930s slogan, "Communism is twentieth-century Americanism."[6] The events of Bulosan's book end at the threshold of a world war against fascism in early 1942. Yet the book itself was first published in 1946, with one war, World War II, concluded, and another, the cold war, on the rise. The ambivalence of the resolution in Bulosan's narrative therefore becomes a moment for reading a historical shift. Bulosan effectively declares his allegiance to America at precisely the moment when America's official control over the Philippines has come to a violent end. (Manila was, of course, occupied by the Japanese early in World War II, prompting General Douglas MacArthur to make his famous promise: "I shall return.")

The resolution of *America Is in the Heart*, rather than presenting problems for the formation of a canon of Asian American literature, has instead become paradigmatic, both for contemporary texts and for earlier, recovered texts. Indeed, Bulosan's autobiography has become one of the most widely taught texts in Asian American studies.[7]

Assimilation Blues: Unhappy Happy Endings

Asian American literary history is a seemingly disorderly heap of things not quite working out. Success stories are not plentiful and they are looked on with suspicion as accomodationist. The paradigmatic "Asian American sensibility," in the terms of the editors of *Aiiieeeee!*, comes not from a comfortable sense of belonging in America or being a part of Asian culture. Rather, their formula for an Asian American literary sensibility was characterized in the following way:

> Asian America, so long ignored and forcibly excluded from creative participation in American culture, is wounded, sad, angry, swearing, and wondering, and this is his Aiiieeee!!! It is more that a whine, shout or scream. It is fifty years of our whole voice.[8]

Asian American literature is concerned with making visible the difficult histories that existing epistemologies are unable to represent. It demands new forms of representation that eschew conventional aesthetic standards, and may indeed aestheticize the eschewing of any conventional standards. To accept a happy ending would be to accept the ways in which you have, or have not, been represented. The editors of *Aiiieeeee!* continue,

> American culture, protecting the sanctity of its whiteness, still patronizes us as foreigners and refuses to recognize Asian-American literature as "American" literature. America does not recognize Asian America as a presence, though Asian-Americans have been here seven generations. For seven generations we have been aware of that refusal, and internalized it, with disastrous effects.[9]

The problematic cultural nationalist tendencies of this moment of forging an Asian American cultural identity have been rightly critiqued. Yet what remains potentially useful, and at times shrilly distracting, is a vigilant refusal of resolution for fear of being whitewashed or being a "banana"—yellow on the outside, but white on the inside. The tradition of Asian American literature is that of suspicion over resolution. The most valorized texts are those that needed recovery, such as John Okada's *No-No Boy* (1957) and the writings of Sui Sin Far (Edith Eaton).[10] And the most suspect texts are those that were popular with mainstream America, such as C. Y. Lee's *Flower Drum Song* (1957).[11] Asian American literature, as it was forming as a canon, would take its cue from these recovered, and by implication, misunderstood texts. The post-*Aiiieeeee!* moment would be able to begin from a refusal to conform to "euphemized white racist love."[12] This refusal is perhaps the one aspect of the preface to *Aiiieeeee!* that has managed to live on usefully in contemporary Asian American cultural politics. We see it in approaches to Fae Myenne Ng's acclaimed first novel, *Bone*.[13]

Bone by Fae Myenne Ng

Lisa Lowe's reading of Fae Myenne Ng's *Bone* (1993) is a now classic example of the Asian American cultural politics of refusal, of even strategic defeat:

> If historical narrative is, as [Walter] Benjamin suggests, a narrative that has "empathy with the victor," the material memory of the unvictorious is not simply repressed by that narrative; it dialectically returns, to pressure and restructure precisely the regimes of uniformity that seek to contain it as representation.[14]

Lowe's analysis of *Bone* proceeds from the failure of Ng's novel to abide by chronology; the novel ends at a point that is actually *earlier* than when it began.

But for this failure to be compelling and instructive, it must *feel* like success. In terms of the conventions of the novel form, the ending of *Bone* is deeply satisfying. Leila declares in the closing paragraph:

> I was reassured. I knew what I held in my heart would guide me. So I wasn't worried when I turned that corner, leaving the old blue sign, Salmon Alley, Mah and Leon—everything—backdaire. (193)

The End. As with *Fifth Chinese Daughter*, *The Woman Warrior*, and *The Joy Luck Club* before it, we are left with a familiar and quite reassuring image from the stock tropes of the Chinatown mothers-and-daughters genre: daughter leaves home with a hard-won sense of self.[15] In those earlier books, we are comforted by the opening of a pottery shop, a coming to voice, or a realization of what it means to be Chinese. If we are caught up in the narrative satisfactions of *Bone*'s ending, we must willingly forget that Ona will kill herself, that Leon and Mah will remain unreconciled, and that Leila herself will move back to Salmon Alley. The novel even ends with a neologism, "backdaire," created and utilized by Leila, derived from a Salmon Alley sign that reads "updaire."

Leila's development as an individual provides the narrative resolution to the book, but in the novel's irresolution, the world in which she lives still cannot be contained by this ending. *Bone* undermines narrative development along an axis of subject formation and in doing so effectively rejects temporality as a conventional coordinate for unifying the narrative. Lowe argues that ultimately the failure of linear, temporal development makes more discernible the ways that local and global space can get mapped by Ng's story of Chinatown mothers and daughters. Such a failed resolution creates a desire to interrogate its reasons for failing.

"In the Land of the Free" by Sui Sin Far

Perhaps the most celebrated act of literary recovery of Asian American literature was the return of Sui Sin Far (1865–1914). Through what Guy Beauregard has usefully called "the politics of reclamation" of the Asian American movement's recovery of Edith Eaton/

Sui Sin Far, her stories were initially recognizable as Asian American literature because of their seemingly anachronistic efforts to assert an Asian American subjectivity in a land where that was virtually unthinkable.[16] As Sui Sin Far became a more canonical figure in Asian American literature, Beauregard compellingly asserts, the complexity of her representations became more appreciated for queerness and for geopolitics, as well as her earlier function as a prescient advocate for a maligned population. If we reframe her stories as connected to the literary and historical conditions of her moment, and connect the literary and historical conditions of her moment to the rise and fall of multiculturalism and the emergence and ascendance of U.S. imperialism, the significance of a lost-and-found cache of sentimental stories from the turn-of-the-century era becomes oddly resonant with matters that the present has been unable to resolve. The crisis of the Chinese immigrants in Sui Sin Far's stories is our own, for it is the crisis of uncontained difference and the contradictions of the institutions that seek to contain them. In the narrative of her literary martyrdom, Far's downfall was her advocacy of a population whose subjectivity no one wanted to recognize. Her seemingly quaint appeals for sympathy for Asian immigrants to North America demanded reconfigurations of subject and object that American culture was profoundly unwilling to entertain.

Judging from the obscurity into which Sui Sin Far's writings fell, Asian American subjectivity at the dawn of the twentieth century was an idea whose time had not yet come. It would take more than sixty years before these articulations from the turn-of-the-century era could be appreciated as distinctly Asian American. Far's literary output, which spoke itself as what we would now call Asian American, found few auditors. Indeed the fact that these texts needed recovery is instructive about the challenges that Asian immigrants faced when seeking recognition as something other than a foreign menace or an industrial reserve army.

Initially recovered mainly because she wrote what are generally perceived as stories sympathetic to Chinese Americans in the West, Far's stories are also documents bearing the specific traces of their time. The canonical function that Far's stories serve, as recovered failures, is multilayered. She is an author before her time, which allows her to be a figure of both her own time and ours, making visible the previously unbridgeable gulf between a readership that could not understand her then and a readership that does understand her today. Annette White-Parks and the late Amy Ling have done important work to recover and republish Far's writings and to place her into American literary history. Their compilation of Far's writings and White-Parks's biography of Edith Eaton/Sui Sin Far have ensured that Far will remain a significant figure of early twentieth-century letters and retain her status as the earliest writer of Asian American literature in English. Almost apologetically, White-Parks writes, "[T]he issue of quality in [Far's] writings cannot be addressed in the absence of the cultural and literary contexts within which she wrote."[17] Yet it is the capacity of Far's writing to show us the intervening ideologies that almost made her lost to history. Through her writing and as a historical figure, Far is therefore immanent evidence of the return of epistemologies that had been repressed.

In Far's most anthologized work of fiction, "In the Land of the Free" (1912), the mother Lae Choo and father Hom Hing are virtually bankrupted by the legal fees incurred for supposedly dealing with all the red tape necessary to recover their son, who is being held in detention.[18] Lae Choo had gone back to China to look after her in-laws, and while away, her son was born. Upon reentering the United States, Little One goes into the custody of the customs officials, due to his lack of paperwork. A protracted legal struggle ensues as they attempt to establish their legal claim to their son.

In a calculatedly heart-wrenching scene, we see the parents nearly bankrupted in their fight. Lae Choo says to their lawyer:

> See, my jade earrings—my gold buttons—my hairpins—my comb of pearl and my rings—one, two, three, four, five rings; very good—very good—all same much money. I give them all to you. You take and bring me paper for my Little One. (100)

James Clancy, their lawyer, still needs to collect more money for his fee. Before Lae Choo goes to get her jewelry to pay the lawyer, she first hands him her gold bracelet. Clancy still prefers cash to Lae Choo's dowry.

> "Oh, look here, I can't accept this," said James Clancy, walking back to Hom Hing and laying down the bracelet before him.
> "It's all right," said Hom Hing, seriously, "pure China gold. My wife's parents give it to her when we married."

"But I can't take it anyway," protested the young man.

"It is all same as money. And you want money to go to Washington," in a matter of fact manner. (100)

As a matter of fact, it is not "all same as money." The value of the jewels is neither as stable nor as fungible as cash. Clancy knows this, as does Hom Hing.

Lae Choo piled up her jewels before the lawyer.

Hom Hing laid a restraining hand upon her shoulder. "Not all, my wife," he said in Chinese. He selected a ring—his gift to Lae Choo when she dreamed of the tree with the red flower. The rest of the jewels he pushed toward the man.

"Take them and sell them," said he. "They will pay your fare to Washington and bring you back with the paper." (100)

In an interesting inversion of the era's preoccupation with monetary convertibility, the lawyer is sent to Washington to turn precious metals into paper. Withholding the ring that commemorated Lae Choo's pregnancy is Hom Hing's attempt to maintain sentimental value and, in the process, to displace his in-laws.

For one moment James Clancy hesistated. He was not a sentimental man; but something within him arose against accepting such payment for his services.

"They are good, good," pleadingly asserted Law Choo, seeing his hesitation.

Whereupon he seized the jewels, thrust them into his coat pocket, and walked rapidly away from the store. (100)

In the end, we see that Clancy does accept the non-cash payment. The narrator tells us that Clancy's hesitation is prompted by his feelings of sympathy for the immigrant couple. Lae Choo, however, interprets the hesitation as anxiety over inconvertibility. That Clancy does take the jewels and successfully obtains the paper from Washington makes Lae Choo's interpretation the more convincing one.

Maudlin sentiment is not the vehicle for understanding the subjectivity of Lae Choo. She is acutely aware of the contradiction between monetary convertibility and all that it implies about the construction of equivalences. Our narrator codes this anxiety as pathos. This is not to say that pathos is not operating in the narrative; this is one of many tortured scenes in the Far oeuvre. Rather, we can see how this climactic moment in the story calls up the terms with which an Asian American subjectivity exceeds the conventional terms of producing identification.

An earlier moment in the story also illustrates Lae Choo's critical perspective on the production of identification. Clancy had stopped by to inspire hope in the Chinese American couple, saying that he was very close to getting their son back. That inspiration was what led the couple to surrender their not-yet-monetary assets to him. Clancy's encouraging news prompts Lae Choo to make an odd statement: "'Oh,' she cried, turning to James Clancy, 'You are a hundred man good!'" But the narrator notes Clancy's discomfort: "The young man felt somewhat embarrassed; his eyes shifted a little under the intense gaze of the Chinese mother" (99). Feeling that he is now the gazed-at, Clancy feels uneasy. On one level, he knows that he is cruelly exploiting the tragedy of this couple; he is a lawyer, after all. But on another level, he has just been placed along an axis of quantification that he neither deserves nor really understands. After Lae Choo realizes that Clancy had been manipulating their suffering for his advantage, her insult is cryptically cutting:

> For a moment Lae Choo gazed wonderingly from one face to the other; then, comprehension dawning upon her, with swift anger pointing to the lawyer, she cried: "You not one hundred man good; you just common white man." "Yes, ma'am," returned James Clancy, bowing and smiling ironically. (99)

He might as well have said, "Whatever." She later even hails Clancy with "Stop, white man; white man, stop!" (99). The gulf between Lae Choo's critical use of a rhetoric of valuation and Clancy's uneasy dismissal of her regard emerges as the point at which an Asian American subjectivity is fashioned. She is more attuned to a conception of the world based on literal and figural forms of monetizing.

In light of these invoked discourses of equivalence, the poignant ending of Far's story has added significance. After ten months in the mission house, Little One has been renamed Little Kim. Not only has he learned to speak, but he speaks English. He is clad like an American, "dressed in blue cotton overalls and white-soled shoes." And, most disturbing of all, is the moment of reunion: "[Lae Choo] fell on her knees and stretched her hungry arms toward her son. But the Little One shrunk from her and tried to hide himself in the folds of the white woman's skirt. 'Go'way, go'way!' he bade his mother" (101).

After all of their sacrifices to obtain a redeemable piece of paper, the paper does not really get them their son back.

This conclusion offers an interesting early portrait of the inter-generational friction so pervasive in countless Asian American family narratives. But juxtaposed with this otherwise trite rendering of the not-Asian/not-American condition of Little One is Lae Choo's critical epistemology of money, and in particular, value, (in)convertibility, and exchange. While the second-generation Little One now has difficulty identifying with the first-generation Hom Hing and Lae Choo, they do both share a tenuous relationship to the failure of American culture to render them abstract and equivalent. Far's success today is tied to her failure a century ago. She can be claimed as virtually a subaltern voice that had to disappear to be meaningful in her return to a present. Asian American cultural politics in the present is now epistemologically equipped to recognize how she was of her day, and how her day is now newly recognized as significant.

Chan Is Missing by Wayne Wang

I now turn to a foundational Asian American cinematic representation of Asian American nonrepresentation: Wayne Wang's 1981 independent film, *Chan Is Missing*.[19] In a tense scene near the end of this revisionist detective film, our two investigators, Jo and Steve, finally begin to give up hope that they will ever find Chan Hung, their friend who had suddenly disappeared. Jo begins by lamenting Chan's inability to find "identity." Chan's lack of identity led to his departure, he argues:

> You know, it's hard enough for guys like us who's been here so long to find identity, I can imagine Chan Hung, somebody from China coming here and trying to find himself.[20]

Steve, however, is unconvinced by this suggestion. He says, "Aw, that's a bunch of bullshit, man. That identity shit, man, that's old news, man. It happened ten years ago" (62). Steve reminds Jo that since the late 1960s and early 1970s, Chinese Americans had become so visible in San Francisco that finding an identity to live with should not have been a problem: "The Chinese are all over this fucking city, man. What do you mean about identity? They got their own identity. I got my identity" (62–63).[21]

As their conversation heatedly continues, the topic makes a curious shift from Chan's presumed failure to find "identity" to the other object of their search: their money. It was becoming apparent that Chan had embezzled four thousand dollars from their abortive taxi venture. Any crisis of identity becomes moot, leaving only the money as their troublesome lack. In the end, their money returns, but Chan Hung remains unseen, if not unseeable, by Jo, Steve, and the viewers of the film.

The inability of Jo, Steve, and the film itself to find Chan Hung is emblematic of the historical shifts this study examines. Jo and Steve are antiheroes of self-determined assimilation. They belong to an older moment when the American dream was to become an owner-operator of a small business and "be our own boss," as Jo says of their doomed enterprise early in the film (17). They fail spectacularly, both to realize this economic goal and to literally and figurally apprehend the thieving Chan Hung. Chan Hung is a new formation of Asian American who eludes "that identity shit." Had Jo's explanations of Chan's fate been accurate, he and Steve would have been able to track Chan down.

Yet Chan remains missing. Chan and their money disappear to become something with which they cannot identify: a free-floating investor in a new age of capital mobility. The money returns, but Chan does not. From the evidence they gather, Jo and Steve learn that Chan Hung essentially used their short-term capital to bankroll his disappearance. Even with their four thousand dollars back, Jo and Steve are left feeling out of step with the capital flow of globalization that was emerging in the 1970s and 1980s.[22] They can only refer to this emergent formation as "the new Chinese money that's coming in now" (15), when they should also understand the new Chinese people that are coming in now. The hapless FOB (fresh off the boat) Chan Hung exercised a mobility that neither his streetwise ABC (American-born Chinese) partners, nor the film itself could envision and he became something new: the impact of emergent international finance capitalism on the politics of late 1970s San Francisco.[23]

And so, with the failure to recover the person of Chan Hung and the success at recovering their money, Jo and Steve find themselves in an epistemological crisis over the terms of their incorporation into America. It is a crisis that defines the limits of cultural identity. That is, the irresolution of the narrative shows the divergence of culture and economy.

As Peter Feng notes, Wang's film was immensely influential on the cinematic formation—and dissolution—of Asian American identity.[24] This was a crisis for multiculturalism, a crisis brought about by its own unresolved internal contradictions, as well as the ascendance of globalization as a new formation that multiculturalism cannot contain. We have seen some of the best minds of our generation reject the idea that multiculturalism is the Promised Land. Breaking silence and then coming to voice is not an end, but a strategic beginning, a beginning that unleashes a Pandora's box of histories that the present finds unresolved, contradictory, and nonetheless true.

This return of the repressed demonstrates how the current era of transition uncannily resonates with a key transition of the past. That is, reading Asian American literature in the era of the ascendance of globalization provides glimpses of another questionable enterprise: the early twentieth-century emergence of American colonialism in the Pacific Rim. The failure of that earlier enterprise—so traumatic to national culture that it had to be repressed—came back to haunt the present at the precise moment that multiculturalism failed to address the emerging contradictions of civil society and globalization. Asian American literature is both a witness to and a product of these historical transitions.

Considering the historical revisionism that Asian American culture has occasioned, it may seem odd that one of the most basic questions of literary scholarship has not really been asked about Asian American literature: namely, what is its period? This question has not come up because Asian American literature was designed to cut through periodizations to see connections and commonalities that made an "Asian American sensibility" discernible.[25] The developmental aesthetics of the novel and of chronological history were less appropriate for Asian American cultural politics than was the logic of the anthology of unearthed and wondrous fragments. Much of this literature had disappeared and had to be disinterred like so many archaeological relics used to reconstruct a formerly unrecognizable past. Historical context was then subordinate to "social context" because the literature had no ordinary relationship to history.[26]

Asian American literature therefore can be said to belong to the era that recovered and read it as much as—or even more than—it does to the moments that saw its creation. Furthermore, the "textual coalition" of Asian American literature is both a document of the contemporary moment and a document of the historical moments it makes visible.[27] These moments may not be limited to that of its production. Asian American literature has become increasingly fractured, yet it retains a useful coherence when understood as both a product of the civil rights era and a vestige of American colonialism and labor recruitment in Asia and the Pacific.

This epistemology is structured around two parallel historical developments: the failure of multiculturalism and the failure of American colonialism. The former failed due to the ascendance of globalization and the latter due to its emergence. These historical failures are parallel not temporally, but conceptually. Despite their different historical moments, identity politics and the civilizing mission both failed to resolve the contradiction between civil society and globalization. To put matters bluntly, whenever we encounter in Asian American literature the structuring trope of failed assimilation to the United States, we encounter the reliving of a repressed idea: American colonialism. The meaning of this failure has changed with the downfall of multiculturalism and its models of incorporating new national subjects. Globalization has fundamentally reconceptualized social and economic relations to make questions of cultural identity newly irrelevant and newly critical.

An offhand question in *Chan Is Missing* articulates this dilemma between political economy and identity politics. Early on in Jo and Steve's search, they go to the Manilatown Senior Center, where Chan was a coworker in food service with Presco. Presco asks Jo and Steve: "You looking for your money or you looking for Mr. Chan?" Presco's question articulates the simultaneous division and comparability of persons and money. He asks the question because Steve had bluntly said, "I'm looking for money, man." Jo, however, in response to Presco's question, asks, "Do you know where he is?" (29). The conflict between Jo's and Steve's motivations for finding Chan again emerge: Jo is looking for Chan and Steve is looking for the money. The ambivalent epistemological desire fueling the mystery narrative of Wang's film erupts in this question that Presco asks early in the film.[28]

More generally, this doomed process is made legible at moments when Asian Americans seek to claim America, an America that had already claimed them by the outset of the twentieth century. Key texts of the Asian American literary canon critically appropriate this assimilation narrative and in doing so, they recuperate lost specificities of America's emergent imperial ethos. That ethos can be recovered in Asian American cultural production by grasping the epistemologies of abstraction and reification that are fundamental to Asian American identity formation. These become visible at moments of failure, when subject or identity formation do not yield the satisfactions they were supposed to.

Chan Is Missing, I argue, is therefore not only a critique of identity formation, but a representation of the new empire. In tracing the terms of this unresolved ending, we find ourselves returning to rethink one of the first scenes in the movie. Late in the film, Jo laments Chan's inability to find "identity," asserting that Chan's lack of identity led to his departure. Steve makes the provocative observation—"That identity shit, man, that's old news, man. It happened ten years ago"—because Chinese Americans are so numerous and visible in San Francisco. Yet the meaning of identity has changed, from that of the individual beset by an identity crisis to another entity they do not know how to recognize: venture capital.

As it dawns on Jo and Steve that they may never find Chan, they turn to the other object of their search: their money, the four thousand dollars that Chan—temporarily, it turns out—took off their persons and out of their pockets. So their efforts to incorporate as a taxicab company fail, and the issue of personal cultural identity falls away as well. Steve sizes up the situation in a train of thought that makes finding Chan's identity a moot issue:

> Hey, I understand the situation, man. Don't tell me I don't understand the situation. I just want to know why you're tripping so heavy on it for. Because obviously to me, man, the facts are the guy is a fucking liar. He's been lying to us. Every time we go to somebody different we hear a different story. Here's how I see it. If you're sick, you go see a doctor, right? If you're going nuts you go see a shrink. If you need some money, man, you go to a bank or a loan company. You know, somebody rips off your money, if you don't have no friends who can take care of it you go to the cops and let them take care of it. (64)

The personal drops away; what matters is their missing capital. Yet a search for identity also ends up being a search for their money. Ultimately they recover their money, but Chan's identity remains in the "negative" column. In an interview, Wayne Wang calls Chan Hung a "negative character"—continually defined more by what he is not, than what he is. They never do find the still warm body of Chan Hung. They never positively identify him, so to speak.[29]

The recoverable "identity"—if we may call it that—that had been missing was the money itself. The only resolution to this ostensible detective narrative happens not at the site of persons, but of money. Steve says, "Eh, we're no closer than when we started, man. In fact, we're—I'm more confused, now I don't even know the guy we're talking about." Jo responds, "Look, he didn't take that money." "Then where's the money?" Steve asks (65).

In their investigation, numerous characters speculated about what kinds of circuits of speculation the four thousand dollars might have traveled in Chan's possession. Yet in the scene that immediately follows, they do get their money back, all four thousand, though they do not know or even care anymore what had happened to it. They just take it back with thanks to Jenny Chan, Chan Hung's estranged daughter.

With the mystery resolved, the inscrutable Chinese immigrant disappears and he is not missed. True, the money has come back, but narratives of the formation of persons, in this case Chan Hung, drop out of the story altogether. Left behind is the recovery of a sum of money: that is the ultimate narrative resolution to this soft-boiled detective story.

While the money has indeed returned, it is not, I argue, the same. The transformations the four thousand dollars might have undergone by the time it is returned to its liquidity for Steve and Jo turn the money into capital after it has probably been temporary capital for speculation in Asia.[30] The four thousand dollars is only the principal; any interest or dividends—or losses for that matter—have been denied to Steve and Jo, along with Chan Hung. With only their principal for their troubles, Steve and Jo are left out of the loop of speculation and finance capital. Asian Americans must be content to remain money, and not capital.

On this matter they are unsentimental. The fact that Chan is still effectively missing is of little import. To them, Chan's substitution by money in the resolution of the narrative returns order to the Asian American community, which had thought it was disrupted by his loss. The impediment to the resumption of life turns out to be a matter of making a balance sheet square, and not a matter of anything personal. The film then fittingly and wryly ends with Pat Suzuki singing "Grant Avenue" from the musical *Flower Drum Song,* over what the screenplay describes as

> [a] montage of sidewalk scenes, Chinese architecture, time-worn buildings, turtles swimming in pans, gung fu posters and giant fortune cookies in store windows. An elderly Chinese woman walks along her balcony, then grasps the railing and rocks back and forth, seemingly in time with the up-tempo soundtrack. Montage continues with an Italian Market, skyscrapers of the neighboring financial district, dim sum restaurant displays, more elderly women on the street, and tinseled window dressing. (75)

Life has indeed gone on and it probably did not pause to consider Chan Hung's vanishing anyway. Instead of resolving at a fully formed Asian American subject as a narrative of ethnic identity would, the film shows us a rather impersonal neighborhood space. We never see Chan Hung at the end, but we do see San Francisco Chinatown with all its vibrant intricacies: adjacent to the waning North Beach Italian American neighborhood on one side and overshadowed by a modern metropolis on the Pacific Rim. The images matter-of-factly satirize the Broadway show-tune rendition of "Grant Avenue" through juxtaposition with the real thing. The two things we are left with are the recovered money and the relatively unfazed space of Chinatown.

In *Chan Is Missing,* money and social space displace people as the center of the universe. This displacement is the triumph of U.S. imperialism. That is, the world has come to be understood as a space for the circulation of money, and people just facilitate the process. Chan Hung does not leave his heart in San Francisco; he leaves his principal.

Such a disappearance flies in the face of identity politics. He never becomes a compositional subject for the strategic use of essentialism. He is an absence that cannot be recognized or even mourned. The actual presence of Chan Hung is appropriately under erasure. He was almost never there at all.

In an early scene from *Chan Is Missing,* we can already begin to see the ways in which Jo and Steve feel left out of the international division of labor. We first see that Jo is a cab driver, a generally abject occupation. He tries to make the best of things by telling us in his voiceover about a "game" he plays: seeing how long it takes non-Asian passengers to ask him, "What's a good place to eat in Chinatown?"

"Under three seconds," he continues, "that question comes up under three seconds 90 percent of the time. I usually give them my routine on the difference between Mandarin and Cantonese food and get a *good* tip" (11–12). While he is self-conscious of the performativity of his routine, he nonetheless performs it regularly for his "*good* tip." Despite his having narrative control over the film, he still interestedly maintains his status as a shuffling menial *Zagat* that would outrage Frank Chin and delight Fred Eng of *The Year of the Dragon*.[31]

The scene immediately shifts to Jo entering the apartment of his nephew and niece, Steve and Amy, where we catch the three of them in media res, engaging in a confusing conversation. The relative opacity of this domestic scene juxtaposed with the utter familiarity of the public cab scene emphasizes our entrance into a private and less overtly performative space. What seems like idle banter actually shows us their frustrating relationship to the changes going on in San Francisco's Chinatown in the late 1970s and early 1980s. Jo did not expect to find them in the kitchen, as he says, "I thought you guys weren't going to eat at home." Steve and Amy did not expect to be there themselves, but they felt out of place in their own neighborhood; as Steve says, "Yeah. I was going to take my mother and sister out. We were going to go to the Golden Lantern. But see, all the people there are from Taiwan, and Gum sing, you know, all the Communists eat there, so we decided to eat at home" (12–13).

In a world they find both familiarly and newly hostile, they all retreat to their home. The familiar hostility is something they have adapted to, as evidenced by Jo's game with his passenger. But the new hostility has these ABCs at a loss. The ominous bogeymen that trouble them are referred to as "the Commie bandwagon" or the "Taiwan competitor" or "the new Chinese money that's coming in now." The global economy has come to their corner of San Francisco and they feel threatened by it. So when Jo finally tells the audience via his voiceover what the story is about, that is, that Chan is missing, we can already understand how it may play out. That is, they really want to recover their lost money, which has been embezzled by an occupationally downgraded immigrant.

Steve's rage in the argument over identity that ends the film then begins to make more sense. When he says, "The Chinese are all over this fucking city, man. What do you mean about identity? They got their own identity. I got my identity," he says it as one who is threatened. The world is moving on and he is not moving with it and he stands to lose more than his identity can recover. But Jo insists on his antiquated notion of the salvation in being Asian American: "You know, it's hard enough for guys like us who's been here so long to find an identity, I can imagine Chan Hung, somebody from China coming over here and trying to find himself." Steve fires back: "Aw, that's a bunch of bullshit, man. That identity shit, man, that's old news, man. It happened ten years ago" (62).

While the Asian American movement did emphasize its solidarity with Third World struggles, it had to balance that alliance with the desire to not have Asian Americans be considered foreigners. The editors of *Aiiieeeee!* repeatedly emphasize their American-born status, and their preface contains an occasional anti-immigrant point of view. The writers feel that recent Asian immigrants are not the Asian Americans they are or who they write about:

> [Francis] Hsu's *The Challenge of the American Dream* may or may not give us insight into the mind of the first-generation upper-middle-class Chinese immigrant scholar, but in terms of the native Chinese American sensibility, we can only note that, in the great tradition of Charlie Chan and Leong Gor Yun, his vision of Chinese America reinforces white racist stereotypes and falls short of the vision Malcolm X and other blacks had for their "minority." (xiii)

Chan Hung, as it turns out, was an upper-middle-class scholar who invented the first word-processing system in Chinese. Jo readily admits this in the hopes of generating Steve's sympathy. Steve, and perhaps also Jo, have come to fear the worst: they have been played by someone who knew the system better than they did and over whom they had thought they could have cultural superiority as Asian Americans. They do get their money back, but that may only point to their having been used up and discarded. They have simply functioned as an interest-free loan company in the new global economy and they are just happy to have their old money back.

Their dreams of "becoming their own bosses" never materialize and it becomes evident that even if they had gone through with getting their taxi license, they would still be the same cabbies doing the same Sambo-esque "routine" for the same hungry tourists. Their relatively unsophisticated and local relationship to the cash they recover marks their inability to envision anything beyond one day owning their own little firm within an insular Chinatown's small producer economy. The "positive" assertion of Asian American identity only emphasizes the "negative": neither they, nor Chan Hung, are what they thought they were. Almost cruelly, Wang's film shows, even as early as 1981, that the comfort that ABCs have earned from their participation in new social movements leaves them unable to envision a new relationship to the changing terms of participation in the new economy.

The failures of America's formal colonial projects in the Philippines taught America that this was not the way things should work. American empire was primarily an economic project, the blessings of capitalism writ large.[32] And a new epistemology became necessary. At the turn of the century, economy came to figure the terms of personhood, of subject status. As literary critic Walter Benn Michaels provocatively notes of the turn-of-the-century period: "Failing to be a person, [the economy] images by the way it isn't a person the condition in naturalism of the possibility of persons."[33] That is, by being in a binary opposition, the personal and the economic newly emerge at this period as mutually constitutive. Only now economy earns the status as the primary category, and persons the one that emerges from it.

What it means to be a subject is built on and against conceptions of market forces. This new cultural formation necessarily shaped the ways that American culture conceives of its empire, or rather, how it avoids conceiving of it. As we have seen, American culture at the turn of the century rendered with a now-forgotten frankness visions of American empire as the unabashed incorporation of the globe and its denizens both under the banner of the United States and into a market economy. Such figurations of empire coupled with and even overshadowed such older notions of the civilizing missions, which came to be called "benevolent assimilation."[34]

Instead of "benevolent assimilation," the more suitable term for the U.S. imperial project was the one used by President (and former governor of the Philippines) William Howard Taft in 1912: "dollar diplomacy." Principally an economic penetration, Taft described the policy as one "substituting dollars for bullets."[35] But we must not wholly buy into this idea by forgetting that the United States did spend many bullets in its "purchase" of the Philippines from Spain.[36]

U.S. material wealth was made possible by cheap, racialized immigrant labor, while simultaneously U.S. dominance abroad was taking the form of foreign investment.[37] The emergence of this foreign investment occurred on the heels of the virtual closure of U.S. borders to immigrant laborers from Asia.[38] Blatantly racist laws disallowed the naturalization of immigrants from Asia, ensuring their subsequent ineligibility to own land under Alien Land laws. Privacy, property, and citizenship went together, as did disenfranchisement and exploitation.

With increasing U.S. investment in Asia, the establishment of military bases in the Far East, and the whitening of the American West, the Pacific Rim as we know it emerged. Today's globalization gestated in "dollar diplomacy." American culture conceived of empire as the expansion of capital, the spread of American money, the scattershot of the decidedly un-bullet-like dollars of dollar diplomacy. The idea that these newly incorporated masses could one day be middle class was both an articulated declaration and an implicit assumption of U.S. imperialism. America's new and improved method of practicing empire meant that money's movements virtually replaced settler colonialism.[39]

From our historical vantage point, the link between the money question and the empire question can be found in nineteenth-century conceptions of mobility—mobility for people and money. For in the discourse of the money question, the mobility of money and the mobility of persons were still considered the same kind of mobility. That is, people carried money.

Portability is a defining characteristic of money: money is not money without it. Marx's formulation quoted earlier in this book bears repeating in this context: "Money is 'impersonal' property. It permits me to transport on my person, in my pocket, social power and social relations in general: the substance of society. Money puts social power in material form into the hands of private persons, who exercise it as individuals."[40] To be money, people must be able to carry you, and perhaps conversely, to be a person, you must be able to carry money.

Today money, in its various morphologies, can move infinitely faster than we the people, in our one morphology, do. But we should remember that it was not always so. In the late nineteenth century, a main argument against specie—and therefore an anti-silver argument—was that its cumbersome physical weight would slow transactions down in an increasingly rapid and large-scale economy.[41] Financial issues and the "managerial revolution" in American business were popularly debated concerns. Historians and economists continue to debate the significance of the gold standard and ponder what might have happened if a silver or bimetallic standard had been adopted.[42] The most curious thing is that ordinary people discussed these issues at all, and they discussed them passionately and allegorically, as we saw in chapter 2.

So much seemed to depend on the form of money and processes of monetizing because they were so palpable and familiar. Human and monetary mobilities were seen as simply differing in degree when now we see them as differing in kind. Money and people had been considered part of the same phenomenon: movement in the noncyber, physical world.[43] As one 1920s commentator on dollar diplomacy remarked: "National boundary lines make the movement of capital more difficult; wars temporarily restrict it, but in the long run it is easier to get a visa for a financial transaction than it is for a passport permitting emigration."[44]

It was believed that the fate of U.S. capitalist development hinged on the physical form that money took, and bimetallism was seen as an anathema to foreign investments, and therefore, to U.S. empire.[45] For a faster economy, American imperialism needed to discursively disconnect persons and capital. Under an older monetary paradigm, bodies and bullion were generally attached, both physically and conceptually.[46]

Culture, then, is the arena for imagining their moment and method of separation. Culture also allows us to imagine the inextricable joinedness of persons and money toward excavating emergent conceptions of American empire. Asian American culture, in particular, with its historical roots in the birth of U.S. empire, allows us to see the beginnings of what sociologist Aihwa Ong calls "ungrounded empire," an empire that builds on and supplants territory as its defining feature.[47]

In the denial of subjectivity to Asian Americans, the price of assimilation, of survival even, has consistently been the forgetting of that colonial history. Asian Americans' status as what can probably be most accurately described as the "formerly colonized" still sidesteps that label in the quest for the American dream.

A century ago, when the United States became an extraterritorial empire, assimilating empire to U.S. national culture faced crises of legitimacy, and it did not succeed in the face of those challenges. Instead, the United States came to practice empire so differently that it ceased to be recognized as one. Denying empire meant coming up with new names, such as *investment in emerging markets, development, strategic military bases, stepping stone to China's limitless markets, the white man's burden,* and perhaps most brilliantly, *decolonization* itself. But America's colonizing failure also meant actually changing the method of colonizing, from the territorial and administrative to the informal and impersonal. Gayatri Spivak's formulation in "Can the Subaltern Speak?" is still the best breakdown of this transition, from the European to the American globe:

> The contemporary international division of labor is a displacement of the divided field of nineteenth-century territorial imperialism. Put simply, a group of countries, generally first-world, are in the position of investing capital; another group, generally third-world, provide the field for investment, both through the comprador indigenous capitalists and their ill-protected and shifting labor force. In the interest of maintaining the circulation and growth of industrial capital (and of the concomitant task of administration within nineteenth-century territorial imperialism), transportation, law, and standardized education systems were developed—even as local industries were destroyed, land distribution was rearranged, and raw material was transferred to the colonizing country. With so-called decolonization, the growth of multinational capital, and the relief of the administrative charge, "development" does not now involve wholesale legislation and establishing educational *systems* in a comparable way. This impedes the growth of consumerism in comprador countries.[48]

American ingenuity turns out not to be a myth, as the Europeans get beaten at their own game. The divided field of the old colonialism becomes a unified one under America's stewardship with the emergence of the international division of labor. Citizen-consumers are its benefactors and that is what we are encouraged to become if we are not that already.

This globality theory makes sense from a global standpoint. But where, then, does a troublesome category such as "Asian American" come into play? Despite physically residing in the first world, Asian Americans' access to its benefits have been dubious. As Trinh T. Minha has pointedly observed, "The West is painfully made to realize the existence of a Third World in the First World, and vice versa."[49] The early Asian American movement in the 1960s and 1970s emphasized the connection of Asian Americans to those questionably decolonized populations in Asia.[50] These protesters were the Asian Americans whose immigration history predated the landmark 1965

Immigration and Naturalization Act. Jo and Steve, Val, and Allos are all pre-1965 Asian Americans who find themselves in a country that is coming to sit atop the international division of labor.

The period before the Asian American movement was a time marked more by what was done to Asian Americans than by what they themselves did. Labor and lawsuits seemed to be the main genres of Asian American expression.[51] We can read the significance of the emergence of American empire through the ways in which we have trouble seeing its emergence. Asian American culture provides these unexpected sites and shows us what is at stake in thinking critically about so pervasive a concept as money.

Knowing the troubled history of money would mean knowing the United States as empire. Asian American culture reminds us of this conception of history because of Asian Americans' shadowy relationship to the beginnings of U.S. imperialism. In and through Asian American literature, we can reframe textual moments to generate genealogies of concepts that we have ceased to question so that we can find this transition's skeleton in globalization's closet.

Chan Is Missing, Bone, "In the Land of the Free," and *America Is in the Heart* are all staples of the Asian American canon. Each of these texts uses its genre and its content to serve the main canonical function of Asian American literature: to assert that there is a distinct category called Asian American literature. Asian American literature as a minority discourse, that is, as a literature serving a minor function to a major language, inherently opens a space for alternative possibility, for histories that do not have a justification of the present as their telos. Yet in addition to providing such narratives of identity-formation, each text reappraises "we are here because you were there" through its representations of assimilation.[52] We see narratives of ethnic identity and analyses of political economy that are not simply juxtaposed, but are shown to be a mutually constituting thematic.

Being able to navigate the discursive, and material, terrain of money and markets means access to, and incorporation into, late capitalism. Each of these pre-1965 Asian Americans—Leila Fu, Carlos Bulosan, and Jo and Steve—fails in this regard as their relationship to the new order has not made a transition to a more cosmopolitan sensibility. They cling to a liberal humanism in the face of overwhelming economic changes that make them seem deluded. Leila retreats to a moment when things were good, "the get long time," even it if is not the present. Bulosan rhapsodizes about a 1930s socialist vision that was fast on the road to paranoid persecution, if not prosecution. Jo and Steve are in full possession of their "identities," which helps Jo in particular feel paternalistic toward Chan Hung. He and Steve are just happy to get their four thousand dollars back, without Chan Hung or any interest.

Lae Choo and Hom Hing, by contrast, are figures whose narrative ends quite unhappily, despite the ostensible return of Little One/Little Kim. In a span of ten months in a missionary house, he has become afraid of his parents, seeking cover in the skirts of his white woman protectress. Sui Sin Far, the earliest of the writers, is profoundly skeptical about the missionary capacity of American culture in the early twentieth century. Crossing historical periods, all of these narratives share a common ambivalence about the meaning of resolution, both the resolution of the narrative forms they take, as well as the resolution of Asian difference to American culture.

Each of these narratives leaves readers and viewers with a sense of productive unease at their failed resolutions. Asian American cultural politics offers a way of making that failure meaningful as a site not only of critique, but of sensibilities for imagining alternatives to the desires for incorporation under existing terms.

These failures allow us to see the convergence of two failures: national culture's capacity to resolve the contradictions of political economy and empire's civilizing mission. By recognizing these failures, we are equipped with a means of turning to a broad range of resonant representations to find connections between historical and cultural formations that have been treated as distinct and unrelated. As the next chapter shows, the canonical failures of Asian American texts to resolve Asian and Asian American subjects to U.S. culture provide us with access to the stakes of perhaps the greatest failure of assimilation in American history: Reconstruction.

4

UPLIFTING RACE, RECONSTRUCTING EMPIRE

> [T]he next morning I sent for the chief engineer of the War Department (our map-maker), and I told him to put the Philippines on the map of the United States (pointing to a large map on the wall of his office), and there they are and there they will stay while I am President!
>
> —President William McKinley, "Remarks to Methodist Delegation," 1899

> I am glad that missionaries go out to the dark corners of the earth; but I ask them not to overlook the dark corners at home.
>
> —Harriet A. Jacobs, *Incidents in the Life of a Slave Girl, Written by Herself,* 1861

CONVENTIONAL AND STILL PERSUASIVE accounts of the modern civil rights movement situate it as the blowback of the failures of Reconstruction.[1] One need look no further than the Reverend Doctor Martin Luther King Jr.'s era-defining "I Have a Dream" speech at the Lincoln Memorial in August 1963 for an overt reference to a century of waiting for the Emancipation Proclamation to be implemented. Dr. King describes how African Americans have come to the "Bank of Freedom" with a "promissory note" and have found that there are "insufficient funds."[2] It should thus be possible to read the desires of the civil rights movement as being resonant with and connected to the desires of Reconstruction. This chapter therefore argues that conceptions of assimilation of the formerly enslaved have a resonance with conceptions of assimilation under U.S. imperialism. Through an examination of the ways in which Asian American texts critique assimilation, we can find links between the so-called Negro Problem and the problem of Asian difference.

"Civilization Begins at Home"

An illustration from an 1898 edition of *The New York Observer* dramatizes one of the key dilemmas of the empire question. In this image, as William McKinley intently ponders a map of the Philippines, the figure of Justice holds her sword and scales in one hand so she can pull back a curtain to reveal the strange fruit of a presumably lynched black body hanging from a tree.[3] The caption reads, "Civilization Begins at Home." This illustration sets up a clear parallel between the unresolved fate of African Americans after emancipation and the unresolved fate of a new population of Filipinos recently incorporated into America through benevolent assimilation. The juxtaposition of these two crises is at once strained and obvious as these two "problems"—"The Negro Problem" and "Our Philippine Problem"—overlapped. That is, the similarities were more than just coincidental; they were ideologically intertwined. For example, the conflation of African and Pacific difference was quite common in the era's popular illustrations. Illustrations of nonwhites, and even non-WASPS, were not known for being anatomically accurate, nor was their clothing or their habitations rendered with thoughtful fidelity. Filipinos, Hawaiians, "Porto Ricans," and the people living in other new possessions were routinely drawn in the style that caricatured African difference.[4] Not surprisingly, the civilizing mission of colonialism and the project of racial uplift invoked similar discourses of managing difference.

Using three Asian American texts that are strategically unlikely sources for apprehending Reconstruction, namely Carlos Bulosan's autobiography *America Is in the Heart* (1946), Darrell Lum's short story "Fourscore and Seven Years Ago" (1994), and Marlon Fuentes's documentary *Bontoc Eulogy* (1995), this chapter looks at the similarities between the discourses of the failures of Reconstruction and the failures of colonization. This chapter does not seek to renarrate the myriad historical and local complexities of what Eric Foner influentially called "America's Unfinished Revolution," but rather to identify lingering traces of Reconstruction's failures as they are manifested in Asian American cultural politics. The three features that have been thematized in this book again appear: (1) projects of liberation, salvation, and education; (2) changing modes of representing difference and thereby incorporating it into America; and (3) the failure of assimilative projects and modes of representation. By examining the ideological connections between these two missions of turn-of-the-century uplift and their different outcomes, we can revise the dominant meanings of both empire and Reconstruction. A chronological and developmental apprehension of these two episodes in American history would presume that the earlier episode set the terms for the latter. But as two notoriously forgotten, misunderstood, and unfinished projects, their meanings are more dialectical. That is, empire emerges as a way of ideologically managing the failures of Reconstruction, rather than as a repetition of them.

Like the colonization of the Philippines, Reconstruction was a test of American civilization's capacity to "do right by" those who had been done wrong by. In this respect, the colonized and the emancipated share a common structure of intelligibility, and they therefore share a common history in relation to mainstream history. Yet at the same time, as two forgotten or misremembered moments in American civilization, they may be said to share common structures of *unin*telligibility and common *gaps* in history. New social movements have made it possible to read for previously unrecognized commonalities between these histories. Newer work in the critical study of race has begun to emphasize the comparative dimensions of different racializations. We can turn to texts that may be overtly about a particular set of histories and questions and find in them undiscovered insights into resonant historical and cultural formations.

Specifically, this chapter revisits the discourse of Reconstruction to establish connections between that failed project and the failed project of U.S. colonization. By most accounts, Reconstruction, officially covering the years from 1863 to 1877, had ended by the turn of the century and it had ended badly. It was the age of the constitutional rise of Jim Crow segregation, the ascendance of the lynch law, and the structural impoverishment of large sectors of the African American population. As Kevin Gaines notes, the passing of Frederick Douglass in 1895 opened a vacuum in black leadership that was undisputedly filled by Booker T. Washington.[5] The great apologia for the failures of Reconstruction is Washington's *Up from Slavery* (1900), an autobiography that includes his 1895 Atlanta Exposition Address and enhances it by showing Washington's life as the embodiment of the address's ideals of "cast[ing] down your bucket where you are" (99–100). Yet *Up from Slavery* contains curious moments that can be read as a critique of colonialism, albeit when read against the grain. In describing the historical impact of slavery on African Americans, for example, Washington writes:

> [W]hen we rid ourselves of prejudice, or racial feeling, and look facts in the face, we must acknowledge that, notwithstanding the cruelty and moral wrong of slavery, the ten million Negroes inhabiting this country, who themselves or whose ancestors went through the school of American slavery, are in a stronger and more hopeful condition, materially, intellectually, morally, and religiously, than is true of an equal number of black people in any other portion of the globe. This is so to such an extent that Negroes in this country, who themselves or whose forefathers went through the school of slavery, are constantly returning to Africa as missionaries to enlighten those who remained in the fatherland.[6]

Such a statement is typical of the conciliatory discourse that catapulted Washington to becoming the representative of his "race." In the face of facts in 1900, the Wizard of Tuskegee could not help but conclude that African Americans were in better shape than the same number of persons of African descent anywhere else in the world. And the "school of American slavery" was responsible for this superior position. Couched, therefore, in this articulation is a backhanded critique of colonialism. That is, the facts of history show that colonialism had placed all other Africans—not only of the diaspora but also in Africa as well—in a less "hopeful condition, materially, intellectually, morally, and religiously." Washington's "cast down your buckets where you are" can therefore be read as a critique of the failures of the civilizing mission abroad.

By that same token, there are certainly ways of reading the irony in statements by Harriet Jacobs, such as her comment in 1861, "I am glad that missionaries go out to the dark corners of the earth; but I ask them not to overlook the dark corners at home."[7] As an instrument to bring about the end of American slavery, Harriet Jacobs's *Incidents in the Life of a Slave Girl* draws on the conventions of sentimental fiction to generate the sympathy and interest of her readers. For sympathy, it invokes the era's ideals of domesticity and "true womanhood" to make her predominantly female readership identify with her story. And for interest, it employs the conventions of the seduction narrative.[8] Until quite recently, this literariness cast the authenticity of Jacobs's narrative into doubt, as it was considered textually too good to be true.

These visions of racial destiny, read against the grain or ironically, recast Reconstruction as a historical development with tragic connections to American colonialism. By examining both the ideals of post-emancipation uplift and the terrorism of lynchocracy, this chapter examines how the emergence of U.S. imperialism was a backhanded effort to manage what Jacobs would call "the dark corners at home."

Two of the thorniest chapters of American history—post–Civil War Reconstruction and early twentieth-century U.S. colonialism in the Pacific—derive their particular prickliness from a common contradiction. Both of these moments saw the failure of the United States to adequately incorporate populations whose absorption would have validated American civilization. This chapter examines how the traumas of a later colonialism gave shape to the ways in which the failures of an earlier moment could make sense. The emerging schism between civil society and globalization was incoherent under Reconstruction, but increasingly obvious under U.S. imperialism.

Teaching America: From Abe Lincoln to Richard Wright

On March 3, 1865, as the Civil War was coming to a conclusion, Abraham Lincoln used his second inaugural address to describe the challenges to social and economic justice that lay ahead of the United States:

> Fondly we do hope—fervently we do pray—that this mighty scourge of war may speedily pass away. Yet, if God wills that it continue until all the wealth piled by the bondman's two hundred and fifty years of unrequited toil shall be sunk, and until every drop of blood drawn with the lash shall be paid by another drawn with the sword, as was said three thousand years ago, so still it must be said, "The judgments of the Lord are true and righteous together."[9]

In other words, he is describing Reconstruction. This vision of social and economic justice in the face of inequality proved to be a crucial part of America's civilizing mission, and the figure of Abraham Lincoln would prove to be an instrumental component in the implementation of that mission. Abraham Lincoln, as history, legend, and myth, has been an important vehicle of Americanism, both at home and abroad.[10] For generations, Lincoln has been the embodiment of all that is right and good and defensible about the United States of America; he is the self-made frontiersman, emancipator of slaves, preserver of the Union, martyr, and honest Abe. In an undecidable yet moving scene from the Americanization of Filipinos under U.S. colonialism, Carlos Bulosan's *America Is in the Heart* (1946) includes a telling episode in Allos's early education. He is in Baguio, a favored spot for tourists and colonizers because it is a cool, dry, high-altitude oasis away from the sweltering heat of Southeast Asia. The young Allos finds himself under the tutelage of the first of many white women he will encounter.[11] Miss Mary Strandon attempts to civilize the young boy with American history and hygiene:

> I will never forget Miss Mary Strandon on the day I pushed the wheelbarrow to her apartment. When I had carefully piled the vegetables and rice in the kitchen, she opened her purse and gave me five centavos.
> "What did you do to your face?" she asked suddenly.
> I was ashamed to tell her that I had hoped the white men and women who came to the market with camera would photograph me for ten centavos. They had always taken pictures of natives with painted faces, and I had hoped that I could fool them with the charcoal marks on my face. I said it must be dirt.[12]

But the great lesson she offers is not one of grooming—as important as sanitation was to colonization.[13] Rather, her lesson in civics and social mobility is the real inspiration for the young ward. This is the conception of America that comes with Allos to the United States. It fuels his idealism in the face of brutality and inequality. By the 1930s, the status of African Americans was no call for celebration. Segregation and sharecropping were emblems of the persistence of racial inequality in America. Yet Allos is led to conclude, as indeed one would from the second inaugural address, that "Abraham Lincoln died for a black person" (70). The specter of the hopes and failures of Reconstruction, this chapter argues, is the occluded prehistory of American colonialism. Yet, importantly, the recognition of this relationship is not one-sided. By understanding the commonalities between African American and Asian and Asian American racialization, our understandings of Reconstruction will necessarily change. The fate of African Americans in the post-Reconstruction era can be conceptualized as having distinct colonial features.[14]

"Who *is* this Abraham Lincoln?" Carlos asks Dalmacio, an Igorot houseboy for an American woman who was teaching him English and American history. The first account of Lincoln is that he was "a homely man." Next he learns that Lincoln was "a poor boy who became president of the United States." This aspect fascinates Carlos, who tells us his feelings upon hearing this information about Lincoln: "Deep down in me something was touched, was springing out, demanding to be born, to be given a name. I was fascinated by the story of this boy who was born in a log cabin and became a president of the United States" (69). This fascination, which was first sparked by Dalmacio, leads him to ask Miss Mary Strandon about Lincoln and she further refines the legend. She tells him, "Lincoln was a poor boy who became a president of the United States." Her identical description of Lincoln provokes Carlos to say "I know that already," and to ask her to tell him more about Lincoln. She continues,

> Well, when he became president he said that all men are created equal. But some men, vicious men, who had Negro slaves, did not like what he said. So a terrible war was fought between the states of the United States, and the slaves were freed and the nation was preserved. But one night he was murdered by an assassin. (70)

Carlos interrupts to ask why. All Miss Strandon can say is, "He was a great man." Carlos then asks a question that likely jarred Miss Strandon as well as his readers, "What is a Negro?" Miss Strandon tells him a Negro is "a black person." So he then asks, "Abraham Lincoln died for a black person?" and Miss Strandon says, "Yes, . . . he was a great man" (70). Bulosan represents Carlos's introduction to conceptions of African Americans as that of being manumitted by Abraham Lincoln. Lincoln serves as Bulosan's introduction to what it means to be an African American. But African Americans were not unknown to the Philippines, nor were the Philippines unknown to them.

In both the Spanish-American War and the ensuing Philippine-American War, the African American soldier in Asia became an important symbol for both imperialism and anticolonialism. For people of color, soldiering has historically been both a means of ready employment and a symbol of undying, or perhaps dying, allegiance to America. And soldiering for America has also, therefore, been something to resist when one disagreed with the war being fought, as did David Fagan, the African American soldier who deserted the American armed forces during the Philippine Insurrection to fight for the Filipinos. The following news item from an African American newspaper in 1901 illustrates this dilemma and is indeed representative of much of the anti-imperialist discourse in African American letters:[15]

> William Simms, a soldier in Bong-a-bong, Philippine Isles whose home is in Muncie, Ind., writing to *The Freeman* says: "I was struck by a question a little boy asked me, which ran about this way—'Why does the American Negro come from America to fight us when we are much friend to him and have not done anything to him? He is all the same as me, and me all the same as you. Why don't you fight those people in America that burn the Negroes, that made a beast of you, that took the child from its mother's side and sold it?'" Simms admits that he was staggered.[16]

In this scene, presumably factual, the newspaper shows how African American struggles in the post-Reconstruction era, on the one hand, and Philippine resistance to American occupation, on the other, converge as resonant forms of liberation. A small boy "stagger[ingly]" articulates the contradiction between the African American soldier's mission in the Philippines and his presumed mission back in the United States. The innocence of this boy's entreaty staggers the soldier, as the legitimacy of his allegiance to the United States becomes questioned and questionable. African American discourse on U.S. imperialism was certainly in circulation. As prominent a figure as W. E. B. DuBois wrote in *The Souls of Black Folk* on the bleakness of the situation for African Americans at the turn of the century:

> And yet, by the irony of fate, nothing has more effectually made [African American emigration] seem hopeless than the recent course of the United States toward weaker and darker peoples in the West Indies, Hawaii, and the Philippines—for where in the world may we go and be safe from lying and brute force?[17]

The white man's burden was not universally embraced; indeed, as discussed in chapter 3, it proved to be an uncomfortable topic for all sides of the debates.

By the 1920s, when Bulosan would have been in Baguio, such a critique of American empire was not quite so overt as articulated by the boy in Bong-a-bong or by DuBois. An explicit critique of empire seems to be quite absent; and Bulosan seems to come across as an apologist for empire. As Bulosan discusses the beneficial influence of Miss Strandon, he describes how he got work in a library in Baguio, and he draws a telling comparison with a fellow traveler, Richard Wright:

I was fortunate to find work in a library and to be close to books. In later years I remembered this opportunity when I read that the American Negro writer, Richard Wright, had not been allowed to borrow books from his local library because of his color. I was beginning to understand what was going on around me, and the darkness that had covered my present life was lifting. I was emerging into sunlight, and I was to know, a decade afterward in America, that this light was not too strong for eyes that had known only darkness and gloom. (71)

Bulosan begins this episode from childhood by identifying with Abraham Lincoln, a poor boy who grew up to be president.[18] Lincoln's greatness is only magnified by his martyrdom as the Great Emancipator of African Americans. Finally, Bulosan has made the final transition to understanding himself as aligned with Richard Wright, particularly from *Black Boy/American Hunger*.[19] But Bulosan even goes beyond Wright to show how, *unlike* Wright, he in the Philippines was permitted to check out books. And this comparison and contrast comes from juxtaposing the failures of Reconstruction with the apparent success of colonialism. In what is an extension of "Coin" Harvey's fantasy about what would happen if Lincoln were president in 1900, Lincoln has been able to "requite the toil of" the Filipino better than the bondsman.

Learning Lincoln and Lynching in Hawaii: Darrell Lum's "Fourscore and Seven Years Ago"

While emancipation offered the blessings of freedom and equality to the bondsmen, it also inaugurated the rise of the lynch law. Ida B. Wells was the leading voice in the crusade against lynching, writing such pamphlets as *A Red Record* and *Southern Horrors*.[20] Central to Wells's campaign was not only a publicizing of the sharp rise in African American lynchings, but also the specious rationales behind them, particularly the protection of white womanhood from black manhood. As a result, her representations of the post-Reconstruction South critically engaged with the politics of race and gender, especially surrounding the figure of the white school teacher from the North and the male student of color who she was there to uplift.

Carlos Bulosan's story, as we have seen, fits this model, as does Darrell Lum's short story, "Fourscore and Seven Years Ago" (1994).[21] Lum's story shows us how the history of the troubled incorporation of African Americans into the post–Civil War United States proved to be an unwitting model of American colonialism in the Pacific.[22] His story, I argue, is about the socialization of Pacific citizens through their desire for, and prohibition from, their white female teacher. In the prestatehood period, the infamous Massie Case of 1931, in which Hawaiian and Asian "beach boys" were accused of sexually assaulting the wife of a U.S. naval officer, effectively condoned a lynching. When the case ended in a mistrial due to an inconclusive case presented by the prosecution, Joseph Kahahawai, one of the defendants, was killed by Massie's husband with accomplices, including his mother. Although the murderers were convicted, the judge sentenced them to serve just a one-hour prison term. The case would go on to influence the terms of American governance in the islands.

As with the lynch law within the United States, anxieties around white womanhood and men of color were shaping policy in the Pacific. But rather than posit a unidirectional and simply chronological cause-and-effect relationship between Reconstruction and U.S. colonialism, I argue that we can see the ways in which American colonialism in the Pacific critically recasts Reconstruction in historical memory via the seemingly anachronistic image of U.S. colonialism. In making these connections newly visible, the stakes of racial uplift and racial menace are newly remembered by different and unintended inheritors of its legacy. After the emergence of U.S. colonialism in Asia and the Pacific, Reconstruction comes to be selectively remembered as a justification for these civilizing policies, or else it is forgotten.

Lum's story of de facto colonial schooling in 1960s Honolulu helps us to appreciate the resonance between African American and Asian American critiques of the U.S. nation-state and the violence that its liberalism not only fails to prevent, but actually puts into specific discourse. That specific discourse is both disseminated through, and given form by, the educational apparatus, particularly the trope of the endangered white woman teacher and the dangerous man of color.[23]

In the history of colonialism, formal education has long been seen as a double-edged sword. For every "pedagogy of the oppressed," there is of course a pedagogy of the oppressor.[24] In the case of U.S. imperialism, individual liberties can serve as ideals of civilization. But you must first capture those "sitting in darkness," to borrow Twain's ironic phrase, and then give them something they did not think they had and are fundamentally unable to acquire.[25]

Literatures of empire frequently feature images of tutelage, both formal and informal. Indeed, the teacher-acolyte dichotomy is one of the great structuring tropes of colonialism, particularly the acquisition of the colonized's language and literature and all that goes with them.[26] A pervasive irony emerges when the language and ideals of the colonizer become the very medium through which an indigenous anticolonial consciousness emerges and is disseminated.[27] In the case of Bulosan, then, his story can certainly be read as ironic. By being made into a good American under colonialism, he has learned to resist.

The story of American educators under American colonialism in Asia and the Pacific in the late nineteenth and early twentieth centuries is a chapter in the history of American education that is only beginning to be told, particularly concerning the Thomasites, the first shipload of teachers from the United States who fanned out across the provinces to spread literacy.[28] While educational systems were certainly established in the Philippines, the more enduring and conspicuous legacy of American colonialism throughout the world has been American mass culture.[29] As U.S. imperialism inaugurated genuine innovations in the practice of empire—particularly its informality—the colonial classroom remained a vestige of occupation and formal colonization. The American colonial classroom can therefore be seen as a liminal institution between the older, administratively cumbersome empires of the past and the newer imperialisms on the rise, which formed compliant subjects through their ironic status as individuated agents.[30] Specifically, we can consider how the colonial classroom is an index for discerning the history of modern individuation as a medium of imperialism.

In Darrell Lum's short story, "Fourscore and Seven Years Ago," we get a glimpse of what it means to be educated in terms of the dialectic of compliance and individuation. Lum's story shows how recalcitrance and submission worked together to form and contain the agency of school children in early 1960s Hawaii. Lum's story examines the formation of desire through an exposure to taboo objects. Ultimately the story explores underappreciated ties between the educative missions of U.S. imperialism and Reconstruction, where teachers supplant soldiers to win the peace.

In *A Red Record*, published in 1895, Ida B. Wells sings the praises of the women educators who brought enlightenment to the recently manumitted slaves in the post–Civil War South. She invokes these

teachers to valorize a group of women who had presumably put themselves in harm's way to uplift the former slaves through education. She
rightly argues that lynch mobs had never thought to defend the honor
of these white women, while they terroristically defended Southern
womanhood with conspicuous brutality.

> When emancipation came to the Negroes, there arose in the northern part of
> the United States an almost divine sentiment among the noblest, purest and
> best white women of the North, who felt called to a mission to educate and
> Christianize the millions of southern ex-slaves. From every nook and corner of
> the North, brave young white women answered that call and left their cultured
> homes, their happy associations and their lives of ease, and with heroic deter-
> mination went to the South to carry light and truth to the benighted blacks.
> It was a heroism no less than that which calls for volunteers for India, Africa
> and the isles of the sea.[31]

Miss Mary Strandon, from Spencer, Iowa, is just such a Wellsian hero-
ine for the self-primitivized Bulosan. At the risk of her own safety, she
takes a sullied and colonized waif under her wing.

Implicit in Wells's formulation is the idea that these schoolmarms
are thought of as presumed, prohibited, and oblivious objects of sexual desire by their pupils on the other side of the color line. Indeed the
erotics of the relationship between teachers and pupils goes back at
least as far as the Athenian academy of Socrates and up to the desk of
many an ombudsperson today. Wells writes:

> Threading their way through dense forests, working in schoolhouse, in the
> cabin and in the church, thrown at all times and in all places among the un-
> fortunate and lowly Negroes, whom they had come to find and to serve, these
> northern women, thousands and thousands of them, have spent more than a
> quarter century in giving to the colored people their splendid lessons for home
> and heart and soul. Without protection, save that which innocence gives to
> every good woman, they went about their work, fearing no assault and suffer-
> ing none.[32]

Wells puts into discourse the notion that white women educators in
this context are inevitably going to be objects of desire by their pupils.
Such an impulse, she implies, is understandable; that these women
have gone South in spite of these presumed conditions makes them
all the more commendable.

While Wells does not explicitly conjecture as to the proper trajectory of the education process vis-à-vis an erotic attachment to one's New England schoolteacher, the presumption is that this feminine virtue *might* need defending but, importantly, it *has not* needed defending. She also notes that slaves left behind to mind the plantations during the Civil War were not considered a threat to Southern womanhood.[33] Wells implicitly asserts that proper individuation has occurred among these free or freed pupils because they have not acted on their libidinous compulsions. These graduates have been incorporated into America successfully, as the safety of these white women teachers from the North mutely attests:

> Before the world adjudges the Negro a moral monster, a vicious assailant of womanhood and a menace to the sacred precincts of home, the colored people ask the consideration of the silent record of gratitude, respect, protection and devotion of the millions of the race in the South, to the thousands of northern white women who have served as teachers and missionaries since the war.[34]

Lum's story, taking place almost a century after Reconstruction, concerns this very same standard for judging the formation and incorporation of new subjects into the United States. Novels and ethnic autobiographies have frequently provided accounts of the formation of properly American subjects out of formerly inappropriate raw materials. For example, we read about Frederick Douglass going from man to slave and back to man again in his 1845 *Narrative* or about June Woo, in Amy Tan's *The Joy Luck Club*, overcoming her low self-esteem as a disappointing daughter (resulting from a traumatic music recital in childhood) by taking a trip to China to become Chinese American. These narrative resolutions occur at ethnic American self-formation, at successful individuation.

While narratives of individual development have long been the stuff of novels—indeed such narratives gave the novel its status as a genre—the short story form can provide glimpses of development from a usefully de-centered perspective.[35] Despite being more brief than a novel, of course, a short story can actually offer a more telling account of a social formation because, generically speaking, it does not need to place *bildung*, or subject formation, at the center of the narrative.

Lisa Lowe and others have persuasively argued that the novel has been a powerful institution of imperialism for this very reason.[36]

Like an "ideological state apparatus," the novel transforms subjects into individuals, frequently but not always as a form of what Etienne Balibar calls "citizen-subjects."[37] The novel produces the compelling terms of post-Enlightenment, bourgeois, metropolitan individualism, whether one identifies with Robinson Crusoe, Elizabeth Bennet, and Jane Eyre, or Huck Finn, Holden Caulfield, and Frank McCourt.[38]

Short stories, on the other hand, can more usefully be interpreted as genealogies of a moment—perhaps "a moment of danger" flashing up, in Benjamin's terms. This moment, by convention, comes at the very end of the story. The major classics of the genre, such as O. Henry's "The Gift of the Magi" and Guy de Maupassant's "The Necklace," involve a late revelation. Even Sui Sin Far's stories abide by these tenets of what makes a good short story: the twist ending.

Lum's story, ironically enough, is concerned with the process of subject formation. The provocative and humorous final line is "Whoa, da spooky." The line appears at the moment when Daniel, the narrator, discovers something quite unexpected about his desires. From this utterance we can disinter the paradox of the colonial classroom as a producer of both rigid conformity and the possibility of profound resistance. And further, this moment allows us to discern a genealogy between the colonial, or even plantation, classrooms of Reconstruction and U.S.-held territories in the Asia Pacific region.

Lum's story takes for its title the famous opening words of what is probably the single most venerated speech in American history: Abraham Lincoln's Gettysburg Address.[39] The oration, officially called in the 1863 event's program, "Dedicatory Remarks, by the President of the United States," rearticulated the mission of the United States of America at a time of national crisis. Five months after a battle that was seen as the turning point in the war and on the occasion of the dedication of the National Cemetery erected on the very battlefield in south-central Pennsylvania, Lincoln sought to ideologically repair a tattered nation.

The speech comes up in Lum's story as one of the elocution exercises that the pidgin-speaking fifth graders had to memorize. The student with the best delivery of the speech was given the honor, or in the case of the students in the story, the shame, of reciting the speech before the fifth-grade class as a sixth grader. Here is how Daniel, our narrator, tells it:

One time, Mrs. Ching went ask me if I like get extra points. She said she would gimme extra points if I get all dressed up like Abraham Lincoln and say da Gettysburg Address to da fift graders. I nevah like but she said I had to go cause I was da best at saying um las year. I still nevah like cause look stoopid when dey pin da black construction paper bow tie and make you wear da tall construction paper hat but she said it was one privilege fo say da speech and dat she would help me memarize um again. Ass cause when I was in da fift grade everybody had to learn da ting and had one contest in da whole fift grade and I went win cause everybody else did junk on purpose so dat dey nevah have to get up in front of da whole school, dressed up like Abe Lincoln. Shoot. I nevah know dat da winner had to go back da next year and say um to do fift graders either. (288–89)

To the students of Mrs. Ching's class, Lincoln's speech is a rote task like any other. And as with any rote task, their main concern is that they don't want to look "stoopid," which in this case means giving a poor performance.

From its very outset, Lum's story is concerned with the disciplining of these Asian American subjects into proper Americans through patriotic drilling: "Sixt grade, we had to give da news every morning aftah da pledge allegence and My Country Tis of Dee" (287). Immediately after these civic exercises, the students engage in "Current events time," an activity that instills in the young Americans a feeling of being "current" with far-distant occurrences that have the status of "events." Frequently, however, the students report the results of professional wrestling matches. But our narrator, good student that he is, reports instead on Yuri Gagarin's historic space flight of 1961. This event allows us to date the events of the story and to get a sense of the prominent and scrutinized role that the American educational system found itself in after Sputnik.

Only two years earlier, in 1959, Hawaii officially became the fiftieth state. What had previously been just a territory, that is, a collection of sugar cane plantations and military bases thousands of miles out in the Pacific, now had to be thought of as part of the United States of America. The Gettysburg Address emerges, then, as a 272-word instrument for interpellating these residents of Hawaii into the American nation, one of many expressions of American national unity. As historian Gary Wills points out, Lincoln's meticulously crafted oration provided a divided nation with an image of its integrity rooted in the Enlightenment ideals of the founding fathers.[40]

But to the students, Lincoln's oration is yet another burden of discipline that they characteristically resist. They resist not out of a protest to annexation and colonialism, but out of a general desire not to be singled out, even if that attention is considered praise. In an ironic inversion of the individuation promised by the education process, they only cling more steadfastly to the opposite, the comfort of anonymity. In either case, the students feel their modern individuality via their ability to perform for or against this state institution.

The final words of the story—"Whoa, da spooky"—emerge as a pivotal moment in Daniel's individuation. Daniel, a seventh-grader, sitting in a barbershop in Honolulu, looks at soft-core porn trying to imagine that the woman depicted is his speech teacher, Mrs. Sherry Sherwin, the young, white teacher all the boys have crushes on. He tries and fails: "I would look at da picture again and try to imagine dat it was Mrs. Sherwin but I only could see Charlene's face in dat picture, bending ovah. Smiling at me, her braces shiny, glistening. Whoa, da spooky" (295). Why would Daniel render this event as spooky? What exactly frightens him?

To interpret this ending, we might well consider again the prominence of Lincoln's speech. The image of Lincoln delivering the Gettysburg Address, or even of Daniel in his construction paper hat and beard, seems the furthest thing from erotic. Indeed that may be the point. What Daniel fears, to be somewhat blunt, is lynching. His object of desire has switched from the forbidden fruit of Mrs. Sherwin, who is older, white, married, and his teacher, to an appropriate one, a Chinese-American peer on the cusp of womanhood just as he is on the threshold of manhood.[41]

The genealogy of this moment can be traced to the process of the managed individuation that Daniel and his classmates learn through varied recitations of the Gettysburg Address. They feel their national identity through the ideological work of Lincoln's speech and the institution that circumstantially, through Mrs. Sherwin, provided them with the ideal objects of desire, the terms of prohibition, with what Foucault would call "the will to know."[42] The students learn desire by learning transgression and punishment.

Daniel is either an inspirational or an absurd image: an eleven-year-old Asian American boy in 1961 Hawaii, wearing construction paper formed into a stovepipe hat and a beard with no moustache. He recites the Gettysburg address to a classroom filled with fifth-graders.

Normally he looks like them (Asian American) and talks like them (Pidgin). But now he does not. He has been placed on a pedestal, the paragon of sixth-grade educatedness. He presumably stirringly tells them, "Fourscore and seven years ago, our fathers brought forth on this continent a new nation, conceived in liberty and dedicated to the proposition that all men are created equal." He solemnly informs them that "[n]ow we are engaged in a great civil war." Then he closes by announcing that "we here highly resolve that these dead shall not have died in vain, that this nation under God shall have a new birth of freedom, and that government of the people, by the people, for the people shall not perish from the earth."[43]

Now cut to a year later: as Daniel's adolescence sets in in an Oahu barbershop, he is jarred by his inability to govern his own desire, to choose his object of sexual fantasy. The genealogy of this moment in Daniel's life has its roots in the genealogy of his very incorporation into American culture, with all the gendering and racialization thereto pertaining to descendants of a plantation labor force.

But the point of recognizing this genealogy for Daniel is not to appreciate his development as an individual. Rather, the new visibility of this now-evident connection between his Hawaii education and the politics of the post–Civil War United States allows for a new appreciation of Reconstruction as a structure serving *and served by* a later imperialism.

Lum's story shifts the terms of lynching to show how it was mobilized for the U.S. civilizing mission in the Pacific. Lynching emerges as the occluded other to America's "empire of laws, and not men," as John Adams might say. At this moment in the story, we see that the specter of lynchocracy powerfully haunts and forms both history and memory.[44]

Indeed, in the history of America's establishment of structures of governance, both civil and military, in Hawaii, as well as in local consciousness and resistance to it, lynching played a central and tragic role. In 1932, Joseph Kahahawai was kidnapped, shot, and killed by Lieutenant Thomas Massie of the United States Navy. Kahahawai and five other young men of Hawaiian and Asian origin were arrested for the alleged rape of Thalia Massie, the lieutenant's wife. Specious evidence, not only concerning the means, motive, and opportunity of the defendants, but even of any crime, resulted in a mistrial. Massie and two accomplices took the law into their own hands, and for their trouble they ultimately received a one-hour sentence for manslaughter.[45]

Yet another American race panic emerged to dictate the terms of the need for civilization: "The situation in Hawaii is deplorable. It is an unsafe place for a white woman. Outside the cities and small towns, the roads go through jungles and in these remote places, bands of dangerous natives lie in wait for a white woman driving by."[46]

Both Daniel's final line from Lum's story and the killing of Joseph Kahahawai give added meaning to Wells's remarks from 1895:

> The government which had made the Negro a citizen found itself unable to protect him. It gave him the right to vote, but denied him the protection which should have maintained that right. Scourged from his home; hunted through the swamps; hung by midnight raiders, and openly murdered in the light of day, the Negro clung to his right of the franchise with *a heroism which would have wrung admiration from the hearts of savages*. He believed that in that small white ballot was a subtle something which stood for manhood as well as citizenship, and thousands of brave black men went to their graves, exemplifying the one by dying for the other.[47]

By the era of American colonialism in the Pacific, the continued failures of American civilization had been instituted through the education apparatus, both through the curriculum and by the apparatus itself. These failures are lived and relived by once and future generations of Americanized schoolchildren. Daniel's journey along the path to proper socialization meets an unexpected bump in that barbershop when this history of American education wrings both fear and admiration from *and for* the "savage" that he is. Such a moment is indeed spooky.

Teaching America: The Reason Why the Asian American Was in the 1904 St. Louis World's Fair

> What is the source of this talent of forgetting?
> —Marlon Fuentes, *Bontoc Eulogy,* 1995

A crucial part of being integrated into a racial hierarchy is the performance of knowing one's place. Bulosan gives just such a performance. As a poor boy in the Philippines who would later grow up to be an American communist, Carlos Bulosan participates in the informal

economy by pretending to be a "native." He is, of course, a native Filipino, but he pretends to be an Igorot, an ethnic group indigenous to
the mountains of Luzon, near the resort city of Baguio. Even to this
day in Baguio, Igorots in g-strings and colorful outfits allow themselves to be photographed for a fee. Bulosan describes how he performed the role of racial spectacle:

> My clothes began to wear out. I was sick from eating what the traders dis-
> carded. One day an American lady tourist asked me to undress before her cam-
> era, and gave me ten centavos for doing it. I had found a simple way to make
> a living. Whenever I saw a white person in the market with a camera, I made
> myself conspicuously ugly, hoping to earn ten centavos. But what interested
> the tourists most were the naked Igorot women and their children. Sometimes
> they took pictures of the old men with G-strings. They were not interested in
> Christian Filipinos like me. They seemed to take a particular delight in photo-
> graphing young Igorot girls with large breasts and robust mountain men whose
> genitals were nearly exposed, their G-strings bulging large and alive.[48]

Taking place in the 1920s, this perception was powerfully formed after the successful displays of Filipinos at the 1904 World's Fair in St.
Louis. But this perception owes a debt, of course, to the vibrant discourses of primitivism and Orientalism circulating in that era.

Marlon Fuentes's *Bontoc Eulogy* involves a similar performance of
playing a primitive Igorot. This 1995 film, produced by PBS's *American Playhouse*, chronicles a search for the remains of Fuentes's grandfather Markod, a bontoc (or mountain) Igorot who came to the United
States as part of the Philippine Reservation of the 1904 World's Fair in
St. Louis. *Bontoc Eulogy* tries to grasp the subjectivity of the not merely
objectified, but sensationalized. In grasping this process of being rendered hypervisible, we find a genealogy with American culture's will
to render invisible the spectacle of African Americans after Reconstruction. The evolving technologies and epistemologies of display
at the turn of the century, particularly world's fairs, emerge as arenas
for making difference intelligible or invisible. The ghosts of African
American exclusion from the influential 1893 Chicago World's Fair
haunt subsequent attempts to use such expositions to contain difference. The inheritors of these modern institutions would become the
liberal form of multiculturalism, which began to wane right around
the time that Fuentes's film emerged.[49]

In a narrative arc similar to many paradigmatic Asian American texts, *Bontoc Eulogy* is a story about looking into the past because the present somehow does not feel right. From Naomi Nakane's sifting through her uncle's attic in Joy Kogawa's *Obasan* to Monique Truong's open letter to a childhood friend about being a Vietnamese refugee in the American South, the recurrent image of an Asian American recovering lost histories and requiring new forms to grasp those histories has made post-traumatic stress syndrome a defining feature of the Asian American condition.[50] Kogawa's haunting novel churns up troubling memories of the treatment of Japanese Canadians during World War II and Truong's short story gives a frank account of the sedimented layers of race, class, and gender that never quite knew what to do with her in Boiling Spring, North Carolina, as the Vietnam War came to an official end. *Bontoc Eulogy* continues that tradition by turning to yet another pre-Asian American movement moment when Asianness had to be dealt with, but then got swept under the rug of history.

The opening shot of Fuentes, seated before an antiquated Victrola listening to scratchy recordings made at the fair, immediately makes us aware of both the technologies of remembering and the remembering of technologies. To recover his grandfather, Fuentes needs to venture into the multimedia colonial archives, to examine the ways in which his grandfather was made knowable. We see the 1904 World's Fair as just one of many institutions that interpellate Markod, albeit a privileged and conspicuous one.

World's fairs, with their explicitly global vision, both produce and reflect modernity. Such an institution has as its project the containment and display of the world in a park, and this architecture necessitates a subjectivity that believes itself capable of a standpoint from which to view and display the entire world. Such a standpoint is the modern subject of knowledge and therefore an imperial one. As with a census, a map, or a museum, a messy totality is functionally and interestedly put into discourse.[51] What modernity meant to the late nineteenth- and early twentieth-century fair goer, then, allows us to have access to the emergence of the colonizer's consciousness.

World's fairs can be used as indices of the state of that colonizing subject, and his colonized object as it developed, as Henry Adams famously did in relation to the Paris Exposition of 1900.[52] In particular, the 1893 and 1904 fairs serve as mileposts for charting the development of U.S. imperialism, not only in the ways the fairs managed difference, but in the reactions provoked by the managed. The tumultuous eleven years between 1893 and 1904 witnessed the emergence of formal U.S. imperialism. In an odd sort of *avant la lettre* "model minority" mythologizing, the different meaning of differences between those two moments is manifested as an unacceptable blackness in 1893 Chicago to an all-too-acceptable Asianness in 1904 St. Louis.

The most notable response to the 1893 fair was Ida B. Wells's 1893 pamphlet, *The Reason Why the Colored American Is Not in the World's Columbian Exposition: Afro-American Contributions to Columbia Literature.*[53] Assembling the work of leading figures including Frederick Douglass, Wells's pamphlet made both a critique of and an argument for America's management of African American difference: lynching on the one hand and black bourgeoisie on the other, with the World's Fair as the arena for its proper contradictory-laden representation. Wells and her contributors simultaneously generated profound critiques of American civilization's continuing unjust treatment of African Americans while arguing that African Americans rightfully wanted to achieve full participation in the political, cultural, and economic life of the country. In making their case for why African Americans were left out of the fair, Wells and her fellow writers necessarily critiqued the form and project of the world's fair as a genre.

A seemingly unrelated development provides a missing link for understanding why African Americans were invisible in 1893 and why Asians were hypervisible: William Wilson's Museum of Commerce. Established in Philadelphia in 1893 by a University of Pennsylvania scientist, Wilson's museum was overtly inspired by the 1893 Chicago World's Fair. However, Wilson's museum distilled what he saw as the most significant aspect of the Chicago fair: its ability to render the world for consumers' taste. Remaining open until 1930, Wilson's museum stripped away the veneer of crass sensationalism to reveal the economic core within every object on display, and indeed, within any displayable object in the world.

In 1904, a taste for the exotic still packed the promenades and pavilions of St. Louis's Exposition, and the architect of the Philippine Pavilion was none other than William Wilson himself. The pagan rituals of Barnum-worthy freaks captivated those who visited the Show-Me State that year. Yet this was an exotic that America had violently made its own. Constellating that fair with the 1893 Chicago one and Wilson's Museum allows us to track the emergence of an economizing of the world that we now take as a matter of course. A closer examination of the articulations by those on display and those excluded from it show us the emerging relationship between difference and a universal system of value measurement. In other words, we see the establishment of wide-scale commodification, a process that performs the ingenious double act of codifying difference and leveling it.

Thus was born the liberal pluralist project of American empire's emergent practice of global capitalism: all can be rendered as a monetary value. This is an idea that Wells knew acutely back in 1893, for the post-emancipation rendering of African Americans with a monetary value was a maneuver the pamphlet shrewdly, and earnestly, made. The pamphlet responds to the Columbian Exposition's exclusion using a prescient logic and arithmetic.

Fuentes's film, *Bontoc Eulogy*, offers a meditation on the links between historic and contemporary reifications of difference. The incorporation of peripheral subjects into the metropole was not merely territorial, but epistemological. Emerging some ninety years after the events in question, the film speaks to an audience schooled in revisionist history and multiculturalist idealism. No doubt the film provides edifying satisfactions to a PBS audience hungering for hidden histories, but the film is also remarkable for taking that approach to diversity awareness to emphasize the epistemological limits to understanding that era's specific concerns. The film asks, how do we grasp what and why the United States did what it did to the Philippines at the turn of the century? And what continuities are there between them then and us now? We can then read the film for its oblique elaboration of crucial connections to the emergence of a distinctly American imperialism and its innovative culture of global commodification.

Fuentes begins:

> I left Manila for America twenty years ago carrying dreams from a past I now barely recognize. In all these years not once have I gone back. These are my children. They were born here in America. It is their home and the only life they know. Perhaps they are fortunate because they do not have to forget what they have never known. In the beginning I lived in two worlds. The sights and sounds of my new life are the flickering afterimage of the place I once called home.

One thing that is immediately noticeable about the narration of *Bontoc Eulogy* is its monotone quality. This black-and-white quasi-documentary chronicles the search for both the story and the physical remains of Fuentes's grandfather, Markod. But Fuentes begins the voice-over with a reference to dreams. Despite showing us images of a smiling college graduate, Fuentes is not referencing the dreams of an immigrant wanting a better life in America. Rather, with the grainy cinematography, hypnotic voice-over, cryptic imagery, and jagged jump cuts, the barely recognized dreams he invokes are more akin to wish-fulfillment night dreams begging psychical interpretation to access what has been repressed.

Whether that unrepression occurs remains profoundly ambiguous. At the conclusion of the film, Fuentes offers a conception of himself as the lost grandfather he had sought:

> After all this I have once again gone back into the hiding places of everyday life. This story has ended but my search has just begun. If I don't find Markod, perhaps my children or my children's children will find him. If they see him, I wonder if they will recognize him.

What links Markod, Fuentes, and Fuentes's grandchildren are these dreams, which grow hazier with each successive generation. The narrative trajectory of the film reaches an impasse at undecidability; what remains is desire, desire for a recognizability that might be unattainable. Fuentes can only look to the next generations for an epistemic shift to remember, and literally re-member, Markod and make him manifest.

Even before these framing statements, the machinery of recognition and remembrance emerges as the central thematic of the film, particularly the recurrent image of Fuentes sitting on the floor of a dreamlike room in front of an antique Victrola. First he winds the handle and we hear Filipino tribal music. The scene is repeated and different tribal music from a different record is heard. The third attempt finds a recorded voice and definition becomes more feasible. He can begin to piece together the history of Markod in a manner similar to that of subaltern historiographers.[54] That is, Markod is made intelligible by the ways that the colonial archive produced him as an object of knowledge. Rising up as "a fragmentary and episodic" history, the gaps and fissures in that archive's seamless garment become the inherently unstable terms of the subjectivity of Markod.[55]

As with a subject of subaltern historiography, Markod's subjectivity is necessarily grasped through hindsight and is always already under erasure. The locus classicus of grasping the subaltern has been unexpected bursts of violence, and Markod's story is no different.[56] His visibility emerges at a moment when that violence was being discursively settled, that is, when he could be rendered as a "possession." Tribal Filipinos erupted into the American national consciousness in a hypervisibility that quickly waned, the most famous of those eruptions being the Philippine Reservation at the St. Louis World's Fair.

The 1904 fair in St. Louis, aptly located when and where it was to commemorate the centennial of the Louisiana Purchase, was for many Americans an introduction to the country's new possessions in the South Pacific. The Philippine Islands had recently been mapped into America after the pacification of the Philippine Insurrection (officially 1898–1902), which immediately followed the briefer and more trumpeted Spanish-American War (1898).[57] Markod was part of that introductory contingent, a representative of the Bontoc Igorots of Luzon. Fuentes's other grandfather, as he tells us, had been one of the insurrectionists, the ostensibly nationalist forces who had tried to establish a Philippine state, first by rising up against the Spanish in 1896 and later by waging a protracted guerilla war against the American occupying forces, but under the banner of a variety of causes.[58]

His nationalist grandfather's history, already somewhat occluded by the educational system installed by the American colonial regime, was differently visible than that of the putatively primitive peoples for whom American imperialism was the justification.[59] For the traditional civilizing discourses of colonialism, these are the people on the periphery to modernity and the modern world system. Even to the colonized in the colonial metropole, these premodern tribal people exist more as an idea than as a material reality. Fuentes describes his education in Manila:

> In our history lessons at school, my teacher talked about the many primitive tribes that populated the islands. . . . I knew that some of my relatives lived in the mountains. But the only way I got to know about them was from the pictures I saw and the books I read. These lessons sparked my interest in learning more about Philippine tribal life. But as the years passed, all these were forgotten.

For the modern Filipino, such tribal peoples became the figures with whom to *dis*identify. Fuentes says, "As a child, when I shared my interest in the Igorots with my friends from school, they asked me if I ever wore a G-string or if I danced around a blazing fire at night beating a brass gong or whether my mother served dog meat at home." Both colonial and nationalist educations consolidated and valorized the modern subject through their production of a denigrated, primitive other at whose difference modernity could marvel. Fuentes is taught to occupy a position resolutely on the side of the gawkers, rather than the gawked at.

This division between gazer and gazed at is inherent to the functioning of world's fairs. A popular form of entertainment since before the middle of the nineteenth century, these expositions were a blending of the fantastical aspects of a carnival with the regional pride of county fairs in displaying the bountiful products of diverse agricultural and manufacturing centers.[60] These two main purposes of expositions cannily intersected with the transitions taking place with the rise of U.S. imperialism. While the extraction of resources had been a central purpose of colonization since ancient times, modern imperialism's methods of producing taxonomies of commodification were literally scientific.

The totalizing logic of colonization was performed with a precision that went beyond making the undiscovered world mappable. World's fairs went even further than hierarchically plotting peoples along a civilized/primitive spectrum; they rendered the world ready for the West's consumption and, importantly, exchange. The fairs were a recreational re-creation of the world in microcosm within the grounds of these increasingly ambitious monuments to civilization. World's fairs and the spectacles and spectators they produced were modernity par excellence, a haven for *les flaneurs*. This spatial rendering of modernity set the stage for what we now call globalization and its new intersection of geography and capitalist speculation, coded as a taste for the exotic.[61]

Inquiring into the curious blend of sensationalism and ethnography allows us access to the ways that alterity was made not only manageable, but profitable. To be managed meant to be rendered profitable, like the continually untapped "China market" that has come to mean any so-called "emerging market." American culture's capacity to absorb otherness was not merely a test of the Enlightenment liberal pluralism on which the United States was founded; it was the next step of capitalist development. American imperialism echoed Benjamin

Disraeli's now-famous quip: "The East is a career."[62] But the methods by which that career was realized occasioned a genuinely new formation under U.S. imperialism.[63]

The road to that career in the East was paved with the different management of other Others. Only eleven years before St. Louis's extremely popular World's Fair, Chicago hosted one of the most successful expositions the world had ever known.[64] But those were two very different fairs in their relationship to the management of difference. That difference can be charted along an axis of capitalist and imperialist development.

The intervening eleven years between the fairs were by any measure a very important period in the development of U.S. imperialism. That stretch of time began with Turner's Chicago-based declaration that the frontier was closed and ended with McKinley's providential reopening of it. The year 1893 was the moment when the notion that there was no more American frontier gained currency, if not wholesale adoption.[65] The year 1904 proved that Turner was somewhat premature in his remarks. These two successful fairs — and not all world fairs were successful — can be used as mileposts for tracking the emergence of America's incipient imperial culture.[66]

The continent had been settled. Now what? If, under the Turner thesis, the frontier functioned as an impetus for growth and a safety valve for overproduction, what would serve this function in lieu of the contiguous territories? How closed the frontier was remained quite debatable, especially if one thinks in more than territorial terms. Frontiers function as spaces for speculation, for possibility and opportunity. The frontier is defined by its sites of potential, by its being incorporated as the not-yet developed.

Reconstruction abortively rendered African Americans as a new frontier for speculation.[67] By 1893, Reconstruction was an acknowledged failure and African Americans were still quite far from being integrated into the social and economic life of the United States in ways other than being structurally exploited. The representation of African Americans at the World's Columbian Exposition, as the fair was officially called in commemoration of 401 years of genocide, was in line with the ways these fairs sought to produce, rather than reflect, the world. Toward that project, there were no exhibits at the Chicago fair that explicitly referenced the history of African Americans. Implicit references necessarily abounded for those with the consciousness to see them, but that was cold comfort to African American leaders in 1893.

Prominent African American activists of the day demanded explicit invocations of the history of African Americans at the fair. As expressed in the pamphlet compiled and published by Ida B. Wells, their wishes for visibility in the face of exclusion were understandable. Wells and her associates knew that their demand for representation in and recognition by the logic of world's fairs needed to be couched in the terms by which a fair would be organized. African Americans were a population whose incorporation into American civilization was in direct contrast to the ideals of a world's fair and its celebration of the resources and values of modernity. They were an alterity that could not be resolved to the nation-state, and the fair's exclusion of them was an all too predictable occurrence. In light of the persuasive and shaming arguments of the pamphleteers, the fair organizers made concessions, such as including a Negro Day. But the damage had been done and the statement about the unrepresentability of African Americans in the "White City" was made quite clear. "[T]he exposition furnishes a magazine for dreams," according to the World's Columbian Exposition President Thomas W. Palmer in 1893. Palmer also stated:

> You have seen Kiralfy's "Around the World in Eighty Days" and read Jules Verne's "Around the World," wherein Mr. Fogg gained a day and saved his fortune by going to the west, so will all people and races here gain more than a day and more than a fortune in getting a more thorough idea of the habitable globe by coming west to Chicago.[68]

Despite this global vision, African Americans were not included.

Even if concessions were made, how would African Americans have been adequately included without manifesting contradictions to the visions of civilization that the fair promoted? The form as well as the content of the fair were designed to render invisible and forgotten that which did not abide by its vision of modernity. African American history would have been devastating to the project of the fair because of the contradictions to America that it made obvious. The nation did not yet want to see as its mission the civilization of Others: slavery, genocide, and exclusion were the order of the day.

By seeming contrast, in 1904 America's capacity to absorb otherness was proudly on display. This stark difference between the two fairs is clearly connected to the emergence of official U.S. colonialism in Asia and the Pacific. It is also an instructive gauge of late capitalism's attempt to maintain concurrent sameness and differentiation, that is, commodification. Commodification was presented as natural and scientific, as is any process discursively produced and indeed practiced as efficient. In this way, pageants of empire occlude empire and the late nineteenth century shows to itself the inevitability of its own progress.

Wells's pamphlet needed to simultaneously explain the exclusion and argue for the inclusion of African Americans in the 1893 World's Fair. The various parts of the pamphlet use different strategies to represent African American critiques of American civilization. These different strategies, though they were devised by dominant members of the African American intelligentsia, assume a wide and at times contradictory array of approaches to arguing for the recognition of African American contributions to "Columbian literature." Frederick Douglass offers a blistering excoriation of the American Enlightenment's hypocrisy when put into practice. Wells herself focuses on the cause for which she is perhaps most well-known: the publicizing of the horrors of lynching. F. L. Barnett focuses specifically on the politics of the 1893 fair itself and the story of what led to African American exclusion. Interestingly, he points not only to the exclusion of African Americans from exhibitions, but to their exclusion from employment at the fair.

Of particular interest to my project is J. Garland Penn's treatise on "The Progress of the Afro-American" since the end of the Civil War. By *progress,* he means the social institutions structuring public and private life for African Americans, such as arts and literature, journalism, the church, and most quantifiably, business. In addition to listing an impressive catalog of patents granted to African American inventors, Penn chooses to represent this last arena of activity with dollar values. Cognizant of the reifying and commodifying logic of American culture, Penn's strategy may seem a concession to the myth of American enterprise.

The impact of Penn's quantification is a canny comment on the relationship between difference and commodification. Constellated with the other essays, Penn's seemingly celebratory vision of the black bourgeoisie becomes a barometer of the balance between exposition recognizability and the real conditions of African American life. African Americans, Penn says, must go from being conceived of as objects of property to being subjects with property: "The total amount of property owned by the race is $263,000,000."[69] Statistics are both an assertion of recognizability and a form of surveilling. Penn is therefore anxious about his arrival at that grand total: "This report, which is an under-estimate, has been going the rounds and accepted as a most remarkable showing." He is cagey about the finality of that figure as there are figures he considers ultimately unknowable and therefore in need of estimate: "With these corrections, we should have an estimated wealth of not less that $275,000,000" (102).

The power to render "the race" as a quantifiable sum exacerbates the contradiction between representation through formal citizenship and representation through economic conditions. The "remarkable showing" that Penn points to is both an assertion of the unexpected largeness and the unacceptable smallness of that sum. He points to financial failures that prevented the figure from being larger, such as the Penny Savings Bank of Chattanooga. Penn's contribution, like the whole pamphlet itself, is necessarily a simultaneous celebration of African American contributions and a critique of the conditions under which those unrecognized contributions were made.[70]

Even at the conclusion of the entire pamphlet, Penn may not have gone far enough in his valuations. Despite the quantifications that Penn makes, Wells offers a slight apologia at the end of the pamphlet: "The haste necessary for the press, prevents the incorporation of interesting data showing the progress of the colored people in commercial lines." Specifically she mentions the Capital Savings Bank, "a flourishing institution conducted by the colored people of Washington, D.C." (82). As Wells's pamphlet abundantly shows, money and violence are two undeniable facts of American life.

As with any ethnicity-based anthology, the pamphlet necessarily juxtaposes different ways of representing what it means to be African American. African American identity meant everything from embodying contradictions to the nation-state and being subject to unpunished vigilante violence to producing alternative social institutions and participating in American capitalism as something other than exploited labor.

The argument that the treatment of African Americans was in

direct contradiction to American political ideals was not a new one. Abolitionist discourse frequently invoked secular and religious arguments that slavery was against liberty, equality, and fraternity. Many a slave narrative argued for the humanity of the enslaved along Douglass's own formulation in his 1845 *Narrative of the Life of Frederick Douglass*: that he would show how a man was made a slave and a slave was made a man.[71]

By 1893, post-emancipation and post-Reconstruction America had to come to terms with the fact that substantive rights were being denied to African Americans, even if procedural rights were formally guaranteed after the Civil War amendments.[72] That is, the economic inequalities that had been set so firmly in place to maintain racialized and gendered populations ready for exploitation could not simply be undone by disintegrating the manacles of enslavement. Not only had so much labor already been stolen, but myriad forms of formal and informal segregation made economic parity a structural impossibility, especially without reparations and other forms of social justice legislation.

Supposedly mitigating this inequality was the era's emerging ideologies of social Darwinism, which rendered these unequal dispensations of economic and social attainment as manifestations of scientific realities. After all, the offending impediment had been removed for three decades and African Americans were not making progress — or so the argument went. The Wells pamphlet, like much of the significant African American intellectual discourse that preceded it, had to tackle this racial thinking head-on by lambasting America while also wanting a well-deserved piece of it. The 1893 World's Fair and its exclusion of African Americans served as an all-too-apt metaphor for the predicament of being an African American.

"A Permanent World's Fair"

The power of representation that the World Fair manifested ushered in an emergent link between liberal pluralism and commodification. Not only were identities such as "Negro" beginning to be seen as sites for the management of difference, but further, these differences evinced a larger sameness on which capitalism and imperialism were waged. The Negro Problem, it was implied, could be solved through economic incorporation, slow though it might be in coming.

The manifestations of this sameness were not always so obvious as an ethnographic catalog. The very salability of the world became a precondition for its knowability. Just as the god of Genesis figured the world as basically a smorgasbord for humans, the world under U.S. imperialism was one incipient emporium of trade waiting to be rendered as such. This incipience fueled and continues to fuel the forms of speculation that have shaped the theory and methods of what we can now recognize as U.S. imperialism. That is, the world was plotted on a narrative of history that had as its end the totality of the free market. Late capitalist modernity began to see itself as operating free of the particularities of any national ideology. That the United States happened to be the regime most well-suited to leading the world into this new order of things was, as McKinley would see it, a serendipitous coincidence.

While this commodifying logic, as well as its practices, may seem more self-evident to us with our hindsight from within an extension of the American Century, this self-evidence is a call to particularize. For we can see the being-made-natural of that which was produced out of specific conditions and with specific interests. We can see the struggle over conceptions of the world by appreciating which epistemologies lost out in the struggle and how their doom was sealed. By seeing as a struggle what we may now take as a given, we can recontextualize the emergence of empire and our relationship to it.

In 1930, William Wilson's Museum of Commerce closed its doors for good; no one seemed to care to visit it anymore. But this failure to attract visitors was actually a sign of its ultimate success. The implicit purpose of a museum is not to present the quotidian, what we already see around us all the time. But that is exactly what Wilson's museum began to do in a culture that saw the entire world as self-evidently fit for commerce. Wilson's museum had happily outlived its usefulness.

The museum sought to codify the dual purposes that U.S. imperialism had for the periphery: as a source of (1) cheaply extractable resources and (2) new consumers for the goods manufactured from those materials.[73] As historian Steven Conn notes, "In Wilson's commercial anthropology, all the world became a market, and all its peoples merely buyers and sellers. In creating a permanent world's fair whose useful lessons would not evaporate, Wilson constructed an epistemology of commercial expansion and he put it on display."[74]

In a 1909 pamphlet, Wilson admired European imperialism's ability to "conform their own ideas to the tastes of semi-civilized people and even barbaric races."[75] The conception of imperialism as the exporting of "taste" necessitates institutions for the inculcation of aesthetic judgments and the Kantian subject of those judgments. Indeed, the notion that the world would profitably be unified by common standards of desire was the Kantian aesthetic community applied to global domination.

The necessary concomitant to the consumerist taste that imperialism sought to generate was the putatively unique productivity that peripheral sites could claim. In an application of Ricardo's theory of comparative advantage, the specificity of different locations was defined by their ability to contribute unique products to the world market. Ironically, the pieces of evidence Wilson used to illustrate this point were the textiles he thought were emerging from Madagascar. The irony was that these fabrics, produced by "savage hands," were in fact European in origin, sold to the islanders under French colonialism. Ultimately, the accuracy of Wilson's claims were not as important as his very project of rendering the world knowable for American enterprise and speculation.

Toward that purpose, the Bureau of Information at Wilson's Museum of Commerce was perhaps the most significant contribution to what we now call consulting. Wilson describes the unique opportunity that had fallen into the laps of American business: "It has served to give the business men of America an unusual opportunity to acquire, in a very short time, a great deal of information concerning the markets of the world; placing them in a position to compete successfully with those who, in a matter of experiences, have had an enormous advantage."[76] Those more experienced folk to whom Wilson referred were the actual colonizers, weighted down with the business of administering colonies while American business interests could focus on more purely profitable endeavors. As Conn aptly notes, "[T]his way, American business would compete in a world colonized by Europeans without becoming colonialists themselves."[77] But America did become a colonialist, and it became one rather proudly judging from the 1904 World's Fair.

Inspired by the ways in which the 1893 World's Fair ordered the world, Wilson's museum was, in a sense, a deliberate reading of "White City," which refined that fair's ability to discipline difference into a more nakedly economic permutation. Wells's pamphlet was a more overt reading of the fair. Both Wilson's museum and Wells's pamphlet, via Garland Penn's contribution, made the connection between economy and taxonomy rather apparent: economic order required taxonomic order and vice versa.

But by 1904, taxonomy appears to have been the main characteristic that the World's Fair emphasized, as popular interest was sparked more by the overtly cultural spectacle of our new primitives and the crisis of incorporation they engendered. Economy actually became less visible for understanding globality as it became more influential. Despite all the attempts to come up with new names like "benevolent assimilation," the mode of colonialism the United States practiced in the Philippines was not so different from the European occupation of other countries. American colonialism was quite similar to that hypocritically described by Teddy Roosevelt as, "the possession of thickly settled districts which, if conquered, will for centuries remain alien and hostile to the conquerors."[78]

How the 1904 fair transformed Wilson's vision and Wells's demands was an epistemology for empire at a moment of transition. Representation of the Other went from invisibility to hypervisibility and back to invisibility again. This hypervisibility served not only an older sensationalist desire to consolidate bourgeois whiteness, but also to render the world as an arena for investment. In other words, 1904 answered Turner's assertion of the closing of the frontier by redefining the frontier as the settlement of the periphery without necessarily having to accommodate actual settlers. As America expanded beyond its contiguous borders, the expansion of markets found colonial apparatuses unnecessary and therefore inefficient. New subjects of this global market did not have to be formally incorporated into an imperialist state. Yet the ones who were formally incorporated, such as Filipinos and immigrants from Asia, embody the confluence of globalization and civil society. Their literary output recuperates the emergence of U.S. imperialism and, in the process, shows us that we need to fashion new interpretive tools for making that emergence visible. *Bontoc Eulogy* points to that need.

"Labeled but Nameless": Anomalous Incorporation

The Asian American canon has served the historical function of being a point of access for what Elaine Kim calls, with refreshing bluntness, "Asian American realities."[79] The political and cultural importance of making such a claim on America cannot be denied. As the rise and critique of identity politics have shown, a formally codified identity position is demanded of any group under liberal pluralism as a necessary response to the gendered and racialized exploitation that has marked the history of American capitalism.

From the earliest articulations of Asian American identity as such, the overtly political act of displacement was a defining thematic of assertions of Asian American subjectivity. *Bontoc Eulogy* continues this tradition of displacing historically sedimented identities, but as a postmodernist text, it does so without necessarily replacing them with anything. For example, the writers of the preface to *Aiiieeeee!* were all too aware of the representations they were writing against, as well as for:

> None of the Chinese, Japanese, and Filipino American works in this volume are snow jobs pushing Asian Americans as the miracle synthetic white people that America's proprietors of white liberal pop . . . make us out to be.
>
> The Asian American writers here are elegant or repulsive, angry and bitter, militantly anti-white or not, not out of any perversity or revenge but of honesty. America's dishonesty—its racist white supremacy passed off as love and acceptance—has kept seven generations of Asian American voices off the air, off the streets, and praised us for being Asiatically no-show.[80]

Not unlike Wells's comrades in 1893 claiming unrecognized African American contributions, the *Aiiieeeee!* editors' 1973 rallying cry of "We are not new here" was their claim for the long-unrecognized and distinctly Asian American contributions to "Columbia literature." Their somewhat ironic use of the familial rhetoric of generations bespoke the fragmentedness that dogged what might otherwise have been a more recognizable succession than a tradition of literary productivity is supposed to possess. Such continuity would have been necessary for wider recognition. The lack of institutions and institutionalization, such as an anthology, and the presence of far more influential disseminations, such as Charlie Chan and Fu Manchu, combined to doom Asian Americans not only to invisibility and silence, but to interested misrepresentation.

The interested misrepresentations that Chin and company point to most angrily are the mass culture representations of our age of mechanical reproduction. But these primarily celluloid representations can be contextualized against the epistemologies that made these silver screen figures so palatable.[81] In particular we can look to the turn-of-the-century ideologies that made America's confrontation with Asian otherness not only undeniable, but even desirable, as it was with the rise of the model-minority myth. Ironically, at a time of immigration exclusion legislation, the 1904 World's Fair needed to settle discursively the matter of the Philippines as American territory and, more challengingly, the Filipino as a new and welcome American subject. These Asians on display can be seen as an ideological point of origin for seeing the great distances that contemporary Asian Americans are said to have come as the "miracle synthetic white people," or as Lisa Lowe would call them, "abstract citizens."

The St. Louis World's Fair was then an early test of what would become multiculturalism, the sameness-in-difference that Lowe usefully rearticulated as the same-enough.[82] By making representable previously unrepresented difference, the St. Louis Fair accommodated the world by obliquely commodifying it. That is, the sameness amid difference upon which the fair was predicated was ready to render difference as radical yet surmountable. Capitalism and its commodifying were that surmounting from which profit would eventually spring.

Marlon Fuentes's *Bontoc Eulogy* remembers the 1904 fair as the management of Asian difference. The triumph of the gold standard in the years between the Chicago and the St. Louis fairs may seem a tangential watershed. But its influence on the epistemology for empire can be seen not only in the project of the fair, but in the ways the fair has been remembered and forgotten. Both the idea of the gold standard and the genre of the world fair unified the world and made it knowable through a blend of economy and taxonomy.

Fuentes ends his film with the following cryptic comment: "[T]his story has ended but my search has just begun." Eschewing a conventional resolution through which the protagonist would be able to achieve wholeness by remembering the past, *Bontoc Eulogy* plays with the affirmative conclusions of ethnic identity narratives. Consider the happy neatness of June Woo's tearful declaration at the end of Amy Tan's *The Joy Luck Club*: "And now I also see what part of me is Chinese. It is obvious. It is my family. It is in our blood. After all these years, it can finally be let go."[83]

Fuentes's ending explicitly adopts for the film the status of a story, yet the resolution ends with the recognition of a lack instead of finding compensation for one. What is located by the detective work in *Bontoc Eulogy* is not a missing object, but rather the methodology by which that object has been rendered invisible. Like Chan Hung of Wayne Wang's *Chan Is Missing*, Markod emerges as a "negative character."[84] That is, his manifest absence at the end of the film demands that we look elsewhere for the actually recovered object. Fuentes finds a curiously adept "talent of forgetting." But what is he actually forgetting?

What Fuentes calls "this talent of forgetting" refers simultaneously to being the forgetter and the forgotten, the curious predicament of those colonized by the United States. U.S. cultural amnesia about its status as an empire was so powerful that the colonized failed to recognize themselves as such. Also, as noted earlier in this chapter, the American colonial and then the Philippine nationalist historiography and even the ethnography in which Fuentes was schooled did not equip him to be able to see his grandfather's subaltern subjectivity. In tracking the reverse-engineered primitivism of Markod and the Bontoc Igorots in 1904, we can piece together Markod's story. But what indeed does he find?

Fuentes's desperate search becomes tragically, almost parodically, physical, as he cannot even locate the remains of Markod:

> For months I hunted the dark corners and attics of anthropology and medical museums trying to follow Markod's trail. My research indicated that by the spring of 1905, months after the World's Fair ended, three Igorot bodies were interred at a private St. Louis morgue. The bodies were embalmed and placed in caskets pending final decision by the federal government. I discovered the Smithsonian collection included three Igorot brains from the Philippine reservation. The brains had been removed for delivery immediately after their deaths. So many objects, identities unknown, labeled but nameless, anonymous stories permanently preserved in a language that can never be understood. I am still not sure of my grandfather's whereabouts. Perhaps his brain lies hidden in a museum somewhere tucked away on some musty shelf, waiting all these years to be discovered.

In this playful use of the rhetoric of discovery, Fuentes is now the explorer/ anthropologist. He knows his attempts to translate these objects into comprehensible languages are futile. Yet the desire remains, or rather, it is produced and put into discourse. His will to know cannot accept the status of "labeled but nameless."

An object's having been "labeled but nameless" means that it has been categorized, but not individuated. Fuentes articulates a liminal category that is not really invisible, but not quite functional either. Analogous to the Philippines itself (as well as Puerto Rico and American Indian reservations), we see an anomalous form of political incorporation that American policy referred to as "domestic to foreign [powers] and yet foreign to domestic matters." That is, Markod's remains lack the specificity of a sovereign subject, but they are still marginally knowable to the present as something not resolved. These remains are made meaningful by a categorization that even in death prevents access to the subaltern consciousness. He never does find the remains, nor does he find the certainty. The very idea that finding the remains would have somehow yielded an answer to his mystery becomes ludicrous.

This inability to comprehend serves a logic similar to the commodification process that brought Filipinos to St. Louis and the Philippines under the U.S. flag. For in the desire to incorporate the Philippines as a U.S. territory and the Filipinos as U.S. subjects, a rationale for empire emerged that had to account for the business sense of empire, as well as the customary civilizing mission. While *Bontoc Eulogy* makes virtually no reference to the commercial interests served by U.S. acquisition of the Philippines, it is the silent and silenced premise of the film.[85] After all, we, along with Fuentes, are left asking, what could it have been like to be this little brown man in St. Louis and where did he go from there? To echo DuBois yet again, how did it feel to Markod to be a problem? Fuentes searches for how the Markod problem was solved.

Fuentes's film fits a genre of films and videos that flowered in the 1980s and 1990s. These films and videos were usually screened at Asian American film festivals, such as the ones still organized by the National Asian American Telecommunications Association (NAATA) in San Francisco, Asian CineVision (ACV) in New York City, and Visual Communications (VC) in Los Angeles. The confluence of good quality and affordable camcorder technology, the emergence of multiculturalism, and the establishment of the annual venues mentioned above put video production in the hands of populations previously relegated to spectator status. They could unprecedentedly show themselves to themselves.

Often made on shoestring budgets, films chronicling generations of Chinese Americans in California, the stories of interned issei and nisei, the lives of Filipino migrant laborers, the Hawaiian sugar plantation experience, and the dreams of Korean convenience store owners, among others, reached and instructed audiences. These earnest oral histories document people whose lives would have been as fragile and inaccessible as memories. Late into this profusion of films entered Fuentes's plaintive inquiry into what it meant to be Filipino at the turn of the century, and what it means to be a Filipino in the late twentieth century.

The familial link between Fuentes and Markod is a common trope of this genre.[86] Yet the film uses this kinship bond not to make connections and continuities apparent, but, on the contrary, to emphasize the profound disconnection and discontinuity between that era and ours. Aside from a few letters, the structures that presumably should have made Markod's story part of Fuentes's memory have failed: "My mother said Markod was a young chieftain known for his skill as a warrior and hunter. That and the fact that he never returned home was all I knew about him." Fuentes then has to rely on the ways in which the colonizer made and makes the colonized knowable to himself.

That the film ends with Fuentes's failure to know Markod points to the inconsistencies, gaps, and contradictions only recognizable as unease and dissatisfaction. *Bontoc Eulogy,* as Jo says at the end of *Chan Is Missing,* "uses the negative to emphasize the positive" (71). But the negative and the positive may not be what we presume them to be. With his use of period footage and physical evidence, Fuentes clearly narrates and documents the early colonial period in the relationship of the United States to the Philippines. The 1904 World's Fair and its abundant archive make sure that history is not forgotten. Indeed, they make sure that the way we remember that history is institutionalized, that history is not what has come to be profoundly forgotten. Rather, I want to suggest, the absence that Fuentes feels is more akin to the absence that gave rise to Wells's pamphlet and its complex of critiques. It is also the absence that Rio Gonzaga felt as she tried to embody McKinley's words and that made Sui Sin Far disappear from American literary history, as discussed in earlier in this chapter.

Like the unknown soldiers anonymously celebrated in their tombs or the vacuums in the cenotaphs described by Benedict Anderson at the opening of *Imagined Communities,* Markod's remains must similarly remain elusive. The emptiness that the film leaves behind makes evident a Markod-shaped hole in our collective memories that we are fundamentally unable to fill. Actually finding a preserved brain or a pile of bones would do little to displace the epistemology of empire.

We should remember that Fuentes's other grandfather, the nationalist freedom fighter, also disappeared: "My grandfather's body was never found. I suspect he died in the trenches and was buried in some mass grave." This grandfather is more easily understood as a martyr to a grateful nation, albeit a neocolonized one. Modernity can make sense of such a loss, as a nation-state is that grandfather's legacy. But Markod's disappearance makes us realize that he may have never really been there at all. We only saw a necessary screen, projected over the failure of American culture to face up to its fundamental dependence on the maintenance of otherness, namely African American contributions that still demand proper tribute beyond multiculturalist representations in the tradition of world's fairs and anthropology museums.

5

"EVERYBODY WANTS TO BE FARRAH"

ABSURD HISTORIES AND HISTORICAL ABSURDITIES

> The one always, as soon as he has stepped from his threshold,
> laughed, the other always wept.
>
> —Juvenal, *Satire X*

> I am clearly for the first humor: not because it is more pleasant
> to laugh than to weep, but because it expresses more contempt
> and condemnation than the other, and I think we can never be
> despised according to our full desert. Compassion and bewailing
> seem to imply some esteem of and value for the thing bemoaned,
> whereas the things we laugh at are by that expressed to be of no
> moment.
>
> —Montaigne, "Of Democritus and Heraclitus"

Civil Society, Globalization, and a Red One-Piece Swimsuit

THIS FINAL CHAPTER offers an extended analysis of a single text
as a closing case study. R. Zamora Linmark's *Rolling the R's* is a darkly
funny and nonlinear assemblage of scenes from the Kalihi section of
Oahu in the 1970s. The text revolves around a group of fifth graders who are simultaneously enamored by and critical of the American
mass culture that structures their queer desires. By abortively seeking
to inhabit the models of proper comportment displayed in the movies
and broadcast over the radio, they subvert those models and imagine
new ones. The subversive mimicry of the unfulfilled visions of American colonialism finds resonance with the structuring feature of Asian
American cultural politics discussed in the previous chapter and in
this book as a whole. While the results may appear tragic, they are
instead darkly comic. Contradiction can be the source of anguish and
tragedy, as indeed we might read the collapse of Rio Gonzaga onto her
bed while reading McKinley, or the image of Marlon Fuentes looking
for the brain of his grandfather preserved in a jar. Or, alternatively,

the strangeness of these images can be darkly funny. In finding the humor in these images, we can see the ways in which contemporary Asian American cultural politics has reckoned with U.S. imperialism by finding absurdity in the project.

Chapters 3 and 4 examined how the ethos of revisionism that motivated the formation of the Asian American literary canon makes it possible to see and feel the transitions of history. From the emblematic disappointments that mark the ends of canonical Asian American literary texts emerges the desire to fashion new ways of seeing the past and its relationship to the present. As Marx wittily quipped at the beginning of *The Eighteenth Brumaire of Louis Bonaparte,* everything in history happens twice, the first time as tragedy and the second time as farce.[1] When empire returned in the contemporary period to make an earlier formation of imperialism visible, we see that it may have been a farce the first time around as well.

The epigraph from Montaigne at the beginning of this chapter shows how finding the humor in a situation can be the most critical, and pleasurable, position to occupy. Humor can build unexpected affiliations and it is precisely with this idea that I conclude this book. For the humor emerging in opposition to empire at the turn of the century finds its way into the humorous moments in Asian American cultural politics. From locating the curious resonance between turn-of-the-century conceptions of American empire and Asian American texts, unnoticed satire emerges.

Satire was a powerful medium of social protest in the debates over imperialism at the turn of the century. Mark Twain was particularly adept at skewering the imperialists, and his "To the Person Sitting in Darkness" is a canonized specimen of satire in general, not just anti-imperialist.[2] Twain was not alone, as many critics of imperialism saw an absurdity in American empire. These critiques of empire saw material in the "Imperialism Stunt" that would likely find its way into the monologues of late night talk show hosts today. Out of these conditions of absurdity, which did after all come to pass, emerged the cultural conditions of Asian American difference.

These voices of dissent from a century ago imagined the manifest strangeness of the incorporation of Asian difference into American culture. The following appeared in an editorial in *The People,* the weekly periodical of the Socialist Labor party, in 1900:

Hence, the Spanish-American War, whereby while fighting Spain in the Antilles, the color of plausibility could be given to the seizure of the Philippines as belonging to the same power. Observe that Manila, so absolutely disconnected from the Cuban question that it lies almost directly straight through the earth from us and Cuba, 8,000 miles beneath our feet, was where the first battle was fought! Cuba was simply the fulcrum of the lever used by the capitalists in prying the "Open Door" of China.[3]

The idea that one could trace the line of U.S. interests in Cuba and the Philippines directly through the crust, mantle, and core of the earth and then back out the other side is something worthy of Jules Verne. It is absurd and funny, but it is true. It is funny because it is true: at the turn of the century, the United States did indeed mount simultaneous military campaigns in these disparate locations, thereby radically altering what territory and territoriality would come to mean.[4] This chapter argues that a form of satire that emerged as the United States became an extraterritorial empire resonates with the dark humor emanating from those who are the pure products of American colonialism. The satiric force of *The People*'s editorial is textual evidence of a critique of empire that did not survive an epistemic shift. That is, these anti-imperialists saw as an emerging absurdity what modernity more readily recognizes as an early moment in the genealogy of globalization under the stewardship of the United States. For most of the twentieth century, the voices of those who saw absurdity in globality were drowned out by the noise-canceling forces of modernity.

The conditions of postmodernity—with its simultaneity of "incredulity toward metanarrative" and undeniable "world order"—have allowed us to reclaim that absurdity through the emergence of cultural formations antagonistic to the totality of modernity.[5] Confrontations with difference are always an ambivalent enterprise, as one is simultaneously parochialized and parochializing. R. Zamora Linmark's *Rolling the R's*, a 1995 queer Asian American text about a community in 1970s Honolulu, uses its bounded locality to assert its translocality. That is, it captures a local place and an innocent time peopled with characters who are unaware of their cosmopolitan translocality and prophetic prescience. At the same time, through literature that depicts a recent period, we can see the current disappointments with unfulfilled promises by seeing those who are not yet disappointed.

In this way, this book is sharply funny because it oddly resonates with turn-of-the-century anti-imperialist satire. But at the same time, that satire from a century ago is also newly humorous because of its strange similarity to a 1995 queer Asian American text. That is, alternative formations such as Linmark's not only reference pasts to which they did not seem to have a direct connection, but also, through that referencing, these alternative epistemologies produce new understandings of those earlier moments as unwittingly setting the stage for a much later exacerbation of contradictions they had only begun to sense. In other words, alternative pasts not only lead to alternative presents, but alternative presents are the sine qua non for making those alternative pasts visible and appreciable in the first place. The present gets the jokes that the past may not have even known it was making. The fractured totality of the contemporary moment has lived through globalization taken to its logical conclusions and found it humorously illogical.

The road to that fractured totality is paved with a growing awareness of the production of gaps where the unrepresentable fail to be wholly incorporated into or repudiated by modernity. As a counterpoint to the mania for producing a grand unifying theory of globality, elegies for the local resurrect how the world felt before modernity reached its current totality.[6] It is a totality measured not only in the Greenwich mean "homogeneous empty time" of the nation, but more precisely in global positioning satellite nanoseconds dutifully ticked off by the U.S. Naval Observatory's master atomic clock. Once upon a time, localities kept their own time until the newfangled railroad demanded standardization. Parochial timekeeping is a relic of a forgotten past.[7]

The affective response to these lost objects, whether of, say, the precapitalist bucolic folk described in Thomas Gray's poem, "Elegy Written in a Country Churchyard," or the vanishing Amerindians of *Ishi, the Last Yahi,* is an appropriately mournful nostalgia.[8] This mourning—or melancholia—evidences a Nietzschean ressentiment for the chain of catastrophes witnessed by Benjamin's "angel of history." Survivor's guilt pries open subaltern histories, and we legitimately weep at the disasters our modernity has wrought. Any grudging claim we make of connection to that past only confirms our complicity in perpetrating another extinction.[9]

Yet lost localities have not only been the fodder of the elegiac; the dustbin of history has also yielded the stuff of brilliant humor. Instead of sobbing at that which has shuffled off its mortal coil, peals of laughter erupt over the idea that things were ever that way at all. And so we have the historically humorous, a category of often pitch-black hilarity, from the confidence in the Maginot line to keep fascists at bay to the solace of duck-and-cover to prevent one's atomic vaporization.

The historically humorous and the elegiac do have important resonances. As with the elegiac, the historically humorous offers a critique of modernity based in an appreciation of local formations. We in the present know that these localities will eventually have to surrender their very souls, that is, their unreconstructed centrism. Local *lebenswelts,* or life-worlds, may ultimately become epistemological ghost towns, ruined cottages for the speculating archaeologists of the future. If any formations survive in an uninterrupted way at all, it is through becoming a minor to the nation's or the empire's major. The result is a dialectic of history and humor, a historical reenactment of a deluded world without end that, alas, actually ended.

The humorous can then be the more critical medium for seizing hold of the past than is the piously elegiac. Gone is the nostalgia, the rose-colored glasses of those in mourning. Instead, the unapologetic melancholic subject throws back its head and laughs with bittersweet delight and newfound purpose. Yet this laughing subject does not produce the aloofly amused Enlightenment subject of whom Montaigne writes. Rather, because of the alternative process of formation in particular historical conditions, the laughing subject avoids reproducing the subject of the liberalism that it found so funny.

R. Zamora Linmark's *Rolling the R's* is just such a historically humorous reenactment. By analyzing the humor of Linmark's justly celebrated text, this chapter examines how a piece of minor literature tells alternative histories that account for alternative presents. Through their contradiction to contemporary ways of knowing, these alternatives smite our funny bones and make us feel the queer sensations of occluded pasts. In apprehending the particular pasts of *Rolling the R's,* we can trace the emergence of U.S. modernity through the ways in which the text contains genealogies of pasts that did not survive their moments in history intact. *Rolling the R's* exacerbates contradictions between a geographically and historically local formation on the one hand and, on the other, the national and imperial terms of coherence that this local formation ultimately fails to meet. The contradictions that emerge at the site of these confrontations ironically and presciently fuel the pleasures of the precocious preadolescents of Linmark's text. These Asian Pacific immigrants to the United States desperately seek to become the Americans that we—and they—see they had already long been under neocolonialism.

In reanimating these impossible children, *Rolling the R's* renders that historical period and those colonial subjects to highlight the irony of what might be called our present's queer modernity, a discontented stasis that may have outlived its usefulness. Queer modernity, like any modernity worth our trouble, is an American formation, or more precisely, it is in the service of the maintenance of the American superpower. *Queer* and *modern* are decidedly antagonistic terms; one seeks order and uniformity, while the other disrupts the same.[10] The odd unification of these manageably recalcitrant terms under the demands of institutionality becomes understandably laughable, and laughably understandable, through the reverse-engineering that Linmark's text performs.

By showing us queers of color before such an idea was codified, Linmark reminds us of the material histories that made the category both important and occluded in ways that make us laugh knowingly at the course that empire and resistance took.[11] Linmark's book reverse-engineers our current cultural politics and our concomitant ways of knowing and studying these subjects by offering a genealogy of that terrain of confrontation through a reenactment of its struggles. We can then see and feel what Kimberlé Crenshaw has usefully termed "intersectionality," not as the unification of competing claims of representation, but as a formation that intersectionality emerged to describe for pragmatic political ends.[12]

And it couldn't have come at a better time. The welcome crises of identity emerged in the wake of rigorous and committed theoretical work, particularly that of Judith Butler's epistemological depth-charge of a book, *Gender Trouble: Feminism and the Subversion of Identity*.[13] Butler's book became the Bible of queer studies. When taken to an absolutist extreme, these critiques of the subject looked to erode the institutional footholds of progressive organizing.[14] Yet there was something undeniably wrong with identity. It became fundamentalist and was used accordingly. There emerged a need for recasting the new social movements of the post–civil rights era without ultimate recourse to the subject of Enlightenment. A simultaneous rethinking of material history and its archives on the one hand, and knowledge and subject formation on the other, set an agenda for new research in all fields of cultural studies.[15]

In literary studies, David L. Eng's *Racial Castration: Managing Masculinity in Asian America* offers a sustained and comprehensive analysis of sexuality's role in producing new subjects and concomitant new histories.[16] Eng synthesizes theories of gender and desire with theories of racialization to demonstrate how the subjects of Asian American literature are not subjects at all in any conventional sense. Eng realigns the Asian American literary canon as a site for accessing deep structures of subjectivity and history that fail to be contained by such liberalist categories as citizenship or liberalism's latest phase, globalization. Eng writes of how Asian American literature offers "tortured model(s) of Asian American citizenship in both the larger global arena and the domestic realm of a liberal, capitalist, U.S. nation-state, which today is rapidly and urgently (re)consolidating itself as the preeminent and unforgiving bastion of economic freedom, straightness, and whiteness" (224). Fittingly, Eng ends his book with a reading of the undeniably patriotic transgender performances of Orlando Domingo, one of the colorful characters of R. Zamora Linmark's *Rolling the R's*. Orling, as he is affectionately known, shows up for school as Farrah Fawcett. Yet, because he is the embodiment of triumphant educational achievement (he is the class valedictorian) and Althusserian "bad subject" formation (he wants to *be,* rather than possess, Farrah), the ideological and repressive state apparatuses do not know how to handle him. The likes of Orling, that is, one who fails to be adequately represented by modernity at modernity's peril, can be found in a cheap domestic labor force or in disease-bearing celestials.[17] *Rolling the R's* is crammed with these, for lack of a better term, queer Asian Americans.

Even before it was published in 1995, *Rolling the R's* had generated an uncommon amount of buzz among the Asian American literati. Linmark's pieces in the *APA Journal*'s *Witness Aloud* (a special gay and lesbian issue from 1994), in *Premonitions: The Kaya Anthology of New Asian North American Poetry*, and in *Charlie Chan Is Dead: An Anthology of Contemporary Asian American Fiction* had whetted the appetites of a readership desiring a new formation at a time of over-easy 1980s multiculturalism and increasingly shrill and worn critiques of hegemony.[18] Anyone who attended even a portion of Linmark's riotously funny readings did not soon forget this emergent voice in Asian American literature.

Embodying a blend of the latest aesthetic strategies, edgy subject matter, and a sense of humor that Asian American literature had never achieved before, or since, the book did not disappoint. The sources of effusive quotes on the dust jacket should have been signal enough to the new formation in our midst: postmodern, postcolonial Jessica Hagedorn and urbanely queer Eve Kosofsky Sedgwick.

Years later, the book simultaneously fractures and unifies the category "Asian American literature" through its form (jump-cut pieces in pidgin without discernible linear chronology) and its content (a revisiting of the pivotal 1970s, but in Hawaii and from the standpoint of queer Filipino immigrants). While many of the critical questions around immigration, gender, sexuality, and cultural nationalism had been simmering for decades, Linmark's text brought together, and to a boiling point, these contentious social, historical, and aesthetic ingredients in a book about schoolchildren in Kalihi, Oahu. As Edgar Ramirez, a ten-year-old, queer, working-class, Filipino mestizo, warns his classmates: "The ground you standin' on is not the freakin' meltin' pot but one volcano. And one day, the thing goin' erupt and you guys goin' be the first ones for burn."[19] Ramirez and his cohorts in "that 70's book" are the ones who would go on to inherit the divided field of Asian American cultural politics today.

The book's naively blunt protagonists anticipate the strains that the politics of identity would face. The book does this by recreating a moment when people still believed in these politics. These children re-present to us the conditions of the moment of emergence for new subjectivities when and where newness and subjecthood were differently valorized. The children become prophets of queer postcoloniality under U.S. imperialism. Like Mark Twain's historical playfulness in *Huckleberry Finn* (revisiting the antebellum 1840s in the post-Reconstruction 1880s), or even Melville's lampooning of eighteenth-century racial hierarchies in *Benito Cereno* (allegorizing the Haitian Revolution, ca. 1792–1804, in antebellum 1852), we end up laughing at the historical gap that emerges when history does not turn out the way the characters had imagined it would. And we laugh even harder when they are dead-on about the new politics of gendered racialization that have come to be emblematic of Asian American cultural politics and the looming contradictions of multiculturalism and globalization.

Finding success in Asian American literature courses that underwent queer and feminist revisionism, the book's publisher, Kaya Production, responded with a cheaper paperback edition that is aptly indicative of a shift in Asian American cultural production. When that more affordable edition of Linmark's book came out, the cover had changed. The dust jacket on the hardcover edition is a somber blood-red collage of images of Kalihi, a fitting double of the textual assemblage within. For the paperback, the seams of collage have departed and now we see one image: Orlando Domingo, the Ivy-League-bound senior, striking the famous, flung-back-and-feathered-hair pose of Farrah Fawcett-Majors in her red one-piece swimsuit. Yet, instead of being a unified representative of modernity, this image of Orlando remains a palimpest of fragments whose seams and layers we can blissful ignore and/or knowingly enjoy.

"The Battle Poem of the Republic"

With one hundred dollars in prize money at stake in the Annual State Poetry Contest, Division III, the students of Miss Takemoto's fifth-grade class at Kalihi Elementary set to work crafting verse. Florante Sanchez, one of the main characters in Linmark's book, gives us a play-by-play description of his classmates' efforts. He saves the following description for last: "Loata Faalele wrote 'bout this road in the deep end of Kalihi Valley diverging and he could not figure out which one to take, so he took the path that was less familiar, and he ended up in Laie" (57).

The humor to many recipients of an American grade-school education is that Loata seems to be plagiarizing Robert Frost's poem, "The Road Not Taken." In the hopes of winning the contest, Loata chooses to copy a venerated monument in the national literature of the United States. Like any canonical text, Frost's poem is a model of behavior, a blueprint for proper subject formation. Loata simply plugs himself and his world into Frost's "yellow wood" and cranks the equation. We almost cannot help picturing Loata, a boy of Samoan extraction, perhaps clutching Frost's poem like a map in his ten-year-old hands, strolling about purposefully on Oahu in an attempt to live out a neo-romantic idyll. The humor of the racialized absurdity is bettered only by the narrative that Loata lives out in his version of poem. He seems to have done Frost one better: he actually arrives somewhere, namely Laie. (Laie happens to be the site of the world-famous Polynesian Cultural Center.[20])

Faalele takes Frost to his logical and literal conclusion on a site profoundly extravagant and ultimately undermining to Frost. For Frost, the choice has made all the existential difference. For Loata, the consequences of that choice end up being unremarkably earthbound and prosaic, literal and palpably material. Frost's poem, long institutionalized in American education as a metaphorical vehicle for (tacitly American) wanderlust and the will to know, is meant to take place in a yearning and maturing American soul. Loata innocently has other uses for the poem that shed light on the particularity of Frost's formerly universal New England deciduous forest. That is, Frost doesn't play in Hawaii. Faalele does.

We are at a historical moment when Frost's poem seeks validation from Loata's, and not the other way around. And it does not receive this validation. The empire has written back and Frost has been found wanting. The juxtaposition of the idealized and the materialized is a by-now common trope of the counterhegemonic force of minor literatures. Witness the uses of the English canon throughout its colonies: the scholarly work of Sara Suleri, Ngugi Wa Thiongo, and Gauri Viswanathan examines the ways in which colonial subjects were repositories for supreme Englishness. And who could forget Macauley's "Minute on Indian Education," with its vision of proper English subjects in all ways except epidermis?[21] The material mimicry of an idealized imperial model subverts the authority of that vision of modernity.

Yet the goal of a minor literature is not necessarily a displacement of imperial hegemony with a similarly totalized improvement. Such was the wrong turn made by many a cultural nationalism with its new state purporting to represent the people it didn't really know. Minor and subaltern formations emerge from, and for, what Fanon tantalizingly called "a zone of occult instability."[22] The fragmentary and episodic features of subaltern culture are perhaps all too recognizable in experimental texts such as Hagedorn's *Dogeaters* and Theresa Hak-kyung Cha's *Dictee*.[23] Minor literatures reflect an education in convention and a productive departure from it. Revisionist literary history is crammed with examples of minor formations. Depending on the historical moment, the subverted convention could be that of Christian missionary incorporation. For example, Phyllis Wheatley's 1773 poem, "On Being Brought from Africa to America," deploys the discourse of Christian salvation to articulate the experience of being captured, transported to the New World, and forced to labor under slavery. The speaker intones: "Once I redemption neither sought nor knew." She had become a Christian and she is resolutely ambivalent about it.[24]

The subverted convention could be that of the more secularized conception of the Enlightenment. For example, Toussaint Louverture invoked the liberty, equality, and fraternity of the French Revolution, which he saw himself and the erstwhile Haitians to be a part of. He declares himself a man, with all the rights and privileges thereto pertaining, and he realizes that that is not enough to secure freedom and prosperity.[25]

Or in the more contemporary moment, subjects under globalization produce a literature that playfully asserts an illusory equality before modernity. Kidlat Tahimik winkingly declares a motto of progress in *The Perfumed Nightmare*, his brilliantly satiric exploration of the discourse of the space age in the underdeveloped world: "Liberté, egalité, fraternité, . . . supermarché!"[26] At the end of that 1977 film, Kidlat renounces his presidency of the Wernher von Braun Fan Club and retreats to a surreally reconstructed traditionalism that would make Jose Martí roll over in his grave.[27]

In each of these examples, a minor text uses its hybridity, that is, its conception of failed incorporation into a previously capacious episteme, to make visible the seams and edges of a modernity on the wane. While the catastrophic proportions of these failures are obvious to us now, we need to remember that these epistemes were not so easy to dismiss. Indeed, as each dominant episteme was overthrown, residue survived in the emergent formations that rose to dominance. Our current post–cold-war totality—the new world order, let's say—is just such a deviously flexible formation.

From Bandung to Stonewall

At the turn of the twentieth century, the United States entered the blood-stained gate of colonialism by waging a "splendid little war" that fittingly annihilated space. For the United States, the Spanish-

American War jubilantly confirmed the sneaking suspicion that the frontier was closed by pushing the United States in multiple and seemingly random directions at once from footholds only familiar to so-called "saltwater empires." Efforts to make sense of the U.S. civilizing mission inaugurated a discourse of a new imperialism. No longer simply "the white man's burden," this mission found a new process and telos: subjugating and then educating not-yet-self-governing peoples.

The benefit of hindsight allows us to trace the genealogy of globalization through this pivotal event in a pivotal era. But at the moment of the emergence of U.S. imperialism, the desire to establish a simultaneous U.S. presence on opposite poles of the earth was not entirely obvious, even as it was being institutionalized and otherwise put into discourse. In understanding the passions and interests of the arguments for and against U.S. imperialism before its triumph, we can better contextualize and appreciate contemporary formations of resistance to late capitalism and its modernity.

American literatures of the post–civil-rights era can then be seen as inheriting these contestations over the meaning of American modernity. Whether under labels ranging from *multicultural, minority, ethnic,* and *subaltern* to *postcolonial, counterhegemonic,* and *antiheteropatriarchal,* what these literatures have in common is the formation of a radical critique of, and importantly, visions of alternatives to, the modernity that rose to dominance a century ago with the emergence of U.S. imperialism.

For certain U.S. populations, it was both voguish and legitimate to claim a connection to people of the third world. From Robert Blauner's conception of "colonized versus immigrant" minorities to the use of the appellation "Third World Liberation Front" to describe hard-fought struggles within institutions of higher education, decolonization possessed compelling explanatory power for a wide range of social relations.[28] The Reverend Dr. Martin Luther King Jr., commonly thought of as an activist purely focused on domestic issues, referred to decolonization struggles in Asia and Africa as inspirational models for African Americans to learn from. As early as his "Letter from Birmingham Jail" (1964), King writes,

> The nations of Asia and Africa are moving with jetlike speed toward gaining independence, but we still creep at horse-and-buggy pace toward gaining a cup of coffee at a lunch counter.[29]

Perhaps the pinnacle of this resistance and simultaneous acknowledgment of globalilzation's totality was the 1955 Bandung Conference, where nonaligned states sought to align themselves as commonly seeking to avoid the hegemony of the United States and the Soviet Union. The daunting diversity of histories and experiences there only ended up driving home the point that the West had won and that the last best hope was an oppositional status called "nonaligned." Those whose narratives seemed extraneous, whose difference seemed immaterial to the emergency at hand, were incorporated into the procrustean bed of the postcolonial nation-state or otherwise swept under the rug of history.

Mobilization in response to a specific incident or issue usefully brings to the surface a commonality around which an identity coheres. The danger lies in the identity being seen as inherent prior to the actions that instrumentalized it. The Stonewall uprising of 1969 is widely regarded as the genesis of the contemporary gay rights movement.[30] But with this newfound uniformity for engaging with state power comes an awareness of that which it does not adequately contain.

New interdisciplinary approaches need to be formed to prevent the reconsolidation of the logics of modernity and its felicitious individualist subject of rights because those whose narratives seemed extraneous, whose difference seemed immaterial to the emergency at hand, were incorporated into a procrustean bed of coalition politics or otherwise swept under the rug of history. But over time that rug has gotten lumpy.

And so we have the return of the repressed: that which could only be suspended, but not expelled.

"I Can't Expel Him. Maybe Suspension."

There is perhaps no better way to provoke simultaneous ridicule and nostalgia for a bygone era than to remind us of its defunct obsessions, especially its sex symbols. For the mid 1970s, Farrah Fawcett was shorthand for a generation's taste. As described in *Rolling the Rs:* "A swimsuit goddess with long graceful legs, pearly white teeth, glossy lips, roller derby hips and a million dollar smile on a king-size waterbed next to none other than the Six Million Dollar Man himself" (22).

For the unsleepy community of Kalihi, Farrah's allure was tranformative and inescapable. The children of Kalihi Elementary formed the "Triple-F C, the Farrah Fawcett Fan Club" with a rigorous regimen of activity that they would never devote to their official studies:

> Once a week, the club met at Edgar's house to: 1) write letters to Farrah Fawcett c/o ABC Network; 2) show off their collections of Farrah memorabilia, including cut-outs from glamour magazines and Farrah's latest swimsuit poster; 3) role play scenes from Charlie's Angels; and 4) discuss sociopolitically charged issues raised by the show, such as prostitution, lesbian undertones, and Orientalism. (23)

These preadolescent children simultaneously abide by and parody the regimentation of organizational disciplining to properly appreciate their objects of desire. Adolescents fuel their autoerotic fantasies with Farrah's phenomenally popular poster:

> Ernesto Cabatbangan, a freshman at Sanford B. Dole Intermediate, doesn't want to be Farrah; he wants to be inside her. He bought all her posters on discount from DJ's Record Store because his calabash cousin manages the Pearlridge branch. He says he can't get it up unless she's there watching over him, smiling. At times, it gets so bad that he sprays the room, bull's-eyeing Farrah's mouth. (22)

But no response to the Farrah phenomenon is as troubling to the authorities as that of Orlando "Orling" Domingo. At first he mimics her famous "flip" hairstyle, in all its feathered allure: "It all started with Charlie's Angels and his addiction to Farrah's blond mane."

> "He's flipped out," Orlando's classmates at Farrington High tell each other the moment he enters the classroom sporting Farrah's hairdo. "The next thing you know, he's goin' be packin' on makeup and dressin' up like her, too." (24)

And he does.

Finally, fearing a transgender epidemic, the teachers demand that Orling stop his schoolyard self-expression:

> "We gotta do something before our boys catch this madness and start huddling in skirts and pom-poms," the football coaches Mr. Akana and Mr. Ching tell Principal Shim. "You gotta do something. Pronto. Suspend him, expel him, we don't care, but you gotta keep him away from our boys if you want the team to bring home the OIA title." (24)

But Principal Shim is in a quandary after he takes one look at Orling's stellar permanent record:

Born in Cebu in 1962; Immigrated to Hawai'i at the age of ten; Lives with mother in Lower Kalihi; Father: deceased; Speaks and writes English, Spanish, Cebuano, and Tagalog; Top of the Dean's List; Current GPA: 4.0; This year's Valedictorian; SAT scores totaling 1500 out of 1600; Voted Most Industrious and Most Likely to Succeed four years in a row; Competed and won accolades in Speech and Math Leagues; Current President of Keywanettes, National Honor Society, and the Student Body Government; Plans to attend Brown University in the fall and eventually take up Law. (25)

Fearing discrimination litigation, the principal comes to the following compromise:

"I can't expel him. Maybe suspension." He squirms at the thought of Orlando turning the tables and charging him, Mr. Akana, Mr. Ching, and the Department of Education with discrimination against a Filipino faggot whose only desire is to be Farrah from Farrington, as in Farrah, the Kalihi Angel. (25)

On a trajectory to become a lawyer, Orlando is not only on a fast track to become an officer of the court; he is also an example of the legal apparatus's inability to contain transgressive formations that exceed direct regulation by the state under liberalism. Sumptuary laws and dress codes would be ultimately unconstitutional. Orling would be able to invoke his status as a proper subject before the law, even though he is an improper subject to nonstate institutions that the state cannot touch in the name of the maintenance of the public/private split. The idea that a disruptive formation such as Orling would fit and indeed claim status as the Enlightenment juridical subject is the liberal turn that queerness may be tempted to take. But it's important to note that Orling never actually invokes this rights-based positionality; rather, it is imputed to him by an agent of the state apparatus, Principal Shim.

Shim is hampered by the very means through which a subject like Orlando is supposed to be regulated, intimidated, and surveilled: the ominously eternal and indelible "permanent record." As documents abiding by what Foucault termed "governmentality," official school records function as a colonial archive for apprehending a kind of subalternity in *Rolling the R's*. The fragment entitled "Tongue-Tied" revisits this very genre.

TO THE PARENTS:

This report is intended to give you an approximation of the progress of your child during the school year 1979-80.

Your interest in, and understanding of the school progress of your son or daughter or twins will be an important factor in his/her/their success. The school cannot accomplish much without the cooperation of the home.

We hope that you will welcome an opportunity to confer with your child's/ children's teacher regarding her/her/their school progress.

Principal Okimura (50)

In the gap between the ability of a teacher's report to represent a student and its ability to function as an against-the-grain archive of queer "occasions" at school, we find ourselves laughing.[31] First, the proper subject's disciplining demands attendance and punctuality, so a record of Presents, Absents, and Tardies is assessed. In the more subjective evaluations, praise is carefully doled out. In particular, good handwriting is a virtue. Mrs. Takemoto and Ms. Takara say that "in our years of teaching, [Vicente De Los Reyes] has the most beautiful and unique penmanship" (51). The teachers also compliment Vicente for being "a happy child, a friendly pupil who is very neat in appearance. Ms. Takara and I especially like his flaming orange and green and purple jumpsuit" (51). We can presume that beauty and uniqueness are valorized to indicate the proper individuation that Vicente is undergoing in his American education. And then, as we read the next report, the teachers say that Mai-Lan Phan, "in our twenty years of teaching, has the most beautiful and unique penmanship" (52). The same compliment is made about Florante Sanchez: "He has the most beautiful and unique penmanship Ms. Takara and I have ever seen" (53). As with Orling's permanent record, these progress reports indicate the proper course of subject formation, as well as the explicit and implied terms of surveillance and regulation.

The criticism and prohibitions put into discourse in these reports convey the means through which these students are being abortively ushered into modernity. Their education is not only their individual incorporation into official national culture, but the systematic erasure of locality. In particular, their use of pidgin is deemed dangerous, both for some intrinsic reason and for the communities it produces: "Ms. Takara and I noticed that the other students Florante does associate with are Katherine Cruz and Edgar Ramirez. Will you discourage him from further associations with the two? Their use of pidgin endangers Florante's appreciation and skillful usage of the English language" (53). To a system of national education, Hawaiian pidgin, a creolized dialect emerging from the unique historical conditions of the plantations, is a disturbing formation. An old joke explains the difference between a language and a dialect—that is, that a language has an army and a navy, and pidgin has neither. But it does have a living tradition that tries to survive in the face of standard "Haolefied" English. Pidgin marks locality over nation, and it is a material trace of a history of inequality and exploitation that national culture might rather forget for the contradictions it ontologically exacerbates.[32] Pidgin, like any regional dialect, is denigrated for being a marker of an absence of education. And it is, for better or for worse, valorized for being an emblem of local resistance.

The vilified and valorized duo are Katrina Cruz and Edgar Ramirez, two students whose blunt recalcitrance seems, to the teachers, to be almost purely malicious. They are the two students who explicitly fail or almost fail. But they are worse than just failures; they are bad influences on otherwise good students, like Vicente, Mai-Lan, and Florante. While they are profoundly precocious, the "ten-year-old-ness" of Edgar and Katrina makes them well-suited to resist the terms of liberalist legitimation for which even Orling might be tempted to opt. If they simply failed and functioned as negative examples to the other students, they would not be a problem to the educational apparatus. Instead, their failure is somehow appealing. They turn their failures—whether literally in the sense of their school work or epistemologically in terms of their being made conventionally knowable—into sites of possibilities that our future did not realize.

The tirade cited earlier in this chapter, when Edgar transforms "the freakin' meltin' pot" into "one volcano," emerges from a seemingly harmless, even celebratory activity initiated by Mrs. Takemoto.[33] The American salad bowl aesthetic gets a dressing down in the chapter "The Two Filipinos," when a census-like accounting of ethnic difference goes horribly wrong. Mrs. Takemoto had "gone row by row asking them their ethnicity." A problem erupts when Nelson Ariola does not want to claim status as a Filipino, possibly the lowest rung on the ethnicity ladder of Hawaii: "Because I was born here . . . because I'm not an immigrant . . . I don't speak English like I got a plugged nose . . . and because my grandfather never came here for cheap labor . . . I'm sick and tired of being called a Filipino. . . . I'm not like them, Mrs.

Takemoto" (67–68). Nelson reaches an epistemological crisis when Stephen Bean, the one white student in the class, pointedly asks him, "'Nelson, if you're such an American, then what am I?'" The narrator says "Nelson opens his mouth," but "no words escape"(69). The gap in knowledge, however, is quickly filled: "Katrina matter-of-factly replies: 'One haole, what else?'"(69). She gives a name to a whiteness that would rather remain the nameless, properly and invisibly unmodified American. Stephen claims the elusive "abstract citizen" category that, as Lisa Lowe reminds us, has been specifically defined over and against Asian immigrants. Histories of gendered racialization make this a profoundly venerated status, which Nelson cannot ever come close to achieving. Mrs. Takemoto immediately tells Katrina, "That's enough" (69). But the conflict is not resolved and more students contribute to the debate.

Edgar's volcanic critique also bursts forth at a moment of silencing and identitarian naming:

> "Edgar, sit down," Mrs. Takemoto says.
>
> "Why only tell me to sit down," Edgar says. "Why no tell the haole for sit down, too."
>
> "Shut up, faggot," Stephen says.
>
> "No tell me to freakin' shut up, halitosis," Edgar says. "And Mrs. Takemoto, you open one case but you no can close 'em, so I goin' close 'em once and for all."
>
> Edgar first points his finger to Nelson. "You, Mr. Haole Wanna-be," then points to Stephen; "and you, Mr. Haolewood. You guys think you so hot-shit, but you know what? The ground you standin' on is not the freakin' meltin' pot but one volcano. And one day, the thing goin' erupt and you guys goin' be the first ones for burn." (70)

In his inability to be granted a happy tile in an American mosaic, Edgar foresees future crises. Indeed, even from the moment Mrs. Takemoto engages the students in this activity of identity formation, contradictions emerge. The narration begins with lucid declarations: "Mai-Lan Phan is Vietnamese" (67). She is ascribed an identity based on a country that was only recently (re)unified as a barely recognized nation-state after an unpopular war. "Jared Shimabukuro is Okinawan" (67). His identity is based on what is basically a polity in the service of the U.S. military. "Judy-Ann Katsura is Japanese" (67). She belongs to the category that is seen as the ruling elite of Hawaii, but she is in a minority in this working-class section of Honolulu. So, too, is the one white student: "Stephen Bean is Caucasian" (69). "Loata Faalele is Samoan" (69). It's unclear whether that means Samoa or American Samoa, which, in a nostalgic allusion to the sun never setting on the British Empire, is proudly known for being the place where the United States begins its day.

And then there's Caroline Macadangdang: "Caroline Macadangdang is one-fourth Filipino, one-fourth Spanish, one-fourth Chinese, one-eighth Hawaiian, one sixteenth Cherokee Indian, and one sixteenth Portuguese-Brazilian" (67). She is an emblem of mestizaje and the absurd use of blood quanta as a meaningful marker of what Michael Omi and Howard Winant call "racial formation." All the other students are Filipino, including Nelson Ariola and probably Caroline herself.

For Edgar, the discursive limits of "Filipino" or "faggot" do not function as an epistemological home base beyond which lies the unknowable; rather, they operate as a standpoint from which to "imagine otherwise."[34] On the first page of the second chapter, the statement "Edgar Ramirez is a faggot" is repeated seven times. We are told that everybody knows it.

> Edgar Ramirez is a faggot. His friends Katrina, Vicente, Loata, Mai-lan, and Florante know it. Even Edgar himself knows it.
> "Since when, Edgar?" Katrina asks.
> "Ever since I saw my father naked," he says.
> "So what are you going to do about it?" Vicente asks.
> "Nothing," Edgar says. "Nothing." (4)

Cognizant of his brownly Oedipal formation, Edgar enjoys being a Filipino faggot and makes no apology to national, imperial, heteropatriachal normativity.[35] The very opening line of the book is Edgar's erotema: "So what?" The second chapter ends the litany of Edgar's openly gay legibility with his self-knowledge as such. In doing so, the book foregrounds the practice of reading and the closet, of a kind of DuBoisian double-consciousness from the soul of a self-named "faggot" and a Filipino. Edgar is not in a latency period. He is not forming his sexuality in preadolescence. He may not even be considered precocious. He is a faggot and everybody knows it and there's nothing that can or should be done about it.

The book then ends with another act of reading and its relationship to using nonnormative sexuality as a site for self-formation, social and historical critique, and, lest we forget, pleasure: Katrina's book report on Judy Blume's *Forever*. In the final chapter, "F for Book Report," Katrina's pidgin-inflected analysis of Blume's novel becomes a retrospective glance at Linmark's project in *Rolling the R's*:

> *Forever* is one of the bestest bestest books I ever read cuz it's so true-to-life and I know it cuz I lived it. I feel like I know Katherine so well, even though I one local and she live all the way east coast side, cuz I can fully relate to the things that happen to her from page one to page two hundred twenty. Was kinda scary actually, reading this book, cuz I felt like I was reading about myself. (145)

Culture texts function as vehicles of identification, traversing geographical and historical spaces. By putting desires and prohibitions into discourse, a book like *Forever* generates the terms of intelligibility for the worlds occupied by their readers. In a relationship of mutual validation, they become provisionally acceptable and useful iterations. The danger lies in believing in the perpetuity of these terms of representability. As Katrina says of her boyfriend Erwin Castillo in the last lines of the book:

> I don't know if he going to be the one shouting I do I do I do to me in front of Father Pacheco. That's too far ahead to be thinking about. But for now, I just gotta make the most of Erwin, cuz for now, Erwin is my forever. (149)

Katrina understands her positionality as the willing embrace of the contradiction between the provisional ("for now") and the eternal ("forever"). And, like Edgar at the beginning of the book, there is nothing that can or should be done about it. She makes no apology and is even downright preachy: "I recommend this book especially for you, Mrs. Takemoto, cuz you might learn a thing or two about love and the painful truth that nothing last forever, not even love. I know you know and everybody know that your husband stay screwing my mother" (148–49).

As with Loata's use of Frost, we witness the power of a piece of literature to both make sense of the world and be made sense of, or not, by other worlds to which it travels. The final poem that Florante describes in the "Battle Poem of the Republic Section" is his own. Suggestively, Florante does not include the poem itself, nor merely its description. He describes the process:

> I wrote 'bout
> Hungry bees eating space, blackdogs losing it first time
> America raiding scotch-taped Kalihi while Pedros drowned in Franco's
> German-spit second time
> Dim in the Philippines, PI Joes missing in Fort DeRussy's dead-end pockets
> third time
> Immigrants coming to Kalihi, dodging the American sham battle fourth time
> Smiles that break evil bones after school, touch-dance brawling in from Kres
> fifth time
> Uninvited priests with dog-tatooed arms, grinding fighting cocks, and
> preaching last words sixth time
> (And I wrote 'bout a pig cap pen bleeding a hundred-dollar poem.) (58)

His final, and presumably submitted, poem is not a modernist solipsistic poem about poetry. By narrating the creative and iterative process, Florante shows us how the last poem he wrote contains within it its own almost irretrievable genesis. Instead of a smoothly textured product, we see a vivid palimpsest of co-mingling alternatives. Like the baroquely grisly paintings of Manuel Ocampo, Florante's poem speaks to a myriad of histories that both acknowledge *and* disavow a will to cohere, acknowledging and disavowing modernity.

Juxtaposed with the absurdity of Loata's poem, and the even greater absurdity of Frost's, Florante's assemblage mimics the experience of reading *Rolling the R's*. In the simultaneity of tragedy and hilarity, the book does not solely claim the bemoaned seeker of justice under liberalism, but also something elusive: that at which we laugh rather than weep, that which seemed to be "of not moment." In this simultaneity, we can link Linmark's humorous look at queer, neocolonized immigrants under globalization to a history they inherited through that sense of humor. Like the early anti-imperialists who found incipient globalization—or more precisely the denial of its emergence—a humorous absurdity, the children of Kalihi feel themselves under the feet, eight thousand miles above them. And from that commonality, we emit uncannily similar laughter. These ghosts of early globalization are not haunting, but hilarious.

Both Orling's race and gender transgressions, as well as the absurdities of the preglobalization explanations of the Spanish-American War, point to a humor based in parochializing that which sees itself as universal and natural. And they share a common and occluded past. From drawing this history into visibility, we have the return of the repressed: the ethos of 1970s Kalihi returns and reminds us of unearthed connections to the turn of the century. For modernity, and its agents, such as Principal Shim, they are things which could only be suspended, but never fully expelled.

PAY ANY PRICE, BEAR ANY BURDEN

In a manner unprecedented in the twentieth century, the Vietnam
War (1959–1975) shook the stability and coherence of America's
understanding of itself. An "unpopular" war contested by social
movements, the press, and the citizenry, a disabling war from
which the United States could not emerge "victorious"—there is
perhaps no single event in this century that has had such power
to disunify the American public, disrupting traditional unities of
"community," "nation," and "culture."
> —Lisa Lowe, *Immigrant Acts: On Asian American Cultural Politics*

EARLY IN LISA LOWE'S *Immigrant Acts,* she reminds us of the tumultuous conditions that occasioned the ethos of revisionism that
brought empire back to American culture. New social movements
collided with entrenched constituencies invested in the status quo
over the reasons for waging war in a former French colony in Southeast Asia. The power of that "event . . . to disunify the American public" is inextricable from the American culture's chronic resistance to
understanding its relation to empire. In the midst of that disunity,
Asian American cultural politics emerged to exacerbate the contradictions of that historical moment, to make visible resonant historical
moments that had previously been invisible or otherwise unrecognizable. The result was a recognition of the emergence of U.S. imperialism, which had actually emerged more than three quarters of a century earlier.

In this book, I have traced the ways in which the return of empire is recognizable through Asian American cultural politics. *Model-
Minority Imperialism* began with a consideration of the underappreciated convergences between postcolonialism and multiculturalism.

Each of those discourses had failed to legitimate ongoing inequalities under the respective neocolonialism and tokenization that have come to pass in the wake of those idealized visions.

With the fall of Saigon in 1975, the failure of the United States to emerge "victorious" presented new but familiar burdens to American civilization. Just as the sweeping immigration reforms of 1965 had begun to radically transform the demographics of Asian America, 1975 was yet again transforming the meaning of Asian difference. An ostensibly new population was being produced: refugees. These refugees were not only coming to the United States because of its status as a safe haven from the ills brought about by the ignorance and repression of despots the United States could readily condemn; they were also coming to the United States because of the ills brought about by the tragic consequences of American activities throughout the world. As American efforts to achieve peace with honor became increasingly difficult to realize, national consensus withered.

American activities abroad were described at the outset of the twentieth century as a burden, and in this new context, the language of burden returned. As John F. Kennedy was winding up his celebrated inaugural address in January 1961, he declared:

> Let every nation know, whether it wishes us well or ill, that we shall pay any price, bear any burden, meet any hardship, support any friend, oppose any foe, in order to assure the survival and the success of liberty. This much we pledge—and more.[1]

This was not the only appearance of burden in what is probably his most famous speech. Kennedy had earlier invoked a biblical reference to imagine an end to the cold war: "Let both sides unite to heed in all corners of the earth the command of Isaiah—to 'undo the heavy burdens . . . and to let the oppressed go free'" (314). The bearing of burdens comes to mean the liberation of the oppressed and, conversely, the liberation of the oppressed is a burden to be borne, by prophetic command. Today we see that this burden became unbearable.

In March 1968, as President Lyndon Johnson told a national audience on television that he would not run for reelection, he echoed Kennedy's words concerning the bearing of burdens:

> Of those to whom much is given, much is asked. I cannot say—and no man could say—that no more will be asked of us. Yet I believe that now, no less

than when the decade began, this generation of Americans is willing to pay any price, bear any burden, meet any hardship, support any friend, oppose any foe, to assure the survival, and the success, of liberty. Since those words were spoken by John F. Kennedy, the people of America have kept that compact with mankind's noblest cause. And we shall continue to keep it.[2]

Despite this ostensible renewed pledge to "the survival, and the success of liberty," early in Johnson's thirty-eight-minute speech, the embattled president had specifically attempted to shrug off the weighty burden that the putative liberty of the Vietnamese had become for hundreds of thousands of non-Vietnamese. Johnson told the nation:

Tonight, we and the other allied nations are contributing 600,000 fighting men to assist 700,000 South Vietnamese troops in defending their little country. Our presence there has always rested on this basic belief: The main burden of preserving their freedom must be carried out by them—by the South Vietnamese themselves.

As his speech drew to a close, Johnson understandably turned to crises nearer at hand, still invoking the language of burden that resonated with the notions of burden that opened the American century:

With American sons in the fields far away, with America's future under challenge right here at home, with our hopes and the world's hopes for peace in the balance every day, I do not believe that I should devote an hour or a day of my time to any personal partisan causes or to any duties other than the awesome duties of this office—the Presidency of your country.

Accordingly, I shall not seek, and I will not accept, the nomination of my party for another term as your President. But let men everywhere know, however, that a strong and a confident and a vigilant America stands ready tonight to seek an honorable peace; and stands ready tonight to defend an honored cause, whatever the price, whatever the burden, whatever the sacrifice that duty may require. Thank you for listening. Good night and God bless all of you.

Johnson does something incredibly rare in the history of the American presidency: he did not seek reelection when he could have. And, as the bulk of his speech essentially makes clear, "America's future under challenge right here at home" led him not to seek a second full term. Managing intense national divisions over Vietnam and over civil rights had become so "awesome" a "duty" to fulfill that it outweighed the partisan politics of running for office.

The prices, burdens, and sacrifices that Kennedy and Johnson envisioned did not end up proving the honor of an "honored cause." Rather these burdens turned out to be the troublesome and perhaps unavoidable burdens that Kipling warned the United States about on the eve of the twentieth century. In 1975, seven years after Johnson's speech, hopes for an "honorable peace" ended with the indelible image of overcrowded helicopters trying to take off from the roof of the United States embassy in Saigon. Such an image, and all that it implied, did indeed shake America's understanding of itself as a liberator, as united, as triumphant.

By the end of the 1980s, this memorable image became a show-stopping sequence in a highly successful musical: *Miss Saigon*. America and the world seemed ready to revisit these painful memories and render them as song, dance, and romance. Premiering on Broadway in 1989, the musical won critical acclaim, huge profits, and a bumper crop of awards, but it was not without controversy.

There are many reasons that *Miss Saigon* would be controversial. It presents a romanticized approach to the Vietnam War. It is an unreconstructed take—as opposed to David Henry Hwang's "deconstructivist" take—on Puccini's *Madame Butterfly* (1904). It is a questionable depiction of the era's sex workers, who presumably did not spontaneously break into choreographed show tunes.

The controversy that did erupt over *Miss Saigon* was over the casting of a Caucasian actor in the role of a Eurasian.[3] With the hard-fought rise of the Asian American movement, yellow-face would no longer be tolerated. Creative cross-casting rarely seemed to benefit struggling performers. We can see how the struggles over representation had become understandably focused on a question of representation in hiring practices, at a moment when affirmative action was suffering crippling assaults that eliminated any hope of its ability to be effective. Questions of artistic freedom were held up as an ideal imperiled by political correctness. Since the Engineer, the character in question, was half-Caucasian, couldn't he just as well be played by a Caucasian performer? An age of interchangeability—"formal equivalence" in Lowe's terms—seemed to be upon us.

Ironically, it seems fitting that interchangeability and substitution would be at the heart of the matter of why this controversy was so compelling. For in these substitutions, we see the simultaneity of interchangeability and untranslatability, what Jean-François Lyotard calls the *differend.* In those moments of comparison and breakdown, we can see the return of prior models for understanding how one mode of understanding had taken the place of another.

A chain of free associations is at once idiosyncratic and symptomatic of the uneven circuits of imperial consciousness in modern American culture. These connections allow us to draw links between locations and periods through the recognition of epistemologies of empire that are epistemologies of our current world order. Specifically, these casting substitutions and their imperfect fidelity to their presumed originals present an opportunity to apprehend new subjects amid old epistemologies, and old subjects amid new epistemologies. We can appreciate the palimpsest of memories of empire that become visible in Asian American cultural politics. The Vietnamese prostitute Kim is the Cio-Cio San figure from Puccini. She was played by the Filipina actress, Lea Salonga, in a Tony-award-winning performance. This is not surprising since the Philippines regularly played the part of "Vietnam" in many films about that conflict, most notably Francis Ford Coppola's *Apocalypse Now* (1979). And it should be noted that Coppola's Mekong River substituted in Joseph Conrad's *Heart of Darkness* for the part of the Belgian Congo, which Marlow reminds us is analogous to the Roman Thames of antiquity.

And so we have another set-piece to go with the one at the outset of this book. The image of a Kim/Lea Salonga, about to commit suicide for the sake of her Eurasian child's better life in America, can be read as an attempt to write over previous and forthcoming empires: American over French transposed to Belgian through British and even Roman. *Heart of Darkness* was first published in 1899, which was also the year Rudyard Kipling's "The White Man's Burden: The United States and the Philippine Islands" was published. Eventually the Philippines would come to be understood anachronistically as a "Vietnam" *avant la lettre.* While Vietnam occasioned the disunification of the American public, new subjects came to articulate their emergence by recognizing themselves as the once-and-future burdens of an evolving American empire.

Preface

1. Jessica Hagedorn, "Notes on the Play," in *Dogeaters* (New York: Theater Communications Group, 2003), viii. Fittingly, Hagedorn also excerpted parts of the play in Angel Velasco Shaw and Luis Francia's important anthology of cultural production and scholarship, *Vestiges of War: The Philippine-American War and the Aftermath of the Imperial Dream,* 1899–1999 (New York: New Press, 2002).

2. Hagedorn, *Dogeaters* (2003), 17.

3. Ibid., 59.

4. This title comes from the heading offered in Hagedorn's novel, *Dogeaters* (New York: Pantheon, 1990), 71. The speech actually was given in 1899 and was published posthumously in January 1903 in *The Christian Advocate*; see William McKinley, "Remarks to the Methodist Delegation," in *The Philippines Reader,* ed. Daniel B. Schirmer and Stephen Rosskamm Shalom, 22–23 (Boston: South End Press, 1987).

5. Gilles Deleuze and Félix Guattari, *Kafka: Notes toward a Minor Literature* (Minneapolis: University of Minnesota Press, 1981). See also Abdul JanMohamed and David Lloyd, "Toward a Theory of Minority Discourse: What Is to Be Done?" in *The Nature and Context of Minority Discourse* (New York: Oxford University Press, 1990), 5–13.

6. Chapter 5, "'Everybody Wants to Be Farrah,'" discusses the uses of humor in the remembering of U.S. imperialism in R. Zamora Linmark's *Rolling the R's* (New York: Kaya Production, 1996).

7. For example, see Stephen Jay Gould's *The Mismeasure of Man* (New York: Norton, 1981). The entire field of anthropology has had to undergo a well-docu-mented reinvention in the wake of poststructuralism, particularly Jacques Der-rida's writings. See his *Of Grammatology* (Baltimore: The Johns Hopkins University Press, 1998), and "Structure, Sign, and Play in the Discourse of the Human Sciences," in *Writing and Difference* (Chicago: University of Chicago Press, 1978), 278–94. The field of anthropology itself has generated some of the most incisive

critiques, such as Clifford Geertz's *Works and Lives: The Anthropologist as Author* (Stanford: Stanford University Press, 1988).

8. Hagedorn, *Dogeaters* (2003), 19.

9. Ibid., viii.

10. *Dogeaters* was reprinted by Penguin in 1990.

Introduction

1. Homi K. Bhabha, "Postcolonial Criticism," in *Redrawing the Boundaries: The Transformation of English and American Literary Studies,* ed. Stephen Greenblatt and Giles Gunn, 465 (New York: MLA, 1992). Said himself notes this influence at the beginning of *Culture and Imperialism* (New York: Vintage, 1994), which is effectively the sequel to his *Orientalism* (New York: Vintage, 1978): "A substantial amount of scholarship in anthropology, history, and area studies have developed arguments I put forward in *Orientalism,* which was limited to the Middle East. So I, too, have tried here to expand the arguments of the earlier book to describe a more general pattern of relationships between the modern metropolitan West and its overseas territories" (xi). Said's work, of course, has been cited as influential for Asian American studies and American studies, particularly his revision of notions of the Oriental as an otherness machine. See Gary Okihiro, *Margins and Mainstreams: Asians in American History and Culture* (Seattle: University of Washington Press, 1994), 10; and Malini Johar Schueller, *U.S. Orientalisms: Race, Nation, and Gender in Literature* (Ann Arbor: University of Michigan Press, 1998), 4–7.

2. Said, *Orientalism,* xii. The quotation comes from Marx's *The Eighteenth Brumaire of Louis Bonaparte.*

3. Williams cites three beliefs that allowed American culture to deny the fact of its own imperialism. The fuller quotation is as follows: "America's traditional view of itself and the world is composed of three basic ideas or images. One maintains that the United States was isolationist until world power was 'thrust upon it,' first to help Cuba, then twice to save the world for democracy, and finally to prevent the Soviet Union and other Communist regimes from overwhelming the world. Another holds that, except for a brief and rapidly dispelled aberration at the turn of the century, America has been anti-imperialist throughout its history. A third asserts that a unique combination of economic power, intellectual and practical genius, and moral rigor enables America to check enemies of peace and progress—and build a better world—without erecting an empire in the process" (William Appleman Williams, *The Tragedy of American Diplomacy* [1959; New York: Norton, 1972], 20).

4. See Garry Wills, *Inventing America: Jefferson's Declaration* (New York: Vintage, 1977). For a precursor to the anticolonial and nationalist sentiment that would manifest itself in the Declaration of 1776, see also Thomas Jefferson's "A Summary View of the Rights of British America," in *Thomas Jefferson: Writings,* ed. Merrill D. Peterson, 103–22 (New York: Literary Classics of the United States, Inc., 1984).

5. Michael Omi and Howard Winant, *Racial Formation in the United States: From the 1960s to the 1990s*, 2d ed. (New York: Routledge, 1993).

6. Michel Foucault's notion of emergence is articulated in "Nietzsche, Genealogy, History," in *Language, Counter-Memory, Practice*, ed. Donald F. Bouchard (Ithaca, N.Y.: Cornell University Press, 1977). Also of related importance is Raymond Williams's notion of "emergent" in *Marxism and Literature* (New York: Oxford University Press, 1977). For Foucault, the notion of emergence emphasizes a nondevelopmental approach to understanding the meaning of historical events: "*Entstehung* designates *emergence*, the moment of arising. It stands as the principle and the singular law of an apparition. As it is wrong to search for descent in an uninterrupted continuity, we should avoid thinking of emergence as the final terms of a historical development. . . . These developments may appear as a culmination, but they are merely the current episodes in a series of subjugations. . . . In placing the present needs at the origin, the metaphysician would convince us of an obscure purpose that seeks its realization at the moment it arises. Genealogy, however, seeks to reestablish the various systems of subjection: not the anticipatory power of meaning, but the hazardous play of dominations." And for Raymond Williams, *emergent* is contradistinguished from *dominant* and *residual* as dynamics of any given historical moment and as features legible within any given text. The emergent makes visible Williams's concept of "new formations" that inaugurate the emergence of new concepts, meanings, and subjects (Williams, *Marxism and Literature* [Oxford: Oxford University Press, 1977], 121–27).

7. Williams, *The Tragedy of American Diplomacy*, 20.

8. "Imperialism," in *Encyclopedia Britannica, Micropaedia V* (Chicago: Encyclopedia Britannica, 1974), 315.

9. Thomas McCormick's *The China Market: America's Quest for Informal Empire* (Chicago: Quadrangle Books, 1967) is a classic history of this notion. The work of William Appleman Williams is also concerned with the persistence in American culture of what he calls "anti-imperial colonialism." See his *The Tragedy of American Diplomacy* and *Empire as a Way of Life* (New York: Oxford University Press, 1980).

10. For example, see Julian Go, "Chains of Empire," in *The American Colonial State in the Philippines: Global Perspectives*, ed. Julian Go and Anne Foster, 323–62 (Durham: Duke University Press, 2003).

11. Amy Kaplan, *The Anarchy of Empire in the Making of U.S. Culture* (Cambridge: Harvard University Press, 2003), 17–18.

12. Said, *Culture and Imperialism*, 114.

13. Histories by Nayan Shah and Warwick Anderson have examined the dialectical relationship between medical science and the various incarnations of the civilizing mission. Shah's analysis of public health in San Francisco's Chinatown and Anderson's discussions of the medical policies of the American colonial administration in the Philippines chart the shift from unassimilable otherness to the other as recipient of benevolent care. See Shah's *Contagious Divides: Epidemics and Race in San Francisco's Chinatown* (Berkeley and Los Angeles: University of

California Press, 2001); and Anderson's "'Where Every Prospect Pleases and Only Man Is Vile': Laboratory Medicine as Colonial Discourse," in *Discrepant Histories: Translocal Essays on Filipino Cultures*, ed. Vince Rafael, 83–112 (Philadelphia: Temple University Press, 1985).

14. Lisa Lowe, in her influential study of Asian American cultural politics, *Immigrant Acts: On Asian American Cultural Politics* (Durham: Duke University Press, 1996), calls this process "Asian American critique." Lowe writes that the question of empire is central to "Asian American critique": "The material legacy of the repressed history of U.S. imperialism in Asia is borne out in the 'return' of Asian immigrants to the imperial center" (16).

15. Ronald Takaki opens his influential *Strangers from a Different Shore: A History of Asian Americans* (New York: Penguin, 1989) by casting it as an overt displacement of Oscar Handlin's midcentury classic, *The Uprooted: The Epic Story of the Great Migrations That Made the American People* (Boston: Little Brown and Co., 1951).

16. Edouard Glissant, *Caribbean Discourse: Selected Essays* (Charlottesville: University of Virginia Press, 1989), 5.

17. Preface to *Aiiieeeee!: An Anthology of Asian American Writers*, ed. Jeffrey Paul Chan, Frank Chin, Lawson Fusao Inada, and Shawn Hsu Wong, xvi (Washington, D.C.: Howard University Press, 1974).

18. Two notable instances of this slogan appearing in black British culture can be found in the writings of Michelle Cliff and Kobena Mercer. Michelle Cliff, in *No Telephone to Heaven* (New York: Dutton, 1987), writes: "A march of the National Front was passing by the windows of the institute, as a seminar on the Hermetic Tradition progressed. Chants. Shouts. Noise slamming against the glass of the well-appointed, high-ceilinged room. KAFFIRS! NIGGERS! WOGS! PAKIS! GET OUT! A banner—white bedsheet with black paint—went past. KEEP BRITAIN WHITE! The voices rose and invaded the room further, forcing the professor to raise his voice, in anachronistic disdain cursing the 'blasted miners.' As if this phrase would embrace any public display which inconvenienced him. Some of the students smiled—miners, fascists, what did it matter?—and the professor continued, attempting in his high-pitched ramble to convey the connection of the Hermetic Tradition to Giordano Bruno and question whether it had been overstated, but the outside jargon smashed clear through his words, louder, louder: NIGGERS, CLEAR OUT! And Clare, seated opposite the windows, looking out, imagined glass breaking, flying; but nothing happened. As if in response, as if there could be a dialogue, a poster appeared the next day on a bulletin board outside the cafeteria in Senate House. 'WE ARE HERE BECAUSE YOU WERE THERE'" (137). See also Kobena Mercer, "The Cultural Politics of Diaspora," in *Welcome to the Jungle: New Positions in Black Cultural Studies* (New York: Routledge, 1994): "The local specificity of [the Brixton riot/rebellion of 1981] said something, too, about the general position of black subjects in Britain: that if we were invisible, marginal and silenced by subjection to a racism by which we failed to enjoy equal protection under the law as common citizens, this was because we were all too visible, all too vocal and

all too central, in Britain's postimperial body politic, as a reminder and remainder of its historical past, and of the paradoxical disadvantage of an early start as one of the key factors of its present-day, post-Empire, decline: *we are here because you were there*" (7).

19. Henry Luce, "The American Century," *Life*, February 17, 1941. See also Neil Smith, *American Empire: Roosevelt's Geographer and the Prelude to Globalization* (Berkeley and Los Angeles: University of California Press, 2003), 2.

20. Most notably, the addition of "Pacific" between "Asian" and "American" has been the main change that has stuck. Historian/activist Haunani Kay Trask has been a vocal critic of the conflation of Asian American and Pacific Islander, particularly in the context of anticolonial struggles of indigenous Hawaiians. See her *From a Native Daughter: Colonialism and Sovereignty in Hawaii* (Honolulu: University of Hawaii Press, 1999).

21. As Sau-ling Wong perceptively notes, literary realism has been the presumed approach to ethnic literatures, at the expense of grasping the formal complexities of texts. Texts are seen as transparently reflective and representative of histories and subjects, when questions of form as well as content are crucial. Through a critique of the a priori presumptions of identity formations, Judith Butler's *Gender Trouble: Feminism and the Subversion of Identity* (New York: Routledge, 1990) rained on the various pride parades of identity politics. See also the Darstellen/Vertreten section of Gayatri Chakravorty Spivak's "Can the Subaltern Speak?" in *Marxism and the Interpretation of Culture,* ed. Cary Nelson and Lawrence Grossberg, 271–313 (Champaign-Urbana: University of Illinois Press, 1988).

22. See Elaine Kim, "Defining Asian American Realities through Literature," in JanMohamed and Lloyd, *The Nature and Context of Minority Discourse*, 146–70. One might even break the phrase down to its constitutive parts to find a wealth of philological intrigues behind *Asian* and *American*. We would see the productively paradoxical and chiasmic structure of the term, hyphenated or not. The interplay of these two concepts is a familiar trope in multiculturalist renderings of "Asian American" that finds all sorts of catchy and colorful ways to describe a fairly superficial hybridity, usually involving references to food or mass culture. This idea is elaborated further here in chapter 1, "Unburdening Empire: The Cultural Politics of Asian American Difference."

23. Raymond Williams, *Keywords: A Vocabulary of Culture and Society* (New York: Oxford, 1983), 87.

24. Louis Althusser, "Ideology and Ideological State Apparatuses (Notes toward an Investigation)," in *Lenin and Philosophy and Other Essays,* trans. Ben Brewster, 127–86 (New York: Monthly Review Press, 1972).

25. Michel Foucault, "Governmentality," in *The Foucault Effect: Studies in Governmentality,* ed. Graham Burchell, Colin Gordon, and Peter Miller, 87–104 (Chicago: University of Chicago Press, 1991).

26. For example, see Stuart Hall, "Cultural Studies and Its Theoretical Legacies" (in *Cultural Studies,* ed. Lawrence Grossberg, Cary Nelson, and Paul Treichler,

277–97 [New York: Routledge, 1992]), in which Hall charts the rise of the study of culture through the work of Althusser and Raymond Williams. Using Williams's "Marx without Guarantees," Hall broaches a critique of Marxian materialism and using Williams's "Gramsci's Relevance for the Study of Race and Ethnicity" (in *Stuart Hall: Critical Dialogues in Cultural Studies* [London: Routledge, 1996]), Hall adapts the tools of Marxist analysis to understandings of racial formations.

27. Two important studies from the 1980s also deploy the notion of "cultural politics": Gayatri Chakravorty Spivak's *In Other Worlds: Essays in Cultural Politics* (Chicago: University of Chicago Press, 1987); and Paul Gilroy's *"There Ain't No Black in the Union Jack": The Cultural Politics of Race and Nation* (New York: Routledge, 1987). For Lowe, what all three of these studies have in common is the convergence of critiques of gendered racialization *and* political economy under capitalist development.

28. See Edna Bonacich and Lucie Cheng's *Labor Immigration under Capitalism: Asian Workers in the United States before World War II* (Berkeley and Los Angeles: University of California Press, 1984); and Alexander Saxton's *The Indispensable Enemy: Labor and the Anti-Chinese Movement in California* (Berkeley and Los Angeles: University of California Press, 1971).

29. See *The Negro Problem: A Series of Articles by Representative American Negroes of To-day,* ed. Booker T. Washington and others (1903; Miami: Mnemosyne Publishing, Inc., 1969).

30. With the need for comparative race studies, scholarship has emerged to draw links between different forms of difference. More often, that has understandably meant the formulation of a black-to-Asian trajectory, asserting that blackness sets the stage for what it means to be Asian American. Other scholarship has strategically inverted that trajectory to show that African American movements were inspired by Asian examples, particularly decolonization as a model for civil rights struggles.

31. One could well argue that the postcolonial field in American studies was inaugurated by Amy Kaplan and Donald Pease's *Cultures of United States Imperialism* (Durham: Duke University Press, 1993). While it was preceded by such important work as Walter LaFeber's *The New Empire: An Interpretation of American Expansion, 1860–1898* (Ithaca: American Historical Association/Cornell University Press, 1963); and Ernest May's *Imperial Democracy: The Emergence of America as a Great Power* (Chicago: Imprint, 1961) and *American Imperialism: A Speculative Essay* (New York: Atheneum, 1968), as well as the work of William Appleman Williams, Kaplan and Pease's volume is more squarely a document of the current ethos of revisionism, which produced the emergent and institutionalized fields that dictate scholarship today.

32. See Matthew Frye Jacobson, *Barbarian Virtues: The United States Encounters Foreign Peoples at Home and Abroad, 1876–1917* (New York: Hill and Wang, 2000).

33. Gauri Viswanathan critiques the presumption of the nation-to-colonizer trajectory, even in committed and progressive criticism; see his "Raymond Williams and British Colonialism: The Limits of Metropolitan Cultural Theory," in

Views from the Border Country: Raymond Williams and Cultural Politics, ed. Dennis Dworkin and Leslie Roman, 217–30 (New York: Routledge, 1993); and *Masks of Conquest: Literary Study and British Rule in India* (New York: Columbia University Press, 1989).

34. Walter Benjamin, "Theses on the Philosophy of History," in *Illuminations* (New York: Schocken Books, 1969), 255.

35. Rudyard Kipling, "The White Man's Burden (The United States and The Philippine Islands)" (1899), in *The Portable Kipling,* ed. Irving Howe, 602–3 (New York: Penguin Press, 1982).

36. Eric Hobsbawm, *The Age of Empire, 1875–1914* (New York: Vintage, 1989).

37. McKinley, "Remarks to the Methodist Delegation," 22.

38. For example, see H. T. Johnson's "The Black Man's Burden" in *The Christian Recorder*, April 1899. Johnson writes, "Pile on the Black Man's burden,/ His wail with laughter drown,/ You've sealed the Red Man's problem/ And now take up the Brown." Such a rendering is actually rather similar to the sentiment expressed by Kipling, that is, that empire is an unpleasantly burdensome proposition.

39. Matthew Frye Jacobson carries on the tradition of historians who right-fully assert with surprise that American colonialism at the turn of the twentieth century remains relatively unknown in proportion to both its significance and its abundant documentary evidence. In the conclusion to *Barbarian Virtues,* his fine history of American colonialism, Jacobson reminds us that the Philippines was a happily accepted arena for the "coming of age" of the United States, not a reluc-tantly held possession.

40. Thomas McCormick argues that the China market idea from the late nineteenth century was itself a cover for a "free trade imperialism" that was vastly preferable to the "political imperialism" of the day. The Philippines was seen as an "American Hong Kong" that "updated the mid-century British system of 'free-trade imperialism' decked out in an Uncle Sam suit" (McCormick, *China Market,* 63).

41. Said, *Orientalism,* 41.

42. Frederick Jackson Turner, *The Significance of the Frontier in American History* (1893; New York: Frederick Ungar Publishing, 1963).

43. Lisa Lowe, "Discourse and Heterogeneity," in *Critical Terrains: French and British Orientalisms* (Ithaca: Cornell University Press, 1991).

44. Ranajit Guha, "The Prose of Counter-Insurgency," in *Culture/Power/His-tory: A Reader in Contemporary Social Theory,* ed. Nicholas Dirks, Geoff Eley, and Sherry B. Ortner, 360–61 (Princeton: Princeton University Press, 1994).

1. Unburdening Empire

1. See James Kyung-jin Lee, *Urban Triage: Race and the Fictions of Multiculturalism* (Minneapolis: University of Minnesota Press, 2004), 86–87, 96, 101–2, 112.

2. See Mae Ngai, *Impossible Subjects: Illegal Aliens and the Making of Modern America* (Princeton: Princeton University Press, 2004), 40, 46–47, 49.

3. *Who's Going to Pay for These Donuts Anyway?* Produced and directed by Janice Tanaka, 58 min., 1985, videocassette.

4. See Victor Bascara, "Cultural Politics of Redress: Reassessing the Meaning of the Civil Liberties Act of 1988 after 9/11," *Asian Law Journal* 10, no. 2 (May 2003): 185–214.

5. David Palumbo-Liu offers a compelling analysis of the "model-minority myth" and the discourse of healing in his appendix to *Asian/American: Historical Crossings of a Racial Frontier* (Stanford: Stanford University Press, 1999), 395–416. See also Viet Nguyen's "Model Minorities and Bad Subjects," in *Race and Resistance: Literature and Politics in Asian America* (New York: Oxford University Press, 2002), 143–71. In the popular press, "model minority" became the face of Asian America. On the explicit occasion of the centenntial of the 1882 Chinese Exclusion Act, *Newsweek* published "Asian Americans: A Model Minority" (December 6, 1982). Citing "thrift, strong family ties, sacrifice for children" and "strong pride in the cultures they left behind" (39), the article sought to explain "remarkable, ever-mounting acheivements" (51). The article usually credited with coining "model minority" is "Success Story: Japanese American Style," in *New York Magazine,* January 9, 1966. Also, "Success Story of One Minority Group in the United States," *U.S. News and World Report,* December 26, 1966, explicitly compares Asian Americans to other minorities.

6. In the 2000 U.S. census, Asian Americans as such constituted approximately 3.6 percent of the total population (http://factfinder.census.gov/servlet/SAFFFacts?_sse=on).

7. U.S. Commission on Civil Rights, *Civil Rights Issues Facing Asian Americans in the 1990s* (Washington, D.C.: U.S. Government Printing Office, 1992).

8. The other six "contributory factors" are, in order: "Perceiving Asian Americans as Foreigners," "Stereotyping Asian Americans as Unaggressive and Lacking in Communication Skills," "Limited English Proficiency," "Cultural Differences," "Religious Diversity," and "Preimmigration Trauma." See ibid., 20–21.

9. A prominent example of this struggle is the work by activists at the University of California at Berkeley to uncover the quota systems that resulted in declining Asian American admissions in the 1980s.

10. See Cheryl Harris, "Whiteness as Property," 106 *Harvard Law Review* 1709 (1993).

11. See Helen Zia, *Asian American Dreams: The Emergence of an American People* (New York: Farrar, Straus, Giroux, 2000), 46–47.

12. Saskia Sassen has argued persuasively that the nation-state was "only a unitary category in political discourse and policy; the modern nation-state has always had economic actors and practices that were transnational" (*Globalization and Its Discontents: Essays on the New Mobility of People and Money* [New York: New Press, 1998], xix). See also her book *The Global City: New York, London, Tokyo* (Princeton: Princeton University Press, 2001); and Fredric Jameson and Masao Miyoshi's *The Cultures of Globalization* (Durham, N.C.: Duke University Press, 1998).

13. See Richard Rodriguez, *Hunger of Memory: The Education of Richard Rodriguez* (New York: Bantam, 1988); and Stephen Carter, *Confessions of an Affirmative Action Baby* (New York: Basic Books, 1991).

14. Stewart David Ikeda offers a comparative analysis of George Bush's and Bill Clinton's apology letters at http://imdcontentnew.searchease.com/Villages/Asian/history_heritage/ikeda_internment_apology.asp.

15. Lowe, *Immigrant Acts,* 27–28.

16. See Neil Gotanda, "A Critique of 'Our Constitution Is Color-Blind,'" 44 *Stanford Law Review* 1 (1991).

17. In the wake of the bombing of Pearl Harbor, the December 22, 1941, issue of *Time* magazine published a visual guide for how to tell the difference between Chinese and Japanese features. For an analysis of race, visibility, and internment, see David Eng, "Primal Scenes: Queer Childhood in 'The Shoyu Kid,'" in *Racial Castration: Managing Masculinity in Asian America* (Durham: Duke University Press, 2001), 104–36. The wearing of "I am Korean" or "I am Chinese" buttons was also a side effect, as dramatized in Hisaye Yamamoto's short story, "Wilshire Bus" (in *Seventeen Syllables and Other Stories* [Brooklyn, N.Y.: Kitchen Table, 1988], 34–38). And being "Japanese" was the impetus for the murder of Chinese American Vincent Chin at the hands and bats of two unemployed Detroit autoworkers in 1982. See U.S. Commission on Civil Rights, *Civil Rights Issues Facing Asian Americans in the 1990s,* 25–26. This incident galvanized the cross-ethnic solidarity of the Asian American movement for two main reasons: (1) the mistaken identity; and (2) the virtual acquittal of the murderers. For the strategic use of "panethnicity," see Yen Le Espiritu, *Asian American Panethnicity: Bridging Institutions and Identities* (Philadelphia: Temple University Press, 1992).

18. See Benjamin, "Theses on the Philosophy of History," in *Illuminations,* 255.

19. The text of HR 442 reads as follows: "The Congress recognizes that, as described in the Commission on Wartime Relocation and Internment of Civilians, a grave injustice was done to both citizens and permanent residents of Japanese ancestry by the evacuation, relocation, and internment of civilians during World War II. As the Commission documents, these actions were carried out without adequate security reasons and without any acts of espionage or sabotage documented by the Commission, and were motivated largely by racial prejudice, wartime hysteria, and a failure of political leadership. The excluded individuals of Japanese ancestry suffered enormous damages, both material and intangible, and there were incalculable losses in education and job training, all of which resulted in significant human suffering for which appropriate compensation has not been made. For these fundamental violations of the basic civil liberties and constitutional rights of these individuals of Japanese ancestry, the Congress apologizes on behalf of the Nation" (133 *Congressional Record* H7555 [1987]).

In an oddly related phenomenon, the rise of neoconservatism also warned the nation, and its others, not to rely on liberal guilt. But of course the point of such an admonition was to advocate a return to values and practices that had long demonstrated their utility as instruments of exploitation. See Shelby Steele, *The*

Content of Our Character: A New Vision of Race in America (New York: St. Martin's Press, 1990).

20. Redress was just the cresting of a wave of popular demand for something to be done about internment. In the early days of the movement, only an apology was sought. The payment of reparations made this a political success of another order. For a description of the laborious and impassioned movement that led to HR 442, see *Achieving the Impossible Dream: How Japanese Americans Obtained Redress,* ed. Mitchell T. Maki, Harry H. L. Kitano, and S. Megan Berthold (Urbana: University of Illinois Press, 1999). See also Robert Shimabukuro's *Born in Seattle: The Campaign for Japanese American Redress* (Seattle: University of Washington Press, 2000). And as a prehistory to the movement, Carolyn Chung Simpson examines the conditions that led to the disappearance of Japanese Americans in the immediate period following World War II in *Absent Presence: Japanese Americans in Postwar American Culture, 1945–1960* (Durham: Duke University Press, 2002).

21. Chris Newfield and Avery Gordon, in the introduction to their collection *Mapping Multiculturalism* (Minneapolis: University of Minnesota Press, 1996), insightfully identify the key role of multiculturalism in the ascendance of globalization. See especially Jon Cruz's chapter, "Reflections on the Reification of Race at Century's End," and the "Multi-Capitalism" section (19–39).

22. Cornel West, "The New Cultural Politics of Difference," in *Out There: Marginalization in Contemporary American Culture,* ed. Russell Ferguson, Marth Gever, Trinh T. Minh-ha, and Cornel West, 19–36 (Cambridge, Mass.: MIT Press, 1990).

23. See Omi and Winant, *Racial Formation in the United States.*

24. Lee, *Urban Triage,* 8.

25. H. Brett Melendy, *The Oriental Americans* (New York: Hippocrene Books, 1972).

26. In "International Context of Asian Immigration," Sucheng Chan's opening chapter to *Asian Americans: An Interpretive History* (Boston: Twayne, 1991), she usefully foregrounds the geopolitical conditions that are frequently forgotten, but have always attended what it means to be Asian American.

27. See David Eng, "'I've Been Re-Working on the Railroad': Photography and National History in *China Men* and *Donald Duck*," in *Racial Castration,* 35–103.

28. As historian William Appleman Willliams noted: "One of the central themes of American historiography is that there is no American Empire. Most historians will admit, if pressed, that the United States once had an empire. They then promptly insist that it was given away. But they also speak persistently of America as a World Power" (quoted by Amy Kaplan in "Left Alone with America: The Absence of Empire in the Study of American Culture" in Kaplan and Pease, *Cultures of United States Imperialism*).

29. For example, see Lisa Lowe's critique of the rise of American multiculturalism in her introduction to *Critical Terrains: French and British Orientalisms.* Lowe coins the notion of "the same enough" to describe the tolerance of some differences and the intolerance of others.

30. See Sucheta Mazumdar, "Asian Studies and Asian American Studies: Rethinking Roots," in *Asian Americans: Comparative and Global Perspectives,* ed. Shirley Hune, 29–44 (Pullman, Wash.: Washington State University Press, 1991).

31. Even though her study has different historical and methodological priorities, King-kok Cheung's skillful readings of Maxine Hong Kingston, Joy Kogawa, and Hisaye Yamamoto in *Articulate Silences: Hisaye Yamamoto, Maxinge Hong Kingston, and Joy Kogawa* (Ithaca: Cornell University Press, 1992) present paradigms for recuperation to which my project is indebted, particularly for its attention to gaps in representation. See also Nguyen, *Race and Resistance.*

32. Lisa Lowe, *Immigrant Acts,* 4.

33. Etienne Balibar, "The Citizen Subject," in *Who Comes after the Subject?* ed. Eduardo Cadava, Peter Connor, and Jean-Luc Nancy, 33–57 (New York: Routledge, 1993). Balibar comes up with the wonderful formulation that "the citizen is the subject who rises up." The rising up of the citizen-consumer, I suggest, finds expression in economic terms.

34. See Spivak, "Can the Subaltern Speak?" 288.

35. The events in Seattle in 1999 were a watershed, but critiques of globalization had been voiced for some time, such as Stephanie Black's film documentary *Life and Debt.* Even books appearing as early as Walter Rodney's *How Europe Underdeveloped Africa* (Washington, D.C.: Howard University Press, 1974) and Frantz Fanon's *The Wretched of the Earth* (New York: Ballantine, 1963) are critiques of neocolonial relations that more or less set the stage for globalization under postcolonialism.

36. The amount of research establishing the connection between race and class is too large to catalog here. Among the more prominent studies is Ronald Takaki's *Iron Cages: Race and Culture in Nineteenth-Century America* (New York: Oxford, 1990).

37. See Lowe, *Immigrant Acts.*

38. Jeff Lesser, "Always 'Outsiders': Asians, Naturalization, and the Supreme Court," *Amerasia Journal* 12, no. 1 (1985–86): 83–100. Lesser recounts the ways in which naturalization has historically been an "inclusive" rather than an "exclusive" category, that is, a category that has needed subjects to be explicitly named to be included, instead of naming the excluded.

39. For a history of this transaction in American civilization, see Leon Wolf, *Little Brown Brother: How the United States Purchased and Pacified the Philippine Islands at the Century's Turn* (New York: Doubleday, 1961). Andrew Carnegie also made a bold suggestion when he famously offered to buy the islands from the United States and then give them to themselves. This move angered the exploited American working class.

40. Glenn Omatsu traces the changing historical circumstances that produced varying coalitions through the history of the Asian American movement. See his "The 'Four Prisons' and Movements of Liberation: Asian American Activism from the 1960–1990s," in *The State of Asian America: Activism and Resistance in the 1990s,* ed. Karin Aguilar-San Juan, 19–70 (Boston: South End Press, 1994).

See also Michael Omi and Howard Winant's seminal study, *Racial Formation in the United States,* for an account of the shifting politics of race in general since the rise of the civil rights era.

41. Giovanni Arrighi's long-wave economic history, *The Long Twentieth Century: Money, Power, and the Origins of Our Times* (London and New York: Verso, 1994) traces the succession of world powers that achieved that status through their ability to practice capitalism most effectively. His theories, as well as those of other world systems theorists, are obviously influential throughout this book. One volume that begins to look at the history of American capitalism's ascendance from radically alternative points of view is David Lloyd and Lisa Lowe's *The Politics of Capital in the Shadow of Culture* (Durham: Duke University Press, 1997). In their introduction, Lloyd and Lowe emphasize that while capitalism did indeed bring about totalizing transformations, inherent to capitalism are its own contradictions, and culture exacerbates those contradictions.

42. The westward expansion across the North American continent has been explained using terms other than imperialism. For example, Teddy Roosevelt: "Of course no one would wish to see these, or any other settled communities added to our domain by force; we want no unwilling citizens to enter our union. . . . European nations war for the possession of thickly settled districts which, if conquered, will for centuries remain alien and hostile to the conquerors; we wiser in our generation, have seized the waste solitudes that lay near us." Quoted in Ernest May, *American Imperialism: A Speculative Essay* (Chicago: Imprint Publications, 1967), 165–66.

43. John Chown, *A History of Money from A.D. 700* (New York: Routledge, 1994), 263. Money, of course, existed before 700 A.D., but 700 A.D. is Chown's starting date because of Charlemagne's reintroduction of silver money in the West.

44. For the official explanation, see Board of Governors, *The Federal Reserve System: Systems and Functions* (Washington D.C.: The Federal Reserve, 1963), especially 1–15.

45. Marcello De Cecco, *The International Gold Standard: Money and Empire* (New York: St. Martin's Press, 1984), 40.

46. Milton Friedman convincingly argues that while the formal adoption of the gold standard was a functional monetary system since 1873, he claims that market forces would have run silver out of the market even if there had been no "Crime of 1873." See his "The Crime of 1873," *Journal of Political Economy* 98, no. 6 (1990): 1159–94.

47. The provocatively familial phrase "dollar of the fathers" comes from pro-gold economist and pamphleteer, David Ames Wells, who wrote a pamphlet called *The Silver Question: The Dollar of the Fathers Versus the Dollars of the Sons* (New York: G. P. Putnam's Sons, 1877).

48. Michel Foucault, "Marx, Nietzsche, Freud," reprinted in *Critical Texts: A Review of Theory and Criticism* 3, no. 2 (1986): 65–66.

49. Karl Marx, *Contribution to the Critique of Political Economy* (New York: International Review Press, 1962).

50. Perhaps the main theorist of the centrality of money in Western culture is Marc Shell; see his *Money, Language, and Thought: Literary and Philosophical Economies from the Medieval to the Modern Era* (Berkeley and Los Angeles: University of California Press, 1982).

51. Jean-Joseph Goux, *The Coiners of Language* (Norman: University of Oklahoma Press, 1984), 3.

52. Corporeal legibility and biological reality (read: race) are also a central and related preoccupation. See Michael O'Malley, "Specie and Species," *American Historical Review* (April 1994): 369–95.

53. The proliferation of new media about internment, some of it funded directly as a result of the Civil Liberties Act of 1988 through the Civil Liberties Public Education Fund (CLPEF), has led to a growing body of insightful criticism. See, for example, Glen Masato Mimura's "Antidote for Collective Amnesia?: Rea Tajiri's *History and Memory*," in *Countervisions: Asian American Film Criticism* (Philadelphia: Temple University Press, 2000), 150–62.

54. In addition to *Who's Going to Pay for These Donuts Anyway?* a growing number of narratives address the question of what to do with reparations checks. For example, Philip Kan Gotanda's 1991 play, *Fish Head Soup,* is about the return of a prodigal son who wants his parents' reparations checks to finance his independent film. Even an episode of the WB network's family drama *Seventh Heaven* involved a storyline in which an elderly nisei woman wants to donate her check to Reverend Eric Camden's church because she cannot in good conscience accept it for herself. (Reverend Camden, of course, cannot in good conscience accept it either.) Prior to the granting of reparations, there was a tradition of Asian American protest art demanding redress. For example, Jon Jang's political jazz suite, *Reparations Now!* (1987), sets to music the congressional testimony of redress activist "Socks" Kitashima.

55. Sau-ling C. Wong, *Reading Asian American Literature: From Necessity to Extravagance* (Princeton: Princeton University Press, 1993).

56. While we now understand U.S. imperialism to be a generally informal affair, late nineteenth-century historical developments necessitated a rather formal conception and practice of American empire in Asia and the Pacific. See McCormick, *China Market.*

57. Although he was writing about his native Italy, Antonio Gramsci's elaborations of hegemony are of unparalleled influence. See his *Selections from the Prison Notebooks* (New York: International Publishers, 1971), especially "Notes on Italian History," 52–120. His ideas have had quite an influence on the study of race and ethnicity. See Takaki, *Iron Cages,* and Stuart Hall, "Gramsci's Relevance for the Study of Race and Ethnicity," *Journal of Communication Inquiry* 10 (Summer 1986): 5–27.

58. Stephen Greenblatt, "Resonance and Wonder," in *Exhibiting Cultures: The Poetics and Politics of Museum Display,* ed. Ivan Karp and Steven D. Lavine, 42–56 (Washington D.C.: Smithsonian Institution Press, 1991).

59. See Walter Benjamin, "Theses on the Philosophy of History," in *Illumina-tions,* 253–64.

60. Elaine H. Kim, *Asian American Literature: An Introduction to the Writings and Their Social Context* (Philadelphia: Temple University Press, 1980).

61. Raymond Williams, "Dominant, Residual, and Emergent," in *Marxism and Literature,* 121–27.

62. In addition to appearing in the scholarship of King-kok Cheung, the theme of gaining voice pervades Asian American literature. For example, Joseph Bruchac's pioneering edition of Asian American poetry, *Breaking Silence: An An-thology of Contemporary Asian American Poets* (Greenfield Center, N.Y.: Greenfield Review Press, 1983), is named after Janice Mirikitani's poem of the same name. Young adult Asian American literature also dramatizes this theme, such as Marie G. Lee's *Finding My Voice* (New York: Harper/Trophy, 2001).

63. Gilles Deleuze and Félix Guattari, "What Is a Minor Literature?" in *Kafka: Toward a Minor Literature,* trans. Richard Brinkley, 16–27 (Minneapolis: Univer-sity of Minnesota Press, 1986). See also JanMohamed and Lloyd, *Nature and Con-text of Minority Discourse.*

64. See Lisa Lowe, "Canonization, Institutionalization, Identity: Asian Ameri-can Studies," in *Immigrant Acts,* 37–59.

2. An Ever-Emergent Empire

The Rumsfeld quotation in the second epigraph was quoted by Paul D. Hutchcroft in an October 24, 2003, article in the *Wisconsin State Journal* head-lined "President's remarks show need for history lesson on Philippines." Thanks to Michael Cullinane for bringing this article to my attention.

1. See Amy Kaplan, *The Anarchy of Empire,* 6.

2. Williams, *The Tragedy of American Diplomacy,* 20.

3. For an analysis of the experience of the recycled innocence in American culture, see Slavoj Zizek, "Welcome to the Desert of the Real," in *Welcome to the Desert of the Real: Five Essays on September 11 and Related Dates* (London: Verso, 2002).

4. See Williams, *Empire as a Way of Life*; Kaplan, "Left Alone with America"; and Campomanes, "Afterword: The New Empire's Forgetful and Forgotten Citi-zens: Unrepresentability and Unassimilability in Filipino American Postcoloni-alities," in *Critical Mass* 2, no. 2 (1995): 145–200.

5. See Henry Parker Willis, *Our Philippine Problem* (New York: Henry Holt and Co., 1905); and "An American Soldier in Love and War," directed by G. W. Blitzer (July 9, 1903), 16 mm., 3 min.

6. See the PBS documentary, *American Experience: TR, The Story of Theodore Roosevelt,* directed by David Grubin, 1999.

7. Jacobson, *Barbarian Virtues,* 264–65.

8. Ibid., 261.

9. John Carlos Rowe, *Literary Culture and U.S. Imperialism: From the Revolution*

to World War II (New York: Oxford University Press, 2000), 6; Kaplan, *The Anar-chy of Empire*, 11.

10. Nevertheless, such books as Stuart Creighton Miller's *Benevolent Assimilation: The American Conquest of the Philippines, 1899–1902* (New Haven: Yale University Press, 1982); Leon Wolff's *Little Brown Brother;* Ernest May's *Imperial Democracy;* Glenn May's *Social Engineering in the Philippines: The Aims, Execution, and Impact of American Colonial Policy, 1900–1913* (Westport, Conn.: Greenwood Press, 1980); and even Stanley Karnow's *In Our Image: America's Empire in the Philippines* (New York: Random House, 1989) are certainly informative. As older studies, they are more implicated in the troublesome divide between area studies and ethnic studies, as they are mainly concerned with the management of geographical zones for the United States and advocacy for new social movements in the United States, respectively; see Mazumdar, "Asian Studies and Asian American Studies." Jacobson's *Barbarian Virtues* effectively employs an approach for understanding American expansionism that allows the narrative to unfold more in terms of markets than as a unified chronology. Such a telling of history, which is both dominant and from below while still reasonably lucid, begins to take seriously the transformations called for by theorists such as Hayden White, Michel de Certeau, Michel Foucault, and of course, Walter Benjamin.

11. Williams, *Tragedy of American Diplomacy,* 18–57.

12. Willis, *Our Philippine Problem,* 5.

13. See May, *American Imperialism.*

14. President William McKinley, *Papers Relating to the Foreign Relations of the United States* (Washington: G.P.O., 1898), 906–7.

15. Ibid., 907.

16. For a history of this concept in economic and diplomatic history, see Robert Snyder, *The Most Favored Nation Clause: An Analysis with Particular Reference to Recent Treaty Practice and Tariffs* (New York: King's Crown Press of Columbia University, 1948).

17. McCormick, *The China Market,* 184.

18. William Pomeroy, *American Neo-Colonialism: Its Emergence in the Philippines and in Asia* (New York: International Publishers, 1970), 11.

19. Willis, *Our Philippine Problem,* 444.

20. William McKinley, "Commercial Reciprocity," in *Commercial Reciprocity and Expansion: As Advocated by William McKinley in His Last Address to His Countrymen and to the World, Delivered at the Pan-American Exposition, Buffalo, N.Y., September 5, 1901* (Chicago: National Business League, 1901), 9.

21. Quoted in Emily S. Rosenberg, *Spreading the American Dream: American Economic and Cultural Expansion, 1890–1945* (New York: Hill and Wang, 1982), 45.

22. Ibid, 45–48.

23. McKinley, "Remarks to the Methodist Delegation," 22.

24. Henry M. Littlefield, "*The Wizard of Oz*: Parable on Populism," *American Quarterly* 16, no. 1 (1964): 47–58.

25. L. Frank Baum, *The Wonderful Wizard of Oz* (Chicago: G. M. Hill Co., 1900).

26. Most recently, see *The Historian's "Wizard of Oz": Reading L. Frank Baum's Classic as a Political and Monetary Allegory*, ed. Ranjit S. Dighe (Westport, Conn.: Praeger, 2002). Thanks to David A. Zimmerman for bringing this work to my attention.

27. For a discussion of this film's influence, see Salman Rushdie, *The Wizard of Oz* (London: BFI, 1992).

28. As mentioned above, the first article to put this claim forward was Littlefield's "The Wizard of Oz: Parable on Populism" in 1964. More recent theorizations along these lines include Hugh Rockoff, "'The Wizard of Oz' as Monetary Allegory" (*Journal of Political Economy* 98, no. 4 [1990]: 739–60); and Gretchen Ritter, "Silver Slippers and a Golden Cap: L. Frank Baum's *The Wonderful Wizard of Oz* and Historical Memory in American Politics" (*Journal of American Studies* 31, no. 2 [1997]: 171–202). The Oz of Baum's book has been read as everything from Australia to South Dakota. See Ritter, "Silver Slippers," 172n1.

29. The main historical studies dealing with these issues are Irwin Unger, *The Greenback Era: A Social and Political History of American Finance, 1865–1879* (Princeton: Princeton University Press, 1964); and Robert P. Sharkey, *Money, Class, and Party: An Economic Study of Civil War and Reconstruction* (Baltimore: The Johns Hopkins University Press, 1967). Bruce Palmer's *"Man Over Money": The Southern Populist Critique of American Capitalism* (Chapel Hill: University of North Carolina Press, 1980) is also a thorough examination of the place of financial issues in national politics.

30. See Gretchen Ritter, *Goldbugs and Greenbacks: The Antimonopoly Tradition and the Politics of Finance in America* (Cambridge: Cambridge University Press, 1997), 288–90. Milton Friedman argues that monetary standards had become a moot question by the 1890s because of mining trends, but that they had been important in the 1870s and 1880s; see Friedman, "Crime of 1873."

31. Contributing to the occlusion of Baum's text's status as a monetary allegory is the switching of Dorothy's silver slippers to ruby in MGM's 1939 adaptation, unless the film was advocating a ruby and gold standard. Salman Rushdie neglects to disinter the colonial legacy of the Oz tale in his book about the movie; see Rushdie, *The Wizard of Oz.*

32. Conspicuously absent is an allegorical representation of African Americans. The troublesome status of recently manumitted African Americans is the focus of chapter 3.

33. Rockoff, "'The Wizard of Oz' as Monetary Allegory," 751.

34. For an analysis of the political maneuvering behind Chinese Exclusion, see Shirley Hune, "Politics of Chinese Exclusion: Legislative-Executive Conflict 1876–1882," in *Amerasia* 9, no. 1 (1982): 5–27. See also Alexander Saxton, "Race and the House of Labor," in *The Great Fear: Race in the Mind of America*, ed. Gary Nash and Richard Weiss, 98–120 (New York: Holt, Rinehart, and Winston, 1970) and *The Indispensable Enemy*; Nayan Shah, "The White Label and the Yellow Peril:

Race, Gender, and Labor in San Francisco in the Nineteenth and Early Twentieth Centuries," in *Clio: Histoire, Femmes et Societes* 3 (1996): 95–115; and Takaki, *Iron Cages*, 215–51. Interestingly, Bret Harte's seemingly anti-Chinese representations, which Takaki analyzes, may have been part of a larger project of Harte's that sought to produce sympathy for the Chinese, not unlike Mark Twain's descriptions of the Chinese in *Roughing It* (1872). Gary Y. Okihiro provides an account of the deep significance of Asianness in American thought in *Margins and Mainstreams: Asians in American History* (Seattle: University of Washington Press, 1994), and Edward W. Said's *Orientalism* is the standard text for elaborating this same tendency in European thought.

35. Generally considered a naive approach to monetary policy, the quantity theory argues that the value of money and its ability to create wealth is directly proportional to how much money is in circulation. Not surprisingly, the Populists wanted more money pumped into the national economy and the free coinage of silver was just the ticket. The silver mining interests in the West were, for understandable reasons, less vocally in favor of bimetallism as well. See Milton Friedman and Anna Schwartz, *A Monetary History of the United States, 1867–1960* (Princeton: Princeton University Press, 1963); John Kenneth Galbraith, *Money: Whence It Came, Where It Went* (Boston: Houghton, Mifflin, 1975); and De Cecco, *The International Gold Standard.*

In addition to Irwin Unger, Robert Sharkey, and Bruce Palmer, for accounts of the rise of late nineteenth-century populism, see John D. Hicks's seminal study *The Populist Revolt: A History of the Farmers' Alliance and the People's Party* (Lincoln: University of Nebraska Press, 1931), especially 301–20; and Norman Pollack's *The Populist Response to Industrial America: Midwestern Populist Thought* (Cambridge: Harvard University Press, 1962).

36. William Jennings Bryan, *Bryan on Imperialism: Speeches, Newspaper Articles and Interviews* (Chicago: Bentley and Company, 1900), 12–13. See also his famous "Cross of Gold" speech in Bryan, *The First Battle* (Chicago: W.B. Conkey, 1896), 205.

37. One of the main instruments of U.S. imperialism was the appeal of the U.S. Constitution itself. See A. Caesar Espiritu, "Constitutional Development in the Philippines," in *Constitutionalism and Rights: The Influence of the United States Constitution Abroad*, ed. Louis Henkin and Albert J. Rosenthal, 260–83 (New York: Columbia University Press, 1990).

38. On the primitivizing of Filipinos pre- and post-1898, see Vincent Rafael, "White Love: Surveillance and Nationalist Resistance in the U.S. Colonization of the Phillipines," in Kaplan and Pease, *Cultures of United States Imperialism*, 185–218.

39. Michael O'Malley offers a fascinating recuperation of the lost meanings of carpetbaggers in "Specie and Species: Race and the Money Question in Nineteenth-Century America," in *American Historical Review* 99 (April 1994): 369–95. In particular he reminds us that carpetbaggers were reviled for bringing satchelfuls of nonlocal currency to redeem at local banks.

40. For an analysis of economic developments in the 1890s, as well as a projection of the possibilities had bimetallism taken hold, see Friedman, "The Crime of 1873."

41. The 1900 Gold Standard Act was the culmination of decades of contestation over monetary policy. After the Coinage Act of 1873 (popularly called the "Crime of 1873"), which demonetized silver, various acts were passed to try to appease silver advocates, including the 1878 Bland-Allison Act and the 1890 Sherman Silver Purchase Act, which both called for rather limited resumption of the coinage of silver. For an overview of key legislation, see Ritter, "Silver Slippers," 286–87; and Herman E. Kroos, ed., *Documentary History of Banking and Currency in the United States* (New York: Chelsea House Publishers, 1983).

42. We might more accurately characterize this transition as only partly abortive because the pro-silver, anti-imperialist platform was indeed the one that the ambivalently Democratic party adopted; they just lost the election on it. See Garland A. Haas, *The Politics of Disintegration: Political Party Decay in the United States, 1840–1900* (Jefferson, N.C.: McFarland and Company, 1994); and Richard Hofstadter, *The Age of Reform: From Bryan to FDR* (New York: Vintage Books, 1955).

43. See William Hope Harvey, *Coin's Financial School* (1894; Cambridge, Mass.: Belknap Press, 1963) and *Coin on Money, Trusts, and Imperialism* (Chicago: Coin Publishing Co., 1899). See also the introduction to Hofstadter, *Age of Reform,* 5.

44. The writings of Horatio Alger are the most prominent and clichéd attempts to produce proper conduct through such adolescent novels as *Ragged Dick* (1868). For a discussion of the anxiety surrounding juvenile delinquency, see Stephen Mailloux, *Rhetorical Power* (Ithaca: Cornell University Press, 1989), 112–20.

45. See "Coin's Financial School," in Hofstadter, *Age of Reform,* 12–14, for a list of the various responses to and parodies of Coin.

46. Harvey, *Coin on Money, Trusts, and Imperialism,* 111.

47. Ibid, 147.

48. The far-reaching legacies of American nonrecognition of Philippine sovereignty are explored in the work of Oscar V. Campomanes; see "The New Empire's Forgetful and Forgotten Citizens: Unrepresentability and Unassimilability in Filipino-American Postcolonialities," in *Critical Mass: A Journal of Asian American Cultural Criticism* 2, no. 2 (Spring 1995): 145–200.

49. Not surprisingly, Filipino nationalism is considered the first modern Asian nationalism; see Benedict Anderson, *Imagined Communities: Reflections on the Origins and Spread of Nationalism,* 2d ed. (New York: Verso Books, 1991), esp. 26–30. In particular, Anderson argues that print culture, from the newspaper to the novel (such as José Rizal's *Noli Me Tangere* [1887; Bloomington: Indiana University Press, 1961]), are examples of the formal cultural production of the nation. See also Anderson's more recent work specifically on Southeast Asia, *Spectres of Comparison: Nationalism, Southeast Asian and the World* (London: Verso, 1998), especially 192–262.

50. The McKinley administration referred to the Philippines as hopefully

becoming an "American Hong Kong," while the anti-imperialists feared it would become an "American India." See Wolff, *Little Brown Brother,* 172.

51. See E. Berkeley Tompkins, *Anti-Imperialism in the United States: The Great Debate, 1890–1920* (Philadelphia: University of Pennsylvania Press, 1970), for a history of the mainstream responses to imperialism. For accounts of how marginalized populations responded to imperialism, see Penny Von Eschen, *Race against Empire: Black Americans and Anticolonialism, 1937–1957* (Ithaca: Cornell University Press, 1997).

52. Alan Trachtenberg, *The Incorporation of America: Culture and Society in the Gilded Age* (New York: Hill and Wang, 1982). Trachtenberg argues that this era can be characterized as a battle between emergent labor and emergent capital over the fate of America. Capital won. Tellingly, a similar but more squarely leftist and empire-centered argument about the history of Great Britain, the dominant nation of this era, can be found in the work of Eric Hobsbawm; see his *The Age of Empire.*

53. Hofstadter dismissed the 1899 text as "suffer[ing] from its lack of concentration on a single theme." See Hofstadter, *Age of Reform,* 70.

54. Immanuel Wallerstein, *The Modern World System* (New York: Academic Press, 1974). See also Arrighi, *The Long Twentieth Century.* Though written from a decidedly different disciplinary perspective, Alfred D. Chandler Jr.'s *The Visible Hand: The Managerial Revolution in American Business* (Cambridge: Harvard University Press, 1977) also tracks these similar trends in the way America was beginning to do business from the middle of the nineteenth century to the beginning of the twentieth. Chandler describes how corporations became "vertically integrated" or centralized transactionally, allowing for diversification. Horizontal corporations, i.e., those dominating a single industry over a great geographical area, were too vulnerable to the status of monopolies under the 1890 Sherman Antitrust Act.

55. Harvey, *Coin on Money,* 132.

56. For an account of the global emergence of economies of scale in this period, see Arrighi, *The Long Twentieth Century,* 159–239, in which he discusses the rise of British capitalism. American capitalism would then go on to displace economies of size with so-called "economies of speed."

57. For an example of the conspiracy theorizing of the silverites, see the story of Ernest Seyd's alleged machinations in Ritter, "Silver Slippers," 190. Hofstadter relates this same story in "The Mind of 'Coin' Harvey," in *Coin's Financial School,* 62–63n37.

58. Harvey, *Coin on Money,* 137.

59. Ibid., 130.

60. For a seminal treatment of the rise of trusts, or "very large corporations" and speculative and finance capitalism in late nineteenth-century America, see Thomas R. Navin and Marian V. Sears, "The Rise of a Market for Industrial Securities, 1887–1902," *Business History Review* 29 (1955): 105–38. Literary scholar Philip Fisher has suggestively argued that postbellum American culture can be

characterized by the rise of "a culture of speculation" that the unprecedented *cultural* centrality of Wall Street today makes nary undeniable. This idea is elaborated further in chapter 6 of this book. See his "American Literary and Cultural Studies since the Civil War," in *Redrawing the Boundaries: The Transformation of English and American Literary Studies,* ed. Stephen Greenblatt and Giles Gunn, 248 (New York: MLA, 1992).

61. While the writings of Pollack (*The Populist Response to Industrial America*) and Hicks (*The Populist Revolt*) have a respectful attitude toward the Populists, Hofstadter's Pulitzer Prize–winning *The Age of Reform* has a tone of sympathetic condescension, especially toward farmers; see *The Age of Reform,* 23–93.

62. One finds echoes of the "era of good feelings" in the Jacksonian antipathy of central financial structures that culminated in Jackson's refusal to renew the charter of the Bank of the United States. See Marvin Meyers, *The Jacksonian Persuasion: Politics and Belief* (Stanford: Stanford University Press, 1957); George Dangerfield, *The Era of Good Feelings* (New York: Harcourt, Brace and Company, 1952); and Leonard D. White, *The Jacksonians: A Study in Administrative History, 1829–1861* (New York: MacMillan, 1954).

63. Hofstadter dismissed the 1899 text as "suffer[ing] from its lack of concentration on a single theme" (70). This lack of focus—and perhaps even the attempts to overproduce an epistemic unity—only showed the degree of complexity that capitalism had reached with the convergence of incorporation and empire-building. See also Trachtenberg, *The Incorporation of America,* and Saxton, *The Indispensable Enemy.*

64. See Turner, *The Significance of the Frontier in American History.*

65. For example, despite being a leftist sympathizer, Charles Beard cautiously avoided being labeled Marxist in *An Economic Interpretation of the Constitution of the United States* (1913; New York: Free Press, 1986). See Michael Denning, *The Cultural Front* (New York: Verso, 1996); and Bonacich and Cheng, *Labor Immigration under Capitalism,* 1–56.

66. For example, Mark Achbar's documentary, *The Corporation* (2003), based largely on the work of Noam Chomsky, is a popular critique of multinational corporations. A modern-day populist figure is Michael Moore, whose documentaries, such as *Roger and Me* (1989), rely on the sentimental production of a folksy left, beginning with himself and his labor union ties.

67. This era is lucidly narrated by Alan Trachtenberg, who makes a good case for the genuine epistemic shift that was inaugurated in this era, an epistemic shift in which we still find ourselves; see his *The Incorporation of America,* especially 70–100 and 140–207.

68. Even W. E. B. DuBois admitted that he was for the gold standard at this time: "I saw the rise of the Free Silver movement, and the beginning of Populism. I was wrong in most of my judgments. My Harvard training made me stand staunchly for the Gold Standard, and I was suspicious of the Populist 'Radicals.' At the same time, I had seen face-to-face something of the social democratic movement in Germany. I had gone to their meetings; and by the time McKinley

got to work on his high tariff and showed his evident kinship to big business, I began to awaken. Certain of my earlier teachings now came into conflict. I had been trained to believe in Free Trade, which the new McKinley high tariff contradicted. I began to realize something of the meaning of the new Populist movement in its economic aspects." See W. E. B. DuBois, "From McKinley to Wallace: My Fifty Years as an Independent" (1948) in *W. E. B. DuBois: A Reader,* ed. David Levering Lewis, 482–94 (New York: H. Holt and Co., 1995).

69. There emerged in the 1870s the beginnings of the weak state in the face of leviathan corporations that set the terms of American political development. See Pacifico Agabin, "Laissez Faire and the Due Process Clause: How Economic Ideology Affects Constitutional Development," *Philippine Law Review* 44 (1969): 709–28. See also Thomas R. Navin and Marian V. Sears, "The Rise of a Market for Industrial Securities, 1887–1902," in *Business History Review* 29 (1955): 105–38.

70. See V. I. Lenin, *Imperialism: The Highest State of Capitalism* (1916; London: Martin Lawrence, 1933); J. A. Hobson, *Imperialism: A Study* (1902; London: Allen and Unwin, 1948); C. K. Hobson, *Export of Capital* (1914; New York: Garland, 1983); and Scott Nearing and Joseph Freeman, *Dollar Diplomacy: A Study in American Imperialism* (New York: Huebsch and Viking Press, 1925); as well as Arrighi, *The Long Twentieth Century.*

71. Walter Benjamin, "The Work of Art in the Age of Mechanical Reproduction," in *Illuminations,* 217–51. Appropriately, Benjamin points to the cinema as the new formation that ushers in this new age. His insights, however, more generally fit accounts of the rise of mass culture. See also Andreas Huyssen, *After the Great Divide: Modernism, Mass Culture, Postmodernism* (Bloomington: Indiana University Press, 1986).

72. Benjamin, "Theses on the Philosophy of History" in *Illuminations,* 253–64.

73. Baum, *The Wonderful Wizard of Oz,* 128.

74. See Booker T. Washington, et al., *The Negro Problem; A Series of Articles by Representative Negroes of To-day* (1903; Miami: Mnemosyne Publishing, Inc., 1969). DuBois's influential "The Talented Tenth" (31–75) is among the essays included in this volume.

75. Cuba is a telling and early counterpoint for how to be a nonaligned compliant state. Oscar Campomanes has written about this undertheorized parallel in "Between Colonialisms" (unpublished manuscript presented at the Bronx Museum of Art, 1998). Campomanes documents the immense carnage inflicted upon the Filipino nationalists by Spain and then the United States as a lesson well-learned by the turn-of-the-century Cuban independence movement.

76. Although the status of Great Britain as a colonial power has been the focus of the field of postcolonial studies, the theorizations of the role of culture in producing empire do have explanatory power for making sense of American imperialism. The customary statement on the immanence of empire is the opening line of Gayatri Chakravorty Spivak's "Three Women's Texts and a Critique of Imperialism": "It should not be possible to read nineteenth-century British literature without remembering that imperialism, understood as England's social mission,

was a crucial part of the cultural representation of England to the English. The role of literature in the production of cultural representation should not be ignored. These two obvious 'facts' continue to be disregarded in the reading of nineteenth-century British literature. This itself attests to the continuous success of the imperialist project, displaced and dispersed onto more modern forms" (*Critical Inquiry* 12, no. 1 [1985]: 262).

77. Exemplary revisionist histories of the American West have been written by Richard White. *"It's Your Misfortune and None of My Own": A History of the American West* (Norman: University of Oklahoma Press, 1991) is a general overview history of the West and his *The Roots of Dependency: Subsistence, Environment, and Social Change among the Choctaws, Pawnees, and Navajos* (Lincoln: University of Nebraska Press, 1983) applies world systems theory to an understanding of the dispossession inflicted on American Indians.

78. This slogan is particularly common in Bryan's speeches. The equating of anti-imperialism with treason was common. In the anti-imperialist chapter of *Coin on Money, Trusts, and Imperialism,* "The Sixth Day," Harvey depicts Coin responding to a rather acrid accusation of sedition.

79. In a different but related context, Frantz Fanon has written about the false promises of de jure postcoloniality amid de facto neocolonialism; see his *The Wretched of the Earth.*

80. The recent writings of literary scholar Lisa Lowe have illuminated the ways that Asian American cultural politics reveals the contradictions of American civil society. See "Immigration, Racialization, Citizenship: Asian American Critique" in *Immigrant Acts,* 1–36.

81. The debunking of the neoconservative model-minority myth has been one of the leading missions of Asian American activism and study. See Harry Kitano and Roger Daniels, *Asian Americans: Emerging Minorities* (Englewood Cliffs, N.J.: Prentice Hall, 1995); and Sucheng Chan, *Asian Americans: An Interpretive History* (Boston: Twayne, 1991).

82. R. Zamora Linmark's *Rolling the R's,* the subject of chapter 5 of this book, is another example of this disciplining at various levels in Hawaiian society, but particularly in Mrs. Takemoto's fifth-grade class in Kalihi Valley Elementary School. Despite, or perhaps because of, its status as a state of the union, Hawaii is no less a site of U.S. colonialism than the Philippines. Filipino-American filmmaker Michael Magnaye's award-winning short film, "White Christmas," brilliantly depicts the disciplining and mimicry that illustrate the depth and breadth of a century of American colonialism in the Philippines, as well as the resistance to that legacy.

83. Ralph Ellison, *Invisible Man* (New York: Vintage, 1952), 568.

3. "The American Earth Was Like a Huge Heart"

1. Especially through the 1980s, battles over the American literary and historical canon became quite visible, appearing in venues from talk shows to protest rallies, as curricula were revised to reflect and produce alternative and corrective

approaches to American culture. Verbs like *redrawing* and *rethinking* and *reimagining* proliferated. For example, see Henry Louis Gates Jr., *Loose Canons: Notes on the Culture Wars* (New York: Oxford, 1992); and David Palumbo-Liu's introduction to *The Ethnic Canon: Histories, Institutions, and Interventions* (Minneapolis: University of Minnesota Press, 1995), 1–27.

2. The body of scholarship that deals with this broad question is too voluminous to recount fully here. Yet some of the key studies that grapple with the question are as follows: in history, Saxton, *The Indispensable Enemy;* Takaki, *Strangers from a Different Shore;* and Shah, *Contagious Divides*; in cultural studies, Kim, *Asian American Literature*; Lowe, *Immigrant Acts*; Patricia Chu, *Assimilating Asians: Gendered Strategies of Authorship in America* (Durham, N.C.: Duke University Press, 2000); and Eng, *Racial Castration*; in social sciences and history, Evelyn Nakano Glenn, *Issei, Nisei, War Bride: Three Generations of Japanese America Women in Domestic Service* (Philadelphia: Temple University Press, 1986); Rhacel Salazar Parreñas, *Servants of Globalization: Women, Migration, and Domestic Work* (Stanford, Calif.: Stanford University Press, 2001); and Ngai, *Impossible Subjects.*

3. See Chan, preface to *Aiiieeeee!*

4. For example, see chapter 2 of Lowe's *Immigrant Acts;* Nguyen's *Race and Resistance* (69–70); chapter 1 of Rachel Lee's *The Americas of Asian American Literature: Gendered Fictions of Nation and Transnation* (Princeton: Princeton University Press, 1999); Marilyn Alquizola's analysis of the irony of Carlos Bulosan's autobiography ("Subversion or Affirmation: The Text and Subtext of *America Is in the Heart*," in Hune, *Asian Americans,* 199–209); and Kenneth Mostern's "Is America in the Heart?" (*Critical Mass* 2, no. 2 [Spring 1995]: 35–65). And the most important early work on Bulosan is E. San Juan Jr.'s *Carlos Bulosan and the Imagination of Class Struggle* (Queza City: University of Philippines Press, 1972).

5. Carlos Bulosan, *America Is in the Heart: A Personal History* (Seattle: University of Washington Press, 1973), 326.

6. Michael Dening, *The Cultural Front: The Laboring of American Culture in the Twentieth Century* (New York: Verson, 1996), 129.

7. *America Is in the Heart* has been a staple on Asian American studies reading lists for as long as there has been Asian American studies. See Amy Tachiki, ed., *Roots: An Asian American Reader* (Los Angeles: Continental Graphics, 1971); and Emma Gee, ed., *Counterpoint: Perspectives on Asian America* (Los Angeles: Asian American Studies Center, 1976).

8. Chan, et al., preface to *Aiiieeee!, viii.*

9. Ibid., viii–ix.

10. See John Okada, *No-No Boy* (Seattle, Wash.: University of Washington Press; 1978); and Sui Sin Far, *Mrs. Spring Fragrance and Other Writings* (Urbana: University of Illinois Press, 1995).

11. C. Y. Lee, *Flower Drum Song* (New York: Penguin, 1957).

12. Chan, et al., preface to *Aiiieeee!, viii.*

13. Fae Myenne Ng, *Bone* (New York: Hyperion, 1993).

14. Lowe, *Immigrant Acts,* 127.

15. Jade Snow Wong, *Fifth Chinese Daughter* (1950; Seattle: University of Washington Press, 1989); Maxine Hong Kingston, *The Woman Warrior: Memoir of a Girl among Ghosts* (New York: Vintage, 1977); Amy Tan, *The Joy Luck Club* (New York: Putnam's, 1989). See also Sau-ling Wong, "'Sugar Sisterhood': Situating the Amy Tan Phenomenon," in Palumbo-Liu, *The Ethnic Canon,* 174–210. Literary critic Wendy Ho has outlined the features and importance of the mother-daughter bond in Asian American literature; see her *In Her Mother's House: The Politics of Asian American Mother-Daughter Writing* (Walnut Creek, Calif.: Alta Mira, 1999).

16. Guy Beauregard, "Reclaiming Sui Sin Far," in *Re-Collecting Early Asian America: Essays in Cultural History,* ed. Josephine Lee, Imogene L. Lim, and Yuko Matsukawa, 340–55 (Philadelphia: Temple University Press, 2002). See also Viet Nguyen's "The Origins of Asian American Literature: The Eaton Sisters and the Hybrid Body" in *Race and Resistance,* 33–59.

17. Annette White-Parks, *Sui Sin Far/Edith Maude Eaton: A Literary Biography* (Urbana and Chicago: University of Illinois Press, 1995), 240.

18. Sui Sin Far, "In the Land of the Free," in *Mrs. Spring Fragrance,* 93–100.

19. *Chan Is Missing,* produced and directed by Wayne Wang, 80 min., 1982.

20. Wayne Wang, *Chan Is Missing: A Film* (Honolulu: Bamboo Ridge Press, 1984), 62.

21. For better or worse, Chinese Americans have consistently been a visible part of San Francisco for 150 years. See Victor Nee and Bret DeBary Nee, *Longtime Californ': A Documentary Study of an American Chinatown* (Stanford: Stanford University Press, 1972), especially part 5, "Radicals and the New Vision," 355–99.

22. *The Fall of the I-Hotel* (1979; produced and directed by Curtis Choy, 90 min., second edition produced in 1993) documents another moment when Asian capital investment in the new San Francisco—in this case a developer from Thailand—displaces the bachelor community of old-timer Filipino Americans. See Grace Kyungwon Hong, "The Fall of the I-Hotel and the Rise of Globalization: Putting the International Back in I-Hotel," paper delivered at the Association for Asian American Studies (AAAS) conference in Toronto, Canada, March 2001.

23. Jo acknowledges in voiceover: "The FOBs, fresh off the boat, as Steve calls them, didn't come off a boat—they came off of jumbo jets" (28). With an emphasis on process over ontology, Wang is quite deliberate with his use of the detective genre to exacerbate epistemological crises. See Diane Mei Lin Mark, "Interview with Wayne Wang," in Wang, *Chan Is Missing,* 101–116, esp. 110–13.

24. Peter Feng, "Becoming Chinese American, Becoming Asian American: *Chan Is Missing,*" in *Screening Asian Americans,* ed. Peter X. Feng, 185–216 (New Brunswick, N.J.: Rutgers University Press, 2002).

25. Chan, preface to *Aiiieeeee!*

26. Kim, *Asian American Literature.*

27. See Wong, *Reading Asian American Literature.*

28. The failure of Marlon Fuentes to recover and remember the story of his grandfather Markod in *Bontoc Eulogy* (see chapter 4) helps us to see how a quest

for persons may be doomed to failure. Both films are concerned with appreciating structures of recognition.

29. He is, as Wang calls him, a "negative character" (111)—one continually defined by what he fails to be. The film *Chan Is Missing* is trapped in Jo's perspective, via his voiceover and his field of vision, literally and figuratively. These limitations are precisely the method by which the film shows the limits of identity at containing its proper subjects.

30. Lisa Lowe has noted that since 1965, Asian immigrants have constituted a split class, as they have been recruited both for their capital (in the form of assets and/or highly trained skills) and for their labor in low-wage work. See Lowe, *Immigrant Acts,* 15–16.

31. Frank Chin, *Chicken Coop, Chinaman, and Year of the Dragon* (Seattle, Wash.: University of Washington Press, 1981).

32. Frantz Fanon's *The Wretched of the Earth* provides an insightful, "stretched" Marxist analysis of the neocolonialism that was necessarily built upon older colonialisms. U.S. colonialism, however, obviates a preexisting settler colonialism, at least its own.

33. Walter Benn Michaels, *The Gold Standard and the Logic of Naturalism: American Literature at the Turn of the Century* (Berkeley and Los Angeles: University of California Press, 1987), 194.

34. William McKinley and Arthur MacArthur proved effective spokesmen for the American actions in the Philippines as a liberatory and economic mission. See Henry Graff, ed., *American Imperialism and the Philippine Insurrection: Testimony Taken from Hearings on Affairs in the Philippine Islands before the Senate Subcommittee on the Philippines—1902* (Boston: Little, Brown, and Co., 1969), 114–28, 135–45, 150–59, 35–50, 89, 121. For conceptions of empire and immigration, the mobilities of money and of person have increasingly diverged. Asian labor, conversely, has, through gendered racialization, been de-anthropomorphized. Asian American historians have noted that orders for work crews were made alongside orders for inanimate objects; "Filipinos" are found listed next to "fertilizer," and "a Chinaman" next to "macaroni" (see Takaki, *Strangers from a Different Shore,* 25). The immigrating Asian laborer can be counterposed with emigrating U.S. capital so that, on one hand, we have the recruitment of Asian labor into the United States and, on the other, we have the "creolization" of U.S. capital abroad.

35. McKinley, *Papers Relating to the Foreign Relations of the United States* (1912), vii–xxvii.

36. See Wolf, *Little Brown Brother.*

37. Critical Marxian accounts of foreign investment include Lenin, *Imperialism*; J. A. Hobson, *Imperialism*; C. K. Hobson, *The Export of Capital*; and Nearing and Freeman, *Dollar Diplomacy*; as well as Arrighi, *The Long Twentieth Century.*

38. The Chinese Exclusion Act of 1882, the Barred Zone Act of 1917, and the Immigration Act of 1924 are the major immigration restriction laws that shaped Asian American history. See Bill Ong Hing, *Making and Remaking Asian*

America through Immigration Policy, 1850–1990 (Stanford: Stanford University Press, 1993).

39. For a convincing account of the major shifts in the past five hundred years of capitalist development, see Arrighi, *The Long Twentieth Century.* Arrighi's analysis builds on the long wave and world system's theories of Fernand Braudel and Immanuel Wallerstein, with a focus on the internalizations of different aspects of capitalist production. The current wave, i.e., the long twentieth century, was a financial revolution ushered in by U.S. internalization of transactions as an improvement over Britain's internalization of production.

40. Karl Marx, "Contribution to the Critique of Political Economy," cited by Suzanna deBrunhoff in *Marx on Money* (New York: Urizen, 1976), 46.

41. The link was actually not all that neat. For example, though he was still against paper money, prolific Goldbugs pamphleteer David Ames Wells looked to, among other things, the recent emancipation of the slaves as evidence of the need for a more portable money; see Wells, *The Silver Question,* 9. With the defeat of the greenbacks in the 1870s, the belief that American money needed to be based on the "intrinsic value" of bullion was only further sedimented.

42. See Chandler, *The Visible Hand;* Friedman and Schwartz, *A Monetary History of the United States;* De Cecco, *The International Gold Standard;* Arrighi, *The Long Twentieth Century;* Pollack, *Populist Response to Industrial America;* and Hofstadter, *Age of Reform.*

43. Despite the electrification of capital, to this day, if you go the Federal Reserve Bank in New York, you will see that bullion moves a few feet via a forklift from one country's vault to another's. Even paper currency became so physically cumbersome that the Fed moved its cash facility out of their Wall Street location to New Jersey.

44. Nearing and Freeman, *Dollar Diplomacy,* 19.

45. As John Kleeberg notes, annexation of the Philippines ironically returned the United States to a limited bimetallism because the Philippine economy had a deeply entrenched silver standard. See his pamphlet, "The Silver Dollar in International Trade: A Study in Failure" (New York: American Numismatic Society, 1995), 100–104.

46. The Federal Reserve publishes a series of comic books to educate youth on the functions and purpose of the Federal Reserve System. These pamphlets also emphasize the need for money to formally transcend the physicality of such past currencies as Chinese chisels, frontier cattle, fish, and of course, gold coins. See Ed Steinberg, *The Story of Money* (New York: Federal Reserve Bank, 1994).

47. Focusing primarily on China, Aihwa Ong's *Ungrounded Empires* (New York: Routledge, 1997) offers compelling theorizations of globality and capitalist disciplining. See also Spivak's "Can the Subaltern Speak?" for an explanation of the downfall of territorial empire and the rise of what would come to be called globalization.

48. Spivak, "Can the Subaltern Speak?" 287–88.

49. Trinh T. Min-ha, *Woman, Native, Other: Writing Postcoloniality and Feminism* (Bloomington: Indiana University Press, 1989), 98.

50. For a useful history of the Asian American movement in higher education, see Mazumdar, "Asian Studies and Asian American Studies."

51. Two major cases that codified legal definitions for Asian Americans are *Yick Wo v. Hopkins* (1886) and *People v. Hall* (1854). For a historical and documentary account of these cases, see Charles McClain, *In Search of Equality: The Chinese Struggle against Discrimination in Nineteenth-Century America* (Berkeley and Los Angeles: University of California Press, 1994); and the following works by Hyung-Chan Kim: *Asian Americans and Congress: A Documentary History* (Westport, Conn.: Greenwood Press, 1996), *Asian Americans and the Supreme Court: A Documentary History* (Westport, Conn.: Greenwood Press, 1992), and *A Legal History of Asian Americans* (Westport, Conn.: Greenwood Press, 1994).

52. For a fine thematic treatment of mobility in Asian American literature, see Sau-ling Wong, "The Politics of Mobility," in *Reading Asian American Literature,* 118–65.

4. Uplifting Race, Reconstructing Empire

1. For example, C. Vann Woodward's *The Strange Career of Jim Crow* (London: Oxford University Press, 1966) turns to the overthrow of Reconstruction and periodizes Jim Crow segregation from 1877 to the 1960s. Kevin Gaines, in *Uplifting the Race: Black Leadership, Politics, and Culture in the Twentieth Century* (Chapel Hill, N.C.: University of North Carolina Press, 1995), describes how modern African American discourses of "uplift" are explicitly a post-Reconstruction phenomenon.

2. Rev. Dr. Martin Luther King, Jr. "I Have a Dream," in *The Norton Anthology of African American Literature,* 2d ed., ed. Henry Louis Gates Jr. and Nellie Y. McKay, 107–9 (New York: Norton, 2004). The exact start of Reconstruction is something of a debate in American historiography. Eric Foner, in his *Reconstruction: America's Unfinished Revolution, 1863–1877* (New York: Harper and Row, 1988), argues for the Emancipation Proclamation as the starting point. King's speech confirms this notion.

3. Neil Smith's *American Empire* examines the role of geographers in the practice and epistemology of U.S. colonization projects. He begins his study with the famously apocryphal, and, in Smith's account, unbelievable story of McKinley's inability to find the Philippines on a map after hearing word of Dewey's naval triumph in Manila Bay. See "The Lost Geography of the American Century" in Smith, *American Empire,* 1–3.

4. Turn-of-the-century cartoon likenesses of Filipinos, Hawaiians, Puerto Ricans, and Cubans were often indistinguishable from minstrelsy figures, particularly children. On the visual cultures of American colonization of the Philippines, see Benito Vergara, *Displaying Filipinos: Photography and Colonialism in Early Twentieth-Century Philippines* (Quezon City: University of the Philippines Press, 1995);

The Forbidden Book: The Philippine American War in Political Cartoons, ed. Abe Ignacio, Enrique de la Cruz, Jorge Immanuel, and Helen Toribio (San Francisco: T'Boli Publishing and Distribution, 2004); and Jacobson, *Barbarian Virtues.*

5. Gaines, *Uplifting the Race,* 39.

6. Booker T. Washington, *Up from Slavery* (New York: Norton, 1996), 13–14.

7. Harriet Jacobs, *Incidents in the Life of a Slave Girl, Written by Herself* (Cambridge: Harvard University Press, 1987), 73.

8. See Hazel Carby, *Reconstructing Womanhood: The Emergence of the Afro-American Woman Novelist* (New York: Oxford, 1987); Val Smith, *Self-Discovery and Authority in Afro-American Narrative* (Cambridge: Harvard University Press, 1987); and Frances Foster, *Witnessing Slavery: The Development of Ante-bellum Slave Narratives* (Madison: University of Wisconsin Press, 1994).

9. Abraham Lincoln, "Second Inaugural Address," March 3, 1865, in *American Literature 1820–1865,* vol. B of *Norton Anthology of American Literature,* 6th ed., ed. Nina Baym. For histories detailing the complexities of Reconstruction in practice, see Foner, *Reconstruction,* and W. E. B. DuBois's *Black Reconstruction in America* (1935; New York: The Free Press, 1998).

10. On the power of the Lincoln narrative, see Richard Hofstadter's "Abraham Lincoln and the Self-Made Myth," in *The American Political Tradition and the Men Who Made It* (1948; New York: Vintage, 1973), 119–74; Robert A. Ferguson's "Lincoln: An Epilogue," in *Law and Letters in American Culture* (Cambridge: Harvard University Press, 1984), 305–17; and Garry Wills's *Lincoln at Gettysburg: The Words That Remade America* (New York: Touchstone, 1992). In a further application of Lincoln's exceptional exemplarity, recent queer revisionism has suggested that Lincoln's longtime companionship with bedfellow Joshua Speed makes the young Abe Lincoln recuperable as nonheteronormative.

11. Rachel Lee compellingly argues that white women function in Bulosan's autobiography as a means of producing notions of fraternity and of occluding Filipinas and other treacherous women. See Lee's "Fraternal Devotions: Carlos Bulosan and the Sexual Politics of America," in *The Americas of Asian American Literature,* 32.

12. Bulosan, *America Is in the Heart,* 69.

13. On the discourse of soap and colonialism, see Anne McClintock, *Imperial Leather: Race, Gender, and Sexuality in the Colonial Contest* (New York: Routledge, 1995). Also, Booker T. Washington's *Up from Slavery* cannot emphasize enough the importance of "the daily bath" as a means of racial uplift and evidence of the disciplinary benefits of civilization. See also Catherine Ceniza Choy's *Empire of Care: Nursing and Migration in Filipino American History* (Durham: Duke University Press, 2003), which examines the role of medical discourse in the colonization of the Philippines.

14. Understanding African Americans as a colonized population was briefly popular during the civil rights era. Malcolm X described the ghetto as a locality from which the wealth is systematically removed. See his "The Ballot or the

Bullet" in Gates and McKay, *The Norton Anthology of African American Literature*, 116–28.

15. See Willard Gatewood, *Smoked Yankees and the Struggle for Empire: Letters from Negro Soldiers, 1898–1902* (Urbana: University of Illinois Press, 1971).

16. Simms's letter, dated May 11, 1901, is quoted in Herbert Aptheker, *A Documentary History of the Negro People in the United States*, vol. 2 (New York: Citadel Press, 1992), 825–26.

17. W. E. B. DuBois, *The Souls of Black Folk* (1903; New York: Washington Square Press, 1970).

18. On this power of this narrative, see Hofstadter, "Abraham Lincoln and the Self-Made Myth."

19. Richard Wright, *Black Boy* (New York: Harper Perennial Modern Classics, 1998).

20. Ida B. Wells. *Southern Horrors and Other Writings: The Anti-Lynching Campaign of Ida B. Wells, 1892–1900* (Boston: Bedford Books, 1997).

21. Darrell Lum, "Four Score and Seven Years Ago," in *Charlie Chan Is Dead: An Anthology of Contemporary Asian American Fiction*, ed. Jessica Hagedorn, 287–95 (New York: Penguin, 1993).

22. In *A History of Negro Revolt* (1938; New York: Haskell House, 1969), C. L. R. James compellingly casts the Civil War as the great bourgeois revolution of American civilization.

23. This dynamic is also important to Frantz Fanon's account of colonialism and culture; see his *Black Skins, White Masks* (New York: Grove Weidenfeld, 1967).

24. Paolo Friere, *The Pedagogy of the Oppressed* (New York: Continuum, 1973).

25. Vicente Rafael, "White Love," in Kaplan and Pease, *Cultures of United States Imperialism*. Filipino nationalist historian Renato Constantino has influentially described the *Miseducation of the Filipino* (1966; Quezon City: Foundation for Nationalist Studies, 1982) under American empire.

26. Ngugi Wa Thiongo, *Decolonising the Mind: The Politics of Language in African Literature* (London: James Currey, 1986); Gauri Viswanathan, *Masks of Conquest: Literary Study and British Rule in India* (New York: Columbia University Press, 1989); Sara Suleri, *The Rhetoric of English India* (Chicago: University of Chicago Press, 1992).

27. See Benedict Anderson, "Third Wave," in *Imagined Communities: Reflections on the Origins and Spread of Nationalism* (London: Verson, 1983).

28. Mary Racelis and Celine Ick, *Bearers of Benevolence: The Thomasites and Public Education* (Pasig City, Philippines: Anvil Publishing, 2001).

29. See Ariel Dorfmann and Armand Mattelart, *How to Read Donald Duck: Imperialist Ideology in the Disney Comic* (New York: International General, 1975).

30. For a discussion of the education state apparatus, see Lowe, "Canonization, Institutionalization, Identity."

31. Wells, *Southern Horrors,* 73–157.

32. Ibid, 81.

33. Angela Davis, "The Myth of the Black Rapist," in *Women, Race, and Class* (New York: Vintage, 1982), 172–201.

34. Wells, *Southern Horrors*, 81.

35. See Ian Watt, *The Rise of the Novel: Studies in Defoe, Richardson and Fielding* (Berkeley and Los Angeles: University of California Press, 1962). Ann du Cille's *Coupling Convention: Sex, Text, and Tradition in Black Women's Fiction* (New York: Oxford University Press, 1993) argues that the bourgeois marriage is the key product of the novel form, starting with Jane Austen's *Pride and Prejudice.*

36. See Lowe, "Decolonization, Displacement, Disidentification: Writing and the Question of History," in *Immigrant Acts,* 97–127.

37. Althusser, "Ideology," and Balibar, "Citizen Subject."

38. Franco Moretti, *The Way of the World: The Bildungsroman in European Culture* (London: Verso, 1987).

39. On the first anniversary of the 9/11 attacks, New York Governor George Pataki chose to read Lincoln's address to commence the ceremonies at Ground Zero.

40. Garry Wills, *Lincoln at Gettysburg.*

41. The recent scandalous case of Seattle schoolteacher Mary Kay LaTourneau's affair with a Samoan thirteen-year-old eerily shows the possible dangers of this very coupling.

42. Michel Foucault, *The History of Sexuality,* vol. 1 (New York: Vintage, 1980). A direct translation of the French title is *The Will to Know.* Foucault's study influentially describes how desire is not inherent, but is produced through prohibition. He displaces what he calls "the repressive hypothesis."

43. For the text of this speech, see Roy P. Bawler, *The Collected Works of Abraham Lincoln* (New Brunswick, N.J.: Rutgers University Press, 1953), 7:22.

44. Avery Gordon, *Ghostly Matters: Haunting and the Sociological Imagination* (Minneapolis: University of Minnesota Press, 1997).

45. From a Hearst newspaper article cited in Roland Kotami, *The Japanese in Hawaii: A Century of Struggle* (Honolulu: Hawaii Hochi, Ltd., 1985), 71.

46. See ibid. Many thanks to Helen Jun for informing me of the case and providing me with the reference. Novelist and playwright Milton Murayama wrote an obscure play on this very subject called *Althea.* In 2005, the PBS documentary series *American Experience* devoted an episode to telling the history of the Massie Case. See *American Experience: The Massie Affair,* produced and directed by Mark Zuonitzer, 60 min., 2005.

47. Wells, *A Red Record,* 77 (emphasis added). Ambivalence over the franchise has a long tradition in African American discourse. See Malcolm X, "The Ballot or the Bullet."

48. Bulosan, *America Is in the Heart,* 67.

49. For a discussion of the production history of Fuentes's film, see Peter Feng, *Identities in Motion: Asian American Film and Video* (Durham: Duke University Press, 2002), 24–33.

50. See Joy Kogawa, *Obasan* (New York: David Godine, 1986); and Monique

Truong, "Kelly," *Amerasia Journal* 17, no. 2 (1991): 41–48. Kogawa has received critical scholarly attention from Sau-ling Wong and King-kok Cheung, and Truong's story figures prominently in chapter 2 of Lisa Lowe's *Immigant Acts.*

51. See Benedict Anderson, "Census, Map, Museum," in *Imagined Communities,* 163–86.

52. The interpretation of world's fairs achieved probably its highest literary treatment in Henry Adams's *The Education of Henry Adams.* See also John Carlos Rowe, "*The Education of Henry Adams* and American Empire," in *New Essays on "The Education of Henry Adams,"* ed. John Carlos Rowe (New York: Cambridge University Press, 1996). See also Paul Kramer's analysis of the fair in "Making Concessions," *Radical History Review* 73 (Winter 1999): 74–114.

53. Ida B. Wells, *The Reason Why,* ed. Robert W. Rydell (Urbana: Univeresity of Illinois Press, 1999).

54. See Ranajit Guha and Gayatri Chakravorty Spivak, *Selected Subaltern Studies* (New York: Oxford University Press, 1988).

55. See Gramsci, *Selections from the Prison Notebooks.*

56. For example, see Guha, "The Prose of Counter-Insurgency."

57. William McKinley's "Remarks to the Methodist Delegation" concludes with his order to the Secretary of the War Department, that is, the official mapmaker, to add the islands to the map of the United States, saying "there they will stay," as long as he was president. Assassinated at the 1901 Buffalo World's Fair, McKinley managed to keep his word.

58. See Rey Ileto's *Pasyon and Revolution* (Quezon City, Philippines: Ateneo de Manila University Press, 1986); and Benedict Anderson's "Cacique Democracy" in *Spectres of Comparison: Nationalism In Southeast Asia and the World* (London: Verso, 1998), 192–226.

59. In *The Language of the Street and Other Essays* (Manila: National Bookstore, 1980), Filipino writer Nick Joaquin describes the systematic vilification of everything Spanish once the Americans set up their colonizing apparatus. In "The Movie Album," Joaquin describes the early power of Hollywood to inculcate American taste.

60. Burton Benedict's *Anthropology of World's Fairs* (Berkeley and Los Angeles: University of California Press, 1986) offers a documentation and theorization of the ideological work performed by the rise of these expositions.

61. David Harvey and Edward Soja each offer useful extensions of world systems theory that emphasize the central role of conceptions of space under late capitalism. See Harvey, "The Geopolitics of Capitalism," in *Spaces of Capital* (New York: Routledge, 1002), 312–44; and Soja, *Postmodern Geographies* (London: Verso, 1987).

62. Quoted in Said, *Orientalism,* xiii.

63. See Arrighi's *The Long Twentieth Century* and Fernand Braudel's *The Wheels of Commerce* (New York: Harper and Row, 1982).

64. According to Burton Benedict's statistics, St. Louis and Chicago were the two most successful fairs in terms of attendance; see his *The Anthropology of*

World's Fairs. For the impact of the Chicago fair, see Trachtenberg's famous analysis of "White City" in *The Incorporation of America,* 208–34.

65. See Henry Nash Smith's *Virgin Land: The American West as Symbol and Myth* (Cambridge: Harvard University Press, 1970), as well as Richard White's works, *Roots of Dependency* and *"It's Your Misfortune,"* and Patricia Nelson Limerick's *The Legacy of Conquest: The Unbroken Past of the American West* (New York: Norton, 1987). Each of these studies proceeds explicitly or implicitly from a confrontation with Turner.

66. William McKinley's assassination at the Buffalo World's Fair led to its miserable gate receipts.

67. Mark Twain and Charles Dudley Warner satirize this culture in *The Gilded Age: A Tale of Today* (1878; New York: Oxford University Press, 1996), with a story of a scam to found a college for African Americans. See also Manning Marable, *How Capitalism Underdeveloped Black America: Problems in Race, Political Economy, and Society* (Boston: South End Press, 1983).

68. Ben Truman, ed., *History of The World's Fair Being a Complete and Authentic Description of the Columbia Exposition From Its Inception* (Philadelphia: Mammoth Publishing Co, 1893), 19–20. The section on the South, "'Way Down Souf 'mong De Fields of Cotton," does not mention African Americans.

69. Ida B. Wells, Frederick Douglass, Irvine Garland Penn, and Ferdinand L. Barnett, *The Reasons Why the Colored American Is Not in the World's Columbian Exposition: The Afro-American's Contribution to Columbian Literature,* ed. Robert W. Rydell (1893; Urbana and Chicago: University of Illinois Press, 1999), 102.

70. The classic post-Reconstruction divide is usually characterized as the divide between W. E. B. DuBois and Booker T. Washington. As early as *The Souls of Black Folk,* DuBois put African Americans in an international frame: "This triple paradox in Mr. Washington's position is the object of criticism by two classes of colored Americans. One class is spiritually descended from Toussaint the Savior, through Gabriel, Vesey, and Turner, and they represent the attitude of revolt and revenge; they hate the white South blindly and distrust the white race generally, and so far as they agree on definite action, think that the Negro's only hope lies in emigration beyond the borders of the United States. And yet, by the irony of fate, nothing has more effectually made this programme seem hopeless that the recent course of the United States toward weaker and darker peoples in the West Indies, Hawaii, and the Philippines—for where in the world may we go and be safe from lying and brute force?

"The other class of Negroes who cannot agree with Mr. Washington has hitherto said little aloud. They deprecate the sight of scattered counsels, of internal disagreement; and especially they dislike making their just criticism of a useful and earnest man an excuse for a general discharge of venom from small minded opponents. Nevertheless, the questions involved are so fundamental and serious that it is difficult to see how men like the Grimkes, Kelly Miller, and J. W. E. Bowen, and other representatives of this group, can much longer be silent" (43).

71. Frederick Douglass, *Narrative of the Life of Frederick Douglass, An American Slave: Written by Himself* (New Haven: Yale University Press, 2001).

72. Some of the earliest legal invocations of the Civil War amendments occurred in cases involving equal rights protections for Chinese immigrants. See Gotanda, "A Critique of 'Our Constitution Is Color-Blind.'"

73. The first section of Matthew Jacobson's *Barbarian Virtues* is precisely about this double-barreled approach to incorporating new subjects as both consumers and laborers.

74. Stephen Conn, "An Epistemology for Empire: The Philadelphia Commercial Museum, 1898–1926," *Diplomatic History* (Fall 1998): 533–63. Thanks to Donald Pease for this reference.

75. Ibid., 544.

76. Ibid., 546.

77. Ibid.

78. Quoted in May, *American Imperialism,* 166.

79. Kim, "Defining Asian American Realities," 146–70.

80. Chan, et al., preface to *Aiiieeeee!* xxi–xxii.

81. Gina Marchetti's *Romance and the "Yellow Peril": Race, Sex, and Discursive Strategies in Hollywood Fiction* (Berkeley and Los Angeles: University of California Press, 1993) and Darrell Hamamoto's *Monitored Peril: Asian Americans and the Politics of TV Representation* (Minneapolis: University of Minnesota Press, 1994) examine the ideological work that televised and cinematic racism have played in Asian American culture.

82. See the introduction to Lowe, *Critical Terrains.*

83. Amy Tan, *The Joy Luck Club* (New York: Putnam, 1989), 288. The book jacket biography quotes Tan echoing this sentiment: "As soon as my feet touched China, I became Chinese."

84. Diane Mark, interview with Wayne Wang in *Chan Is Missing,* 101–16. Carolyn Chung Simpson's notion of "absent presence" for Japanese Americans in the immediate post–World War II era is a further elaboration of this similar idea.

85. Daniel B. Schirmer notes that one of the least known American motivations for occupying the Philippines was the opening of shipping lanes to the Persian Gulf. See Schirmer and Shalom, *The Philippines Reader,* 140–49.

86. Rumor has it that Fuentes is not really the grandson of any of the St. Louis World's Fair Igorots and that he invented this tale to make his support by PBS more likely. Such inauthenticity only makes the film a more brilliant performance. In any case, the detail with which Markod recounts his experiences and his feelings in his "letters" stretches credibility.

5. "Everybody Wants to Be Farrah"

1. Karl Marx, *The Eighteenth Brumaire of Louis Bonaparte* (New York: International Publishers, 1969), 15.

2. Mark Twain, *Mark Twain's Weapons of Satire: Anti-Imperialist Writings on the*

Philippine American War, ed. Jim Zwick (Syracuse, N.Y.: Syracuse University Press, 1992).

3. Editorial, *The People,* October 14, 1900, quoted by Philip Foner and Richard C. Winchester in *The Anti-imperialist Reader: A Documentary History of Anti-Imperialism in the United States* (New York: Holmes and Meier, 1984), 1:140.

4. The literature on geopolitical space theory is too numerous to recount comprehensively in a single footnote. But among the most influential works are those by Edward Soja, David Harvey, Saskia Sassen, and Henri Lefebvre.

5. See Jean-François Lyotard, *The Postmodern Condition: A Report on Knowledge* (Minneapolis: University of Minnesota Press, 1988); and Michael Hardt and Antonio Negri, *Empire* (Cambridge: Harvard University Press, 2000).

6. In addition to the works already cited, globalization has seized an astoundingly wide range of work in the academy as a puzzle to be solved. Not surprisingly, a concomitant formation has been the reassertion of the local, such as the sovereignty movement in Hawaii.

7. James Gleick, in *Faster: The Acceleration of Just About Everything* (New York: Vintage, 2000), explains how global positioning satellites demand time in the nanoseconds because a nanosecond translates to roughly one foot, which is especially important for finding your way around in a rental car and bombing enemies.

8. Robert F. Heizer and Theodora Kroeber, eds., *Ishi, the Last Yahi: A Documentary History* (Berkeley: University of California Press, 1979).

9. Subaltern studies has produced groundbreaking historical work on the colonial archives of South Asia, as well as controversial application of its methods in other contexts. See Guha and Spivak's *Selected Subaltern Studies.*

10. The use of the term *queer,* as with *subaltern,* has not been without controversy over unreasonably wide application. In both cases, the term usefully denotes a limit point of normativity and modernity. For a discussion of the political deployment of *gay, lesbian,* and *queer,* see Mark Blasius's introduction of a *GLQ* special issue on "Identity/Space/Power: Lesbian, Gay, Bisexual, and Transgender Politics" (*GLQ* 3, no. 4 [1997]: 337–56). See also Social Text Collective's *Fear of a Queer Planet,* ed. Michael Warner (Minneapolis: University of Minnesota Press, 1993).

11. See Kimberlé Crenshaw, "Demarginalizing the Intersection of Race and Sex: A Black Feminist Critique of Anti-Discrimination Doctrine, Feminist Theory, and Antiracist Politics," *University of Chicago Legal Forum* (1989): 139–68.

12. For an insightful analysis of the cultural politics of race and sexuality, see Roderick Ferguson, *Aberrations in Black: Toward a Queer of Color Critique* (Minneapolis: University of Minnesota Press, 2004).

13. There were many books on the critique of the subject and the critique of that critique, such as *Who Comes after the Subject?* ed. Eduardo Cadava, Peter Connor, and Jean-Luc Nancy (New York: Routledge, 1991). That Judith Butler's *Gender Trouble* emerged as the most prominent is ironically significant because it was championed by the movements it critiqued.

14. Even before Butler's book, the late great Barbara Christian voiced an

articulate polemic warning about the pitfalls of theory's alleged annihilation of subjectivity. See Barbara Christian, "The Race for Theory," in JanMohamed and Lloyd, *The Nature and Context of Minority Discourse,* 37–49.

15. Some of the resulting scholarship in Asian American cultural studies has been breathtakingly resistant to these critiques of identity for their methodological ingenuity and historical rigor. Two recent books, in different but related ways, confront the nexus of civil society, globalization, and Asian American critique. Rhacel Salazar Parreñas's *Servants of Globalization,* even from its very title, shows us the emergence of new subjects at the site of the contradiction between civil society and globalization. That is, the promises held out by civil society are clearly no match for the unprecedentedly international market in reproductive labor. This legitimated market has generated a neofeudal subject position that can only be understood as a new servant to a new master. In apprehending the ill fit of these women to their niche in globalization, fundamentally new critiques of the new world order become traceable. And, because of the distanced relationship of these women to conventional forms of political representation under modernity, namely nation-states or even global feminist nongovernmental organizations, they cannot be championed by liberalism.

What Parreñas does with testimony and statistics to articulate the newness of new critical subjects under globalization, Nayan Shah does with official historical archives. In *Contagious Divides: Epidemics and Race in San Francisco's Chinatown,* Shah reintroduces us to urban, national, and global space and the unintended subjects that emerge. By reading the public health records of late nineteenth and early twentieth century San Francisco against the grain, Shah locates a new subject of history that demands new ways of looking at the past. Shah demonstrates how alternative and previously unrecognizable forms of socialization exceed containment by the governmentality of medical modernity. Further, by using these records to make visible the terms of the deeply sustaining homosociality of Chinatown bachelor communities, Shah eschews the cultural nationalist sorrow and pity for these men and boys, who were thought to be victims of history that the normatively nostalgic Asian American subject champions as a lamented forefather who never got to be one.

16. Eng, *Racial Castration.*

17. See Parreñas, *Servants of Globalization;* and Shah, *Contagious Divides.*

18. Chi Tsang, ed., *The APA Journal* 2, no. 1 (New York: Asian American Writers Workshop, 1993); Walter K. Lew, *Premonitions: The Kaya Anthology of New Asian North American Poetry* (New York: Kaya Production, 1995); Hagedorn, *Charlie Chan Is Dead.*

19. Linmark, *Rolling the R's,* 70.

20. For a lively cultural studies analysis of the Polynesian Cultural Center, see Andrew Ross, *The Chicago Gangster Theory of Life: Nature's Debt to Society* (London: Verso, 1995), 21–98.

21. In postcolonial cultural studies, Macauley's "Minute on Indian Education" is regarded as infamous. Macauley wrote of the desired outcome of British

education in India: "a class of interpreters between us and the millions whom we govern—a class of persons Indian in blood and colour, but English in tastes, in opinions, in morals and in intellect." Cited in Homi K. Bhabha, *The Location of Culture* (New York: Routledge, 1994), 87.

22. Fanon, *The Wretched of the Earth,* 227.

23. Hagedorn, *Dogeaters* (1990); Theresa Hak-Kyang Cha, *Dictee* (New York: Tanam Press, 1982).

24. Phillis Wheatley, *Poems of Phillis Wheatley* (Bedford, Mass.: Applewood Books, 1995), 12. "On Being Brought from Africa to America" was first published in 1773.

25. Toussaint Louverture, "Notes and Proclamations," in *The Heath Anthology of American Literature,* ed. Paul Lauter, 4th edition (New York: Houghton Mifflin, 2002), 1:1023–29. See also C. L. R. James, *Black Jacobins* (1938; New York: Vintage, 1963).

26. *The Perfumed Nightmare*, produced and directed by Kidlat Tahimik, 92 min. (Flower Films, 1977).

27. "How can the universities produce a governing subject, if there is not a single university in America that teaches the rudimentary basics of the art of government, to wit, the analysis of the elements peculiar to the peoples of America? Like guesswork, out in the world wearing Yankee or French spectacles, young men aspire to govern a nation they do not know." José Martí, "Nuestra America" (1891), in *Our America: Writings on Latin America and the Struggle for Cuban Independence,* ed. Philip Foner, 87 (New York: Monthly Review Press, 1977).

28. See Robert Blauner, "Colonized and Immigrant Minorities," in *Racial Oppression in America* (New York: Harper and Row, 1972), 51–81.

29. Martin Luther King Jr., "Letter from Birmingham Jail," in Gates and McKay, *Norton Anthology of African American Literature,* 1854–65.

30. See, for example, Eric Marcus, *Making History: The Struggle for Gay and Lesbian Equal Rights, 1945–1990* (New York: Harper Collins, 1992).

31. I borrow this useful term, "occasion," from Judith Halberstam as an alternative to the fraught concepts of subject, identity, or position, for their reliance on a human(ist) agent.

32. The formation of any creole dialect is inevitably a trace of historical conditions of encounter in a "contact zone." Hawaiian pidgin in particular formed out of the interethnic divisiveness of antiunion labor practices. The dialect's surviving usage, and struggles around its being recognized as a legitimate language, continue to be the source of lively debate. Recent years have seen the resurgence of local sovereignty movements in Hawaii and pidgin is a particularly volatile issue. See Elizabeth Carr, *Da Kine Talk: From Pidgin to Standard English in Hawaii* (Honolulu: University of Hawaii Press, 1972); Ronald Takaki, *Pau Hana: Plantation Life and Labor in Hawaii, 1835–1920* (Honolulu: University of Hawaii Press, 1983); Haunani Kay Trask, *Notes of a Native Daughter: Colonialism and Sovereignty in Hawaii* (Honolulu: University of Hawaii Press, 1999); and Rob Wilson, *Reimagining the American Pacific: From South Pacific to Bamboo Ridge and Beyond* (Durham: Duke

University Press, 2000). For a discussion of the literary history of Hawaii, see Stephen Sumida, *And the View from the Shore: Literary Traditions of Hawai'i* (Seattle: University of Washington Press, 1991).

33. Even before the American acquisition of the geothermally active atolls of Hawaii, the volcano was a common symbol of the racial unrest of the United States.

34. I take this phrase from Kandice Chuh's book on Asian American literature, *Imagine Otherwise: On Asian American Critique* (Durham: Duke University Press, 2004). Chuh borrows the phrase from Avery Gordon's *Ghostly Matters.*

35. The dynamics of race and oedipalization are elaborated in David Eng, "Primal Scenes: Queer Childhood and 'The Shoyu Kid,'" in his *Racial Castration.*

Epilogue

1. John F. Kennedy, "Inaugural Address, January 20, 1961, Capitol Steps, Washington, D.C.," in *The Presidents Speak: The Inaugural Addresses of the American Presidents from Washington to Clinton,* ed. Davis Newton Lott, 312–15, 313 (New York: Henry Holt and Co., Inc., 1994).

2. For the text of this speech, see www.americanrhetoric.com/speeches/lbjvietnam.htm.

3. For a discussion of this *Miss Saigon* controversy, see Helen Zia, *Asian American Dreams: The Emergence of an American People* (New York: Farrar Straus Giroux, 2000), 109–35.

VICTOR BASCARA is associate professor of English and Asian American studies at the University of Wisconsin, Madison. He has published in *MELUS, Amerasia, Asian Law Journal,* and anthologies on Asian American cultural politics.

www.ingramcontent.com/pod-product-compliance
Lightning Source LLC
Chambersburg PA
CBHW071739270326
41928CB00013B/2733